FREE Study Skills Videos/DVD Offer

Dear Customer,

Thank you for your purchase from Mometrix! We consider it an honor and a privilege that you have purchased our product and we want to ensure your satisfaction.

As part of our ongoing effort to meet the needs of test takers, we have developed a set of Study Skills Videos that we would like to give you for FREE. These videos cover our *best practices* for getting ready for your exam, from how to use our study materials to how to best prepare for the day of the test.

All that we ask is that you email us with feedback that would describe your experience so far with our product. Good, bad, or indifferent, we want to know what you think!

To get your FREE Study Skills Videos, you can use the **QR code** below, or send us an **email** at studyvideos@mometrix.com with *FREE VIDEOS* in the subject line and the following information in the body of the email:

- The name of the product you purchased.
- Your product rating on a scale of 1-5, with 5 being the highest rating.
- Your feedback. It can be long, short, or anything in between. We just want to know your impressions and experience so far with our product. (Good feedback might include how our study material met your needs and ways we might be able to make it even better. You could highlight features that you found helpful or features that you think we should add.)

If you have any questions or concerns, please don't hesitate to contact me directly.

Thanks again!

Sincerely,

Jay Willis
Vice President
jay.willis@mometrix.com
1-800-673-8175

NYSTCE

School Building Leader (109/110)

Secrets Study Guide

NYSTCE Exam Review and Practice Test for the New York State Teacher Certification Examinations

Copyright © 2025 by Mometrix Media LLC

All rights reserved. This product, or parts thereof, may not be reproduced, stored in a retrieval system, or transmitted in any form or by any means—electronic, mechanical, photocopy, recording, scanning, or other—except for brief quotations in critical reviews or articles, without the prior written permission of the publisher.

Written and edited by Mometrix Test Prep

Printed in the United States of America

This paper meets the requirements of ANSI/NISO Z39.48-1992 (Permanence of Paper).

Mometrix offers volume discount pricing to institutions. For more information or a price quote, please contact our sales department at sales@mometrix.com or 888-248-1219.

Mometrix Media LLC is not affiliated with or endorsed by any official testing organization. All organizational and test names are trademarks of their respective owners.

Paperback
ISBN 13: 978-1-5167-1649-4
ISBN 10: 1-5167-1649-3

Dear Future Exam Success Story

First of all, **THANK YOU** for purchasing Mometrix study materials!

Second, congratulations! You are one of the few determined test-takers who are committed to doing whatever it takes to excel on your exam. **You have come to the right place.** We developed these study materials with one goal in mind: to deliver you the information you need in a format that's concise and easy to use.

In addition to optimizing your guide for the content of the test, we've outlined our recommended steps for breaking down the preparation process into small, attainable goals so you can make sure you stay on track.

We've also analyzed the entire test-taking process, identifying the most common pitfalls and showing how you can overcome them and be ready for any curveball the test throws you.

Standardized testing is one of the biggest obstacles on your road to success, which only increases the importance of doing well in the high-pressure, high-stakes environment of test day. Your results on this test could have a significant impact on your future, and this guide provides the information and practical advice to help you achieve your full potential on test day.

Your success is our success

We would love to hear from you! If you would like to share the story of your exam success or if you have any questions or comments in regard to our products, please contact us at **800-673-8175** or **support@mometrix.com**.

Thanks again for your business and we wish you continued success!

Sincerely,
The Mometrix Test Preparation Team

Need more help? Check out our flashcards at:
http://MometrixFlashcards.com/NYSTCE

Copyright © 2025 by Mometrix Media LLC. All rights reserved.
Written and edited by the Mometrix Exam Secrets Test Prep Team
Printed in the United States of America

TABLE OF CONTENTS

INTRODUCTION	1
SECRET KEY #1 – PLAN BIG, STUDY SMALL	2
SECRET KEY #2 – MAKE YOUR STUDYING COUNT	3
SECRET KEY #3 – PRACTICE THE RIGHT WAY	4
SECRET KEY #4 – PACE YOURSELF	6
SECRET KEY #5 – HAVE A PLAN FOR GUESSING	7
TEST-TAKING STRATEGIES	10
INSTRUCTIONAL LEADERSHIP FOR STUDENT SUCCESS	**15**
CULTURE OF HIGH STANDARDS AND EXPECTATIONS	15
IDENTIFYING AND RESPONDING TO ACHIEVEMENT GAPS	16
CURRICULUM AND INSTRUCTION	18
ASSESSMENT AND ACCOUNTABILITY	23
COMMUNICATING PROGRESS TOWARD GOALS	26
PROFESSIONAL INFLUENCE FOR SYSTEMIC CHANGE	27
IDENTIFYING AREAS IN NEED OF IMPROVEMENT	28
ADVOCATING FOR CHANGE	30
TRENDS IN EDUCATION	31
CHAPTER QUIZ	37
SCHOOL CULTURE AND LEARNING ENVIRONMENT TO PROMOTE EXCELLENCE, EQUITY, AND SOCIAL JUSTICE	**38**
CULTURE OF LEARNING	38
SCHOOL VISION AND GOALS	39
DATA-INFORMED GOALS AND VISION	40
INVOLVING STAKEHOLDERS IN DEVELOPING VISION	42
GOALS THAT MEET DIVERSE NEEDS	43
IMPLEMENTING VISION AND GOALS	43
MEASURABLE EXPECTATIONS AND GOALS	46
LOCAL, STATE, AND FEDERAL POLICY	48
RELATIONSHIP BETWEEN VISION AND GOALS WITH LEGAL RESPONSIBILITIES	49
COMMUNICATING AND IMPLEMENTING VISION AND GOALS	50
LEADERSHIP MODELS AND STYLES	53
DISTRIBUTING RESPONSIBILITY THROUGH ROLES AND DELEGATION	54
MONITORING AND COMMUNICATING ABOUT PROGRESS TOWARD THE GOAL	56
ADJUSTING AND REVISING GOALS	56
IMPLEMENTING CHANGES	59
CHAPTER QUIZ	60
DEVELOPING HUMAN CAPITAL TO IMPROVE TEACHER AND STAFF EFFECTIVENESS AND STUDENT ACHIEVEMENT	**61**
RECRUITING STAFF MEMBERS	61
EVALUATING STAFF PERFORMANCE	62

    Professional Development and Staff Performance Standards _____ 63
    Collaborative Teaching and Learning _____ 65
    Resources for Effective Instruction _____ 67
    Chapter Quiz _____ 69

Family and Community Engagement _____ 70
    Using Community Resources _____ 70
    Communication with Family and the Public _____ 74
    Shared Decision-Making and Stakeholder Involvement _____ 76
    Chapter Quiz _____ 77

Operational Systems, Data Systems, and Legal Guidelines to Support Achievement of School Goals _____ 78
    Managing Operational Systems _____ 78
    Improving Organizational Systems _____ 80
    Physical Plant Safety and Compliance _____ 80
    Acquisition and Maintenance of Equipment and Technology _____ 81
    Allocating Resources and Budgeting _____ 82
    Recruiting Highly Qualified Personnel _____ 84
    Safe Environments _____ 85
    Disciplinary Expectations and Behavior Management _____ 87
    Emergency Preparedness and Response _____ 88
    Promoting the Welfare of Staff and Students _____ 90
    Disciplinary Policy _____ 94
    Personal and Professional Ethics _____ 97
    Protecting and Advocating for Students _____ 101
    Motivating Students _____ 102
    Transparent Decision-Making _____ 103
    Feedback and Reflection _____ 104
    Chapter Quiz _____ 106

NYSTCE Practice Test #1 _____ 107
    Part 1 _____ 107
    Part 2 _____ 141

Answer Key and Explanations for Test #1 _____ 158
    Part 1 _____ 158
    Part 2 _____ 164

NYSTCE Practice Test #2 _____ 168
    Part 1 _____ 168
    Part 2 _____ 204

Answer Key and Explanations for Test #2 _____ 222
    Part 1 _____ 222
    Part 2 _____ 233

How to Overcome Test Anxiety _____ 241

Additional Bonus Material _____ 247

Introduction

Thank you for purchasing this resource! You have made the choice to prepare yourself for a test that could have a huge impact on your future, and this guide is designed to help you be fully ready for test day. Obviously, it's important to have a solid understanding of the test material, but you also need to be prepared for the unique environment and stressors of the test, so that you can perform to the best of your abilities.

For this purpose, the first section that appears in this guide is the **Secret Keys**. We've devoted countless hours to meticulously researching what works and what doesn't, and we've boiled down our findings to the five most impactful steps you can take to improve your performance on the test. We start at the beginning with study planning and move through the preparation process, all the way to the testing strategies that will help you get the most out of what you know when you're finally sitting in front of the test.

We recommend that you start preparing for your test as far in advance as possible. However, if you've bought this guide as a last-minute study resource and only have a few days before your test, we recommend that you skip over the first two Secret Keys since they address a long-term study plan.

If you struggle with **test anxiety**, we strongly encourage you to check out our recommendations for how you can overcome it. Test anxiety is a formidable foe, but it can be beaten, and we want to make sure you have the tools you need to defeat it.

Secret Key #1 – Plan Big, Study Small

There's a lot riding on your performance. If you want to ace this test, you're going to need to keep your skills sharp and the material fresh in your mind. You need a plan that lets you review everything you need to know while still fitting in your schedule. We'll break this strategy down into three categories.

Information Organization

Start with the information you already have: the official test outline. From this, you can make a complete list of all the concepts you need to cover before the test. Organize these concepts into groups that can be studied together, and create a list of any related vocabulary you need to learn so you can brush up on any difficult terms. You'll want to keep this vocabulary list handy once you actually start studying since you may need to add to it along the way.

Time Management

Once you have your set of study concepts, decide how to spread them out over the time you have left before the test. Break your study plan into small, clear goals so you have a manageable task for each day and know exactly what you're doing. Then just focus on one small step at a time. When you manage your time this way, you don't need to spend hours at a time studying. Studying a small block of content for a short period each day helps you retain information better and avoid stressing over how much you have left to do. You can relax knowing that you have a plan to cover everything in time. In order for this strategy to be effective though, you have to start studying early and stick to your schedule. Avoid the exhaustion and futility that comes from last-minute cramming!

Study Environment

The environment you study in has a big impact on your learning. Studying in a coffee shop, while probably more enjoyable, is not likely to be as fruitful as studying in a quiet room. It's important to keep distractions to a minimum. You're only planning to study for a short block of time, so make the most of it. Don't pause to check your phone or get up to find a snack. It's also important to **avoid multitasking**. Research has consistently shown that multitasking will make your studying dramatically less effective. Your study area should also be comfortable and well-lit so you don't have the distraction of straining your eyes or sitting on an uncomfortable chair.

The time of day you study is also important. You want to be rested and alert. Don't wait until just before bedtime. Study when you'll be most likely to comprehend and remember. Even better, if you know what time of day your test will be, set that time aside for study. That way your brain will be used to working on that subject at that specific time and you'll have a better chance of recalling information.

Finally, it can be helpful to team up with others who are studying for the same test. Your actual studying should be done in as isolated an environment as possible, but the work of organizing the information and setting up the study plan can be divided up. In between study sessions, you can discuss with your teammates the concepts that you're all studying and quiz each other on the details. Just be sure that your teammates are as serious about the test as you are. If you find that your study time is being replaced with social time, you might need to find a new team.

Secret Key #2 – Make Your Studying Count

You're devoting a lot of time and effort to preparing for this test, so you want to be absolutely certain it will pay off. This means doing more than just reading the content and hoping you can remember it on test day. It's important to make every minute of study count. There are two main areas you can focus on to make your studying count.

Retention

It doesn't matter how much time you study if you can't remember the material. You need to make sure you are retaining the concepts. To check your retention of the information you're learning, try recalling it at later times with minimal prompting. Try carrying around flashcards and glance at one or two from time to time or ask a friend who's also studying for the test to quiz you.

To enhance your retention, look for ways to put the information into practice so that you can apply it rather than simply recalling it. If you're using the information in practical ways, it will be much easier to remember. Similarly, it helps to solidify a concept in your mind if you're not only reading it to yourself but also explaining it to someone else. Ask a friend to let you teach them about a concept you're a little shaky on (or speak aloud to an imaginary audience if necessary). As you try to summarize, define, give examples, and answer your friend's questions, you'll understand the concepts better and they will stay with you longer. Finally, step back for a big picture view and ask yourself how each piece of information fits with the whole subject. When you link the different concepts together and see them working together as a whole, it's easier to remember the individual components.

Finally, practice showing your work on any multi-step problems, even if you're just studying. Writing out each step you take to solve a problem will help solidify the process in your mind, and you'll be more likely to remember it during the test.

Modality

Modality simply refers to the means or method by which you study. Choosing a study modality that fits your own individual learning style is crucial. No two people learn best in exactly the same way, so it's important to know your strengths and use them to your advantage.

For example, if you learn best by visualization, focus on visualizing a concept in your mind and draw an image or a diagram. Try color-coding your notes, illustrating them, or creating symbols that will trigger your mind to recall a learned concept. If you learn best by hearing or discussing information, find a study partner who learns the same way or read aloud to yourself. Think about how to put the information in your own words. Imagine that you are giving a lecture on the topic and record yourself so you can listen to it later.

For any learning style, flashcards can be helpful. Organize the information so you can take advantage of spare moments to review. Underline key words or phrases. Use different colors for different categories. Mnemonic devices (such as creating a short list in which every item starts with the same letter) can also help with retention. Find what works best for you and use it to store the information in your mind most effectively and easily.

Secret Key #3 – Practice the Right Way

Your success on test day depends not only on how many hours you put into preparing, but also on whether you prepared the right way. It's good to check along the way to see if your studying is paying off. One of the most effective ways to do this is by taking practice tests to evaluate your progress. Practice tests are useful because they show exactly where you need to improve. Every time you take a practice test, pay special attention to these three groups of questions:

- The questions you got wrong
- The questions you had to guess on, even if you guessed right
- The questions you found difficult or slow to work through

This will show you exactly what your weak areas are, and where you need to devote more study time. Ask yourself why each of these questions gave you trouble. Was it because you didn't understand the material? Was it because you didn't remember the vocabulary? Do you need more repetitions on this type of question to build speed and confidence? Dig into those questions and figure out how you can strengthen your weak areas as you go back to review the material.

Additionally, many practice tests have a section explaining the answer choices. It can be tempting to read the explanation and think that you now have a good understanding of the concept. However, an explanation likely only covers part of the question's broader context. Even if the explanation makes perfect sense, **go back and investigate** every concept related to the question until you're positive you have a thorough understanding.

As you go along, keep in mind that the practice test is just that: practice. Memorizing these questions and answers will not be very helpful on the actual test because it is unlikely to have any of the same exact questions. If you only know the right answers to the sample questions, you won't be prepared for the real thing. **Study the concepts** until you understand them fully, and then you'll be able to answer any question that shows up on the test.

It's important to wait on the practice tests until you're ready. If you take a test on your first day of study, you may be overwhelmed by the amount of material covered and how much you need to learn. Work up to it gradually.

On test day, you'll need to be prepared for answering questions, managing your time, and using the test-taking strategies you've learned. It's a lot to balance, like a mental marathon that will have a big impact on your future. Like training for a marathon, you'll need to start slowly and work your way up. When test day arrives, you'll be ready.

Start with the strategies you've read in the first two Secret Keys—plan your course and study in the way that works best for you. If you have time, consider using multiple study resources to get different approaches to the same concepts. It can be helpful to see difficult concepts from more than one angle. Then find a good source for practice tests. Many times, the test website will suggest potential study resources or provide sample tests.

Practice Test Strategy

If you're able to find at least three practice tests, we recommend this strategy:

UNTIMED AND OPEN-BOOK PRACTICE

Take the first test with no time constraints and with your notes and study guide handy. Take your time and focus on applying the strategies you've learned.

TIMED AND OPEN-BOOK PRACTICE

Take the second practice test open-book as well, but set a timer and practice pacing yourself to finish in time.

TIMED AND CLOSED-BOOK PRACTICE

Take any other practice tests as if it were test day. Set a timer and put away your study materials. Sit at a table or desk in a quiet room, imagine yourself at the testing center, and answer questions as quickly and accurately as possible.

Keep repeating timed and closed-book tests on a regular basis until you run out of practice tests or it's time for the actual test. Your mind will be ready for the schedule and stress of test day, and you'll be able to focus on recalling the material you've learned.

Secret Key #4 – Pace Yourself

Once you're fully prepared for the material on the test, your biggest challenge on test day will be managing your time. Just knowing that the clock is ticking can make you panic even if you have plenty of time left. Work on pacing yourself so you can build confidence against the time constraints of the exam. Pacing is a difficult skill to master, especially in a high-pressure environment, so **practice is vital**.

Set time expectations for your pace based on how much time is available. For example, if a section has 60 questions and the time limit is 30 minutes, you know you have to average 30 seconds or less per question in order to answer them all. Although 30 seconds is the hard limit, set 25 seconds per question as your goal, so you reserve extra time to spend on harder questions. When you budget extra time for the harder questions, you no longer have any reason to stress when those questions take longer to answer.

Don't let this time expectation distract you from working through the test at a calm, steady pace, but keep it in mind so you don't spend too much time on any one question. Recognize that taking extra time on one question you don't understand may keep you from answering two that you do understand later in the test. If your time limit for a question is up and you're still not sure of the answer, mark it and move on, and come back to it later if the time and the test format allow. If the testing format doesn't allow you to return to earlier questions, just make an educated guess; then put it out of your mind and move on.

On the easier questions, be careful not to rush. It may seem wise to hurry through them so you have more time for the challenging ones, but it's not worth missing one if you know the concept and just didn't take the time to read the question fully. Work efficiently but make sure you understand the question and have looked at all of the answer choices, since more than one may seem right at first.

Even if you're paying attention to the time, you may find yourself a little behind at some point. You should speed up to get back on track, but do so wisely. Don't panic; just take a few seconds less on each question until you're caught up. Don't guess without thinking, but do look through the answer choices and eliminate any you know are wrong. If you can get down to two choices, it is often worthwhile to guess from those. Once you've chosen an answer, move on and don't dwell on any that you skipped or had to hurry through. If a question was taking too long, chances are it was one of the harder ones, so you weren't as likely to get it right anyway.

On the other hand, if you find yourself getting ahead of schedule, it may be beneficial to slow down a little. The more quickly you work, the more likely you are to make a careless mistake that will affect your score. You've budgeted time for each question, so don't be afraid to spend that time. Practice an efficient but careful pace to get the most out of the time you have.

Secret Key #5 – Have a Plan for Guessing

When you're taking the test, you may find yourself stuck on a question. Some of the answer choices seem better than others, but you don't see the one answer choice that is obviously correct. What do you do?

The scenario described above is very common, yet most test takers have not effectively prepared for it. Developing and practicing a plan for guessing may be one of the single most effective uses of your time as you get ready for the exam.

In developing your plan for guessing, there are three questions to address:

- When should you start the guessing process?
- How should you narrow down the choices?
- Which answer should you choose?

When to Start the Guessing Process

Unless your plan for guessing is to select C every time (which, despite its merits, is not what we recommend), you need to leave yourself enough time to apply your answer elimination strategies. Since you have a limited amount of time for each question, that means that if you're going to give yourself the best shot at guessing correctly, you have to decide quickly whether or not you will guess.

Of course, the best-case scenario is that you don't have to guess at all, so first, see if you can answer the question based on your knowledge of the subject and basic reasoning skills. Focus on the key words in the question and try to jog your memory of related topics. Give yourself a chance to bring the knowledge to mind, but once you realize that you don't have (or you can't access) the knowledge you need to answer the question, it's time to start the guessing process.

It's almost always better to start the guessing process too early than too late. It only takes a few seconds to remember something and answer the question from knowledge. Carefully eliminating wrong answer choices takes longer. Plus, going through the process of eliminating answer choices can actually help jog your memory.

Summary: Start the guessing process as soon as you decide that you can't answer the question based on your knowledge.

How to Narrow Down the Choices

The next chapter in this book (**Test-Taking Strategies**) includes a wide range of strategies for how to approach questions and how to look for answer choices to eliminate. You will definitely want to read those carefully, practice them, and figure out which ones work best for you. Here though, we're going to address a mindset rather than a particular strategy.

Your odds of guessing an answer correctly depend on how many options you are choosing from.

Number of options left	5	4	3	2	1
Odds of guessing correctly	20%	25%	33%	50%	100%

You can see from this chart just how valuable it is to be able to eliminate incorrect answers and make an educated guess, but there are two things that many test takers do that cause them to miss out on the benefits of guessing:

- Accidentally eliminating the correct answer
- Selecting an answer based on an impression

We'll look at the first one here, and the second one in the next section.

To avoid accidentally eliminating the correct answer, we recommend a thought exercise called **the $5 challenge**. In this challenge, you only eliminate an answer choice from contention if you are willing to bet $5 on it being wrong. Why $5? Five dollars is a small but not insignificant amount of money. It's an amount you could afford to lose but wouldn't want to throw away. And while losing

$5 once might not hurt too much, doing it twenty times will set you back $100. In the same way, each small decision you make—eliminating a choice here, guessing on a question there—won't by itself impact your score very much, but when you put them all together, they can make a big difference. By holding each answer choice elimination decision to a higher standard, you can reduce the risk of accidentally eliminating the correct answer.

The $5 challenge can also be applied in a positive sense: If you are willing to bet $5 that an answer choice *is* correct, go ahead and mark it as correct.

Summary: Only eliminate an answer choice if you are willing to bet $5 that it is wrong.

Which Answer to Choose

You're taking the test. You've run into a hard question and decided you'll have to guess. You've eliminated all the answer choices you're willing to bet $5 on. Now you have to pick an answer. Why do we even need to talk about this? Why can't you just pick whichever one you feel like when the time comes?

The answer to these questions is that if you don't come into the test with a plan, you'll rely on your impression to select an answer choice, and if you do that, you risk falling into a trap. The test writers know that everyone who takes their test will be guessing on some of the questions, so they intentionally write wrong answer choices to seem plausible. You still have to pick an answer though, and if the wrong answer choices are designed to look right, how can you ever be sure that you're not falling for their trap? The best solution we've found to this dilemma is to take the decision out of your hands entirely. Here is the process we recommend:

Once you've eliminated any choices that you are confident (willing to bet $5) are wrong, select the first remaining choice as your answer.

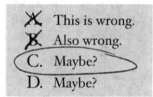

Whether you choose to select the first remaining choice, the second, or the last, the important thing is that you use some preselected standard. Using this approach guarantees that you will not be enticed into selecting an answer choice that looks right, because you are not basing your decision on how the answer choices look.

This is not meant to make you question your knowledge. Instead, it is to help you recognize the difference between your knowledge and your impressions. There's a huge difference between thinking an answer is right because of what you know, and thinking an answer is right because it looks or sounds like it should be right.

Summary: To ensure that your selection is appropriately random, make a predetermined selection from among all answer choices you have not eliminated.

Test-Taking Strategies

This section contains a list of test-taking strategies that you may find helpful as you work through the test. By taking what you know and applying logical thought, you can maximize your chances of answering any question correctly!

It is very important to realize that every question is different and every person is different: no single strategy will work on every question, and no single strategy will work for every person. That's why we've included all of them here, so you can try them out and determine which ones work best for different types of questions and which ones work best for you.

Question Strategies

⊘ READ CAREFULLY

Read the question and the answer choices carefully. Don't miss the question because you misread the terms. You have plenty of time to read each question thoroughly and make sure you understand what is being asked. Yet a happy medium must be attained, so don't waste too much time. You must read carefully and efficiently.

⊘ CONTEXTUAL CLUES

Look for contextual clues. If the question includes a word you are not familiar with, look at the immediate context for some indication of what the word might mean. Contextual clues can often give you all the information you need to decipher the meaning of an unfamiliar word. Even if you can't determine the meaning, you may be able to narrow down the possibilities enough to make a solid guess at the answer to the question.

⊘ PREFIXES

If you're having trouble with a word in the question or answer choices, try dissecting it. Take advantage of every clue that the word might include. Prefixes can be a huge help. Usually, they allow you to determine a basic meaning. *Pre-* means before, *post-* means after, *pro-* is positive, *de-* is negative. From prefixes, you can get an idea of the general meaning of the word and try to put it into context.

⊘ HEDGE WORDS

Watch out for critical hedge words, such as *likely*, *may*, *can*, *sometimes*, *often*, *almost*, *mostly*, *usually*, *generally*, *rarely*, and *sometimes*. Question writers insert these hedge phrases to cover every possibility. Often an answer choice will be wrong simply because it leaves no room for exception. Be on guard for answer choices that have definitive words such as *exactly* and *always*.

⊘ SWITCHBACK WORDS

Stay alert for *switchbacks*. These are the words and phrases frequently used to alert you to shifts in thought. The most common switchback words are *but*, *although*, and *however*. Others include *nevertheless*, *on the other hand*, *even though*, *while*, *in spite of*, *despite*, and *regardless of*. Switchback words are important to catch because they can change the direction of the question or an answer choice.

⏱ Face Value

When in doubt, use common sense. Accept the situation in the problem at face value. Don't read too much into it. These problems will not require you to make wild assumptions. If you have to go beyond creativity and warp time or space in order to have an answer choice fit the question, then you should move on and consider the other answer choices. These are normal problems rooted in reality. The applicable relationship or explanation may not be readily apparent, but it is there for you to figure out. Use your common sense to interpret anything that isn't clear.

Answer Choice Strategies

⏱ Answer Selection

The most thorough way to pick an answer choice is to identify and eliminate wrong answers until only one is left, then confirm it is the correct answer. Sometimes an answer choice may immediately seem right, but be careful. The test writers will usually put more than one reasonable answer choice on each question, so take a second to read all of them and make sure that the other choices are not equally obvious. As long as you have time left, it is better to read every answer choice than to pick the first one that looks right without checking the others.

⏱ Answer Choice Families

An answer choice family consists of two (in rare cases, three) answer choices that are very similar in construction and cannot all be true at the same time. If you see two answer choices that are direct opposites or parallels, one of them is usually the correct answer. For instance, if one answer choice says that quantity x increases and another either says that quantity x decreases (opposite) or says that quantity y increases (parallel), then those answer choices would fall into the same family. An answer choice that doesn't match the construction of the answer choice family is more likely to be incorrect. Most questions will not have answer choice families, but when they do appear, you should be prepared to recognize them.

⏱ Eliminate Answers

Eliminate answer choices as soon as you realize they are wrong, but make sure you consider all possibilities. If you are eliminating answer choices and realize that the last one you are left with is also wrong, don't panic. Start over and consider each choice again. There may be something you missed the first time that you will realize on the second pass.

⏱ Avoid Fact Traps

Don't be distracted by an answer choice that is factually true but doesn't answer the question. You are looking for the choice that answers the question. Stay focused on what the question is asking for so you don't accidentally pick an answer that is true but incorrect. Always go back to the question and make sure the answer choice you've selected actually answers the question and is not merely a true statement.

⏱ Extreme Statements

In general, you should avoid answers that put forth extreme actions as standard practice or proclaim controversial ideas as established fact. An answer choice that states the "process should be used in certain situations, if..." is much more likely to be correct than one that states the "process should be discontinued completely." The first is a calm rational statement and doesn't even make a definitive, uncompromising stance, using a hedge word *if* to provide wiggle room, whereas the second choice is far more extreme.

⊘ BENCHMARK

As you read through the answer choices and you come across one that seems to answer the question well, mentally select that answer choice. This is not your final answer, but it's the one that will help you evaluate the other answer choices. The one that you selected is your benchmark or standard for judging each of the other answer choices. Every other answer choice must be compared to your benchmark. That choice is correct until proven otherwise by another answer choice beating it. If you find a better answer, then that one becomes your new benchmark. Once you've decided that no other choice answers the question as well as your benchmark, you have your final answer.

⊘ PREDICT THE ANSWER

Before you even start looking at the answer choices, it is often best to try to predict the answer. When you come up with the answer on your own, it is easier to avoid distractions and traps because you will know exactly what to look for. The right answer choice is unlikely to be word-for-word what you came up with, but it should be a close match. Even if you are confident that you have the right answer, you should still take the time to read each option before moving on.

General Strategies

⊘ TOUGH QUESTIONS

If you are stumped on a problem or it appears too hard or too difficult, don't waste time. Move on! Remember though, if you can quickly check for obviously incorrect answer choices, your chances of guessing correctly are greatly improved. Before you completely give up, at least try to knock out a couple of possible answers. Eliminate what you can and then guess at the remaining answer choices before moving on.

⊘ CHECK YOUR WORK

Since you will probably not know every term listed and the answer to every question, it is important that you get credit for the ones that you do know. Don't miss any questions through careless mistakes. If at all possible, try to take a second to look back over your answer selection and make sure you've selected the correct answer choice and haven't made a costly careless mistake (such as marking an answer choice that you didn't mean to mark). This quick double check should more than pay for itself in caught mistakes for the time it costs.

⊘ PACE YOURSELF

It's easy to be overwhelmed when you're looking at a page full of questions; your mind is confused and full of random thoughts, and the clock is ticking down faster than you would like. Calm down and maintain the pace that you have set for yourself. Especially as you get down to the last few minutes of the test, don't let the small numbers on the clock make you panic. As long as you are on track by monitoring your pace, you are guaranteed to have time for each question.

⊘ DON'T RUSH

It is very easy to make errors when you are in a hurry. Maintaining a fast pace in answering questions is pointless if it makes you miss questions that you would have gotten right otherwise. Test writers like to include distracting information and wrong answers that seem right. Taking a little extra time to avoid careless mistakes can make all the difference in your test score. Find a pace that allows you to be confident in the answers that you select.

⏱ KEEP MOVING

Panicking will not help you pass the test, so do your best to stay calm and keep moving. Taking deep breaths and going through the answer elimination steps you practiced can help to break through a stress barrier and keep your pace.

Final Notes

The combination of a solid foundation of content knowledge and the confidence that comes from practicing your plan for applying that knowledge is the key to maximizing your performance on test day. As your foundation of content knowledge is built up and strengthened, you'll find that the strategies included in this chapter become more and more effective in helping you quickly sift through the distractions and traps of the test to isolate the correct answer.

Now that you're preparing to move forward into the test content chapters of this book, be sure to keep your goal in mind. As you read, think about how you will be able to apply this information on the test. If you've already seen sample questions for the test and you have an idea of the question format and style, try to come up with questions of your own that you can answer based on what you're reading. This will give you valuable practice applying your knowledge in the same ways you can expect to on test day.

Good luck and good studying!

Instructional Leadership for Student Success

Transform passive reading into active learning! After immersing yourself in this chapter, put your comprehension to the test by taking a quiz. The insights you gained will stay with you longer this way. Scan the QR code to go directly to the chapter quiz interface for this study guide. If you're using a computer, simply visit the bonus page at **mometrix.com/bonus948/nystcescbl109110** and click the Chapter Quizzes link.

Culture of High Standards and Expectations

COMMITMENT TO HIGH STANDARDS FOR ALL STUDENTS
EQUITY VS. EQUALITY

All students are expected to meet the standards outlined by the state and federal governments. School leaders are responsible for providing students with the instruction, resources, and support necessary to meet these standards. **Equality** refers to providing all students with the same resources and support, regardless of their needs. **Equity** refers to providing students with the resources and support that meet their individual needs. An example of equality would be that all students receive ninety minutes of reading instruction each day. An example of equity would be that students who have shown deficiencies in reading receive an extra thirty minutes of reading instruction each day. When leaders implement equity in schools, this may mean that some students receive more **resources and support** than others, or different support and resources. Leaders must be aware of what students need so that the right resources and support can be used to support these students. This need may be due to a lack of educational opportunity, physical or intellectual disabilities, or other circumstances. All students need resources and support to enrich their education, but practicing equity means that students will receive appropriate resources based on their identified needs.

> **Review Video: Equality vs Equity**
> Visit mometrix.com/academy and enter code: 685648

CREATING A CULTURE OF HIGH EXPECTATIONS

A culture of high expectations means that staff and students strive toward high goals and excellence. A leader can create a **culture of high expectations** by setting campus goals **above minimum standards**. For example, if the required student attendance rate is 90%, the leader can set a goal for a 95% attendance rate for the campus. The leader can also **reward** student and staff performance that exceeds expectations. For example, the leader may publicly celebrate students who achieve Honor Roll. Another strategy for creating a culture of high expectations is to provide **models of excellence** for students and staff. These models can be effective programs on other campuses, role models in the community, or exemplary staff and students on campus. To create a culture of high expectations, a leader must also **address performance that does not meet expectations** in an effective manner. It must be clear to staff and students that performing below expectations is not acceptable. The leader must also **provide the resources necessary** for staff and students to meet the high expectations that have been set.

EVIDENCE OF A CULTURE OF HIGH EXPECTATIONS ON SCHOOL CAMPUSES

It is evident that a school has a culture of high expectations by what is seen and heard on campus. The culture of high expectations is evidenced by the **campus appearance**, including its cleanliness, organization, and posted materials. Bulletin boards and other visual aids in the hallways and in classrooms should demonstrate high expectations for academic achievement, character, and behavior. For example, a school may post college pennants and posters in the hallways to demonstrate an expectation that students are college-ready. Also, the **instruction** that is observed in the classroom should be evidence of high expectations for students and their ability to perform academically. The culture of high expectations is also evidenced by how **students and staff speak**. When there are high expectations, teachers and students speak positively about learning and meeting goals. There is little to no negative talk in regard to learning and performance. Instead, there is problem-solving, brainstorming, and action-planning to meet academic goals. A culture of high expectations on campus is evidenced by the **performance**, which is indicated by goal attainment and student performance data.

EVIDENCE OF A CULTURE OF HIGH EXPECTATIONS IN CLASSROOMS

Within the classroom, a culture of high expectations is evident by the **appearance** of the classroom and the **behavior** of teacher and students. First, the classroom will be neat, organized, and conducive to learning. Posted materials will be academically relevant, positive, and encouraging. In a classroom with a culture of high expectations, the teacher begins class on time and is prepared for the lesson. Materials and technology are ready for the start of class and there is a clear objective for the day's lesson. The teacher makes an effort to engage all students and uses a variety of instructional strategies to do so. In this classroom, students are eager to participate and remain engaged in the lesson throughout its entirety. Students demonstrate engagement in and mastery of the content by engaging in discussion with the teacher and their peers. There are few, if any, behavioral problems in this type of classroom, and if they do arise the teacher addresses them quickly and appropriately. There is evidence in the classroom of a good relationship and rapport between the teacher and the students, and no students are allowed to disengage from the lesson.

Identifying and Responding to Achievement Gaps

ACHIEVEMENT GAPS

The term "achievement gap" refers to the disparity in educational performance of students of low socioeconomic status, minority students, and female students. **Educational performance** is measured by many indicators such as course grades, pass/fail rates and promotion, standardized test performance, course selection, graduation rates, college enrollment rates, and many other indicators. The achievement gap exists as a national phenomenon but is also observed at the state level, district level, and even within campuses. The achievement gap was identified over fifty years ago and continues today. There is an abundance of research regarding why it exists and how to address it at all educational levels, but so far there has not been any success in eliminating it. As a result, leaders should be prepared to **identify and address** achievement gaps on their campuses.

PERFORMANCE INDICATORS

The best way to determine the existence of an achievement gap on campus is to analyze **student performance indicators**. Leaders can use a variety of performance indicators to identify if an achievement gap exists on their campus and, if so, for whom. Leaders can analyze performance data for **standardized tests** administered over the past 2–3 years to identify any disparities. The data should be compared based on socioeconomic status, race and ethnicity, gender, special education status, limited English proficiency status, and any other subgroups that are relevant to the campus.

If an achievement gap exists, students in a particular **subgroup** will consistently perform at a lower rate when compared to the other groups of students. This method of analysis should be repeated for other performance indicators such as grades, pass/fail rates, promotion and retention, graduation, and any others that are relevant to the campus goals.

COMPARING PERFORMANCE WITH OUTSIDE STANDARDS

A school leader may evaluate data on campus and determine that all students, regardless of demographics, are performing academically at **comparable rates**. This is often the case in schools with little to no diversity. However, a lack of evidence of an achievement gap within a campus does not mean that students are not affected by it. The school leader should **compare** the performance of students on his or her campus to other schools in the surrounding area, both within and outside of the school district. The leader may then find that his or her students are not performing at the same level as students in other schools. For example, a school leader may find that the majority of students on his or her campus are demonstrating a proficiency of 76% in math, while students in other schools are demonstrating a proficiency of 88%. Consequently, the school leader may realize that students at his or her school need to improve in math to remain on pace with their academic peers.

REDUCING THE ACHIEVEMENT GAP

To reduce the achievement gap on campus, leaders should **assess** the needs of the underperforming groups of students and **align resources and support** in an equitable manner. Leaders can provide **targeted interventions** to these students based on their identified needs. For example, the leader may schedule math and reading tutorials for a particular subgroup of students who have demonstrated deficiencies in that area. A leader should also set **campus goals** that specifically address the performance of underperforming groups of students. This will ensure that there is an action plan for addressing the needs of these students, as well as specific resources dedicated to their performance. Finally, a leader should **track data** for the performance indicators that show the achievement gap. This data should be collected and analyzed at regular intervals so that additional interventions, resources, and support can be implemented, if necessary. In order to reduce the achievement gap, the leader should target these students with resources and support and monitor their progress on a regular basis.

ADDRESSING THE ACHIEVEMENT GAP THROUGH GOAL SETTING AND DATA-MONITORING

GOAL-SETTING

Goal-setting can help to address the achievement gap because it focuses attention on the groups of students who need extra support and helps to target resources in those areas. Areas in which school leaders create goals receive **attention and targeted resources**. When goals are developed that specifically address areas of the school programming with evidence of an achievement gap, the school leader can turn the focus of students, staff, and the community to these areas. Additionally, when goals are created, there is a **determination** to accomplish those goals, so if a goal is related to the achievement gap, it is more likely that the gap will be addressed. For example, if the school leader has seen evidence in the data that Hispanic students with limited English proficiency are lagging behind their peers in reading performance, the school leader can develop a school goal that specifically addresses the reading performance of Hispanic students with limited English proficiency. As a result, there would be increased focus on all Hispanic students with limited English proficiency, including the dedication of time, effort, and resources.

DATA MONITORING

Data monitoring can be used to address the achievement gap because it can help to **identify** areas of the school program where the gap exists and to **monitor changes** in the achievement gap on campus. First, data should be used to identify where an achievement gap is present. The achievement gap is typically present in **reading and math content areas**, but can vary among other subject areas, as well as by groups of students. For example, a school leader may find that there is a gap in math performance between African American students and their peers, but that the gap is largest among African American males. Additionally, the data can show the school leader where the gap may be **narrowing** due to the instructional strategies and changes in school programming, or where the gap has **shifted** to another group of students. Therefore, data monitoring is key in identifying the achievement gap, determining the efficacy of strategies implemented to address the achievement gap, and assessing changes in the achievement gap among other student populations.

Curriculum and Instruction

RIGOROUS AND RELEVANT CURRICULUM DESIGN

A cornerstone of the educator's role in cultivating effective student learning experiences is the development of a rigorous and relevant **curriculum design**. This approach not only pushes educators to reconsider their perspectives on how students learn but also encourages the adoption of innovative instructional methods. By recognizing the diverse array of learning styles and cultural backgrounds among students, educators can adeptly tailor their approaches, fostering an inclusive and captivating classroom atmosphere. Moreover, a robust curriculum design establishes a structured **framework** for instructional goals, providing educators with a clear roadmap for effective teaching. This helps to ensure both consistency in delivery and the flexibility needed for differentiation, accommodating for the diverse learning needs of students. As educators engage in targeted professional development opportunities centered on these principles, they can acquire the essential skills to craft and deliver instruction that is rigorous, differentiated, and culturally relevant, thereby enriching the overall educational experience for all students.

RIGOR

Rigor in academic instruction refers to **challenging curriculum and instruction**. Rigorous instruction challenges students not only academically, but also intellectually, and even personally. Rigorous instruction is often complex and challenges students to think deeply and critically. Through rigorous instruction, students are able to develop the **soft skills** necessary for success in college, career, and adulthood, such as problem-solving, critical thinking, inferring, studying, time management, self-discipline, working in teams, and many others. Rigor does not mean something is excessively hard or difficult. However, rigor does involve stimulating, engaging instruction. Rigorous instruction often requires students to make connections **across academic content areas** and apply concepts to the **real world**. For example, if a high school English teacher wanted to assign a rigorous assignment based on a reading of *To Kill a Mockingbird*, he or she could assign a project in which students discuss the impact of the political setting in the United States at the time of the story on the plot. In contrast, a non-rigorous assignment could be a worksheet of multiple-choice questions.

ENSURING RIGOR

A school leader must ensure that all students have access to a rigorous instructional program. First, a leader must evaluate the curriculum for **alignment to state standards**. This ensures that all curriculum is designed to instruct students based on the expectations set by the state. This prevents the lowering of standards in the classroom, which could lead to students falling behind. Next, a leader must determine that curriculum is taught in a **rigorous manner**. This includes creating lessons that require students to think critically. A leader may encourage instructional strategies such as differentiated instruction, project-based learning, and collaborative learning to help foster rigorous instruction in the classroom. Finally, the school leader must ensure that **assessment** of instruction is rigorous. This may mean encouraging the use of projects and other creative means that allow students to demonstrate mastery of standards and objectives. A rigorous instructional program avoids reliance on worksheets and other assessment activities that do not align with a rigorous instructional program.

SUPPORTING RIGOROUS INSTRUCTION

Rigorous instruction is challenging yet feasible for students. Campus goals can support rigorous instruction by motivating instructional staff to have **high expectations** for teaching and learning. When a goal is set high, it challenges instructional staff to work harder and with greater urgency, which requires utilizing **rigorous instruction**. For example, if a campus has had prior reading performance of 65%, a campus goal of 70% would not require significant change from the prior year's strategies and practice. However, setting a reading performance goal of 80% for the school year would encourage teachers to provide rigorous instruction to students to meet the higher performance expectation. Low expectations in goal setting will result in low expectations in instruction and high expectations in goal setting will result in high expectations in instruction. Similarly, when campus goals include all populations and sub-populations of students, rigorous instruction is supported. This ensures that low-performing students and high-performing students receive instruction at their appropriate level of rigor.

CROSS-CURRICULAR INSTRUCTION

Cross-curricular instruction is the deliberate making of connections between **various content areas** so that students may apply their knowledge in more than one content area at a time. For example, students may examine the historical setting of a story in a reading class, utilize math strategies in a science class, or discuss geometric principles in an art class. Cross-curricular instruction is beneficial for students because it demonstrates the **relevance** of their content knowledge. When students understand that the instruction is not isolated to one particular area, but has applicability in other areas, students find the knowledge to be more **meaningful**. Additionally, utilizing concepts and skills in different contexts helps students to **master and retain** those skills. Cross-curricular instruction also aids students in their critical thinking skills such as inferring, drawing conclusions, predicting, and so forth. Cross-curricular instruction benefits teachers as well as students because it facilitates **collaboration** among colleagues. Teachers can plan together when lessons align across content areas and even team-teach lessons.

SUPPORTING CROSS-CURRICULAR INSTRUCTION

Leaders can support cross-curricular instruction by facilitating collaboration and providing resources for teachers. Cross-curricular instruction can be done independently but is more effective when teachers can **collaborate in lesson planning**. Leaders can provide time during the school day or at other times for teachers of different content areas to collaborate and examine the curriculum for opportunities for cross-curricular instruction. Also, leaders can support cross-curricular instruction by providing the appropriate resources. Teachers may have ideas that require books, supplies, or other materials to facilitate these lessons. Additionally, teachers may need **training or professional development resources** to help them present cross-curricular lessons effectively. Leaders can cultivate an environment where cross-curricular instruction is supported, encouraged, and praised.

ALIGNMENT OF CURRICULUM AND INSTRUCTION TO ASSESSMENT

Curriculum and instruction must be aligned to assessment because what is taught must be measured and what is measured must be taught. If instruction is not aligned to the assessment, there will likely be no **measurement** of how well students mastered what was taught. Additionally, if instruction is not aligned to the assessment, students will likely be assessed on concepts and material they have **not been taught**. Neither scenario is fair or beneficial to students. In the case of district- or campus-created assessments, the **assessment** is often created first because this defines what students should know at the conclusion of the given time period. Then, based on the assessment's expectations, teachers can plan the order and pacing of the concepts and skills to teach. On state-mandated tests, students are expected to have mastered all skills and objectives provided by the state, but no one is aware of the test content until its administration.

RIGOR AND DIFFERENTIATED INSTRUCTION

Rigorous instruction is challenging to students, but not impossible. However, classrooms are diverse and not all students perform at the same academic levels. As a result, teachers must provide an appropriate level of rigorous instruction to students based on their **current performance**. When teachers **differentiate instruction** for students, they cater to the individual needs of students, such as identifying the appropriate level of rigor for particular students or groups. For example, an eighth-grade math teacher would not give the same assignment to a struggling student as he or she would to a student who is performing above grade level. Each student needs a **unique level of rigorous instruction**. The teacher may identify that adding and subtracting fractions is a rigorous activity for the struggling student whereas the high-performing student may be able to solve algebraic equations that include fractions.

RELEVANCE IN INSTRUCTION

Relevance in instruction refers to how content is related to other content and to the real world, as experienced by the students in the classroom. When instruction is **not relevant**, students may have difficulty making connections to the instruction, identifying or connecting any background knowledge they may have, or retaining the information. In contrast, when instruction is **relevant**, students understand how the content connects to what they already know, what they are learning in other areas, and to the world around them. For example, a math teacher may explain to students how using an algebraic function can help them calculate their weekly paycheck on a job. An English teacher may compare a plot from classic literature to a modern-day movie or story to help students to make connections. Teachers make instruction relevant by demonstrating how the new content **connects** with old content, with the content they are learning in other courses, and with the real world as they experience it.

SUPPORTING STUDENT ENGAGEMENT AND PERFORMANCE

When instruction is relevant to students, they are more likely to engage in it and demonstrate better academic performance. Students are better able to **engage in relevant instruction** because they understand how the new content **relates** to what they already know, which can build their interest and provide them with a way to contribute to the lesson. For example, if the students are reading a story in which a character spends a day at the beach, a student who has never been to the beach may have difficulty engaging in the lesson, whereas a student who has visited the beach is more eager to share experiences and connections to the lesson. Similarly, when students are taught **abstract concepts**, they may have difficulty grasping and retaining them if they are not relevant. In contrast, when students understand how concepts are applied in the **real world**, they are more likely to retain them. For example, students may learn about chemical reactions in a science course, but if they are shown how these chemical reactions occur in everyday life, such as cooking, they will have a deeper understanding of the concept and be more likely to retain it.

School-Wide Practices and Focus on Standards-Based Instruction
Differentiated Instruction

Differentiated instruction refers to providing **customized or tailored instruction** to students to meet their diverse learning needs. These learning needs can be determined by previous academic performance, special needs such as a physical or learning disability, learning style, or other means. Based on the identified needs, teachers can **differentiate** the content, process, or product of the instruction. When teachers differentiate **content**, they provide different content to students, such as a math teacher instructing one group of students on fractions and another group on algebraic equations. When teachers differentiate by **process**, a teacher provides different modes of instruction, such as video or media, field experiences, exploratory discovery, or other means. When a teacher differentiates by **product**, she provides different ways for students to demonstrate mastery of the content such as through writing, performance, or projects, among others. Teachers may differentiate instruction in all of these areas or in selected areas, based on the needs of the students.

Using Data to Support Differentiated Instruction

Instruction is differentiated based on **students' needs**. Data can be used to identify these needs, especially in the area of academic performance. **Historical student performance data** as well as current **formative and summative assessments** can help to determine the type of instruction a student may need. For example, the data may show that a certain group of students has deficits in reading. These students may benefit from not only reading a text, but additional methods of instructional delivery, as well as specific instruction that helps to build their reading skills. Data may inform campus leaders on what **courses** to offer. For example, if historical data demonstrates that many students have achieved advanced performance on state assessments, the leader may consider offering advanced classes in certain academic areas such as Advanced Placement, Gifted and Talented, Honors, and others. Other data that can be used to identify ways of differentiating instruction for students includes learning styles inventories, personality assessments, and observational data. These types of data can help teachers determine how to tailor instruction in a way that will support student learning and increase their academic performance.

Monitoring Curricular Programs
Ensuring Student Needs Are Met

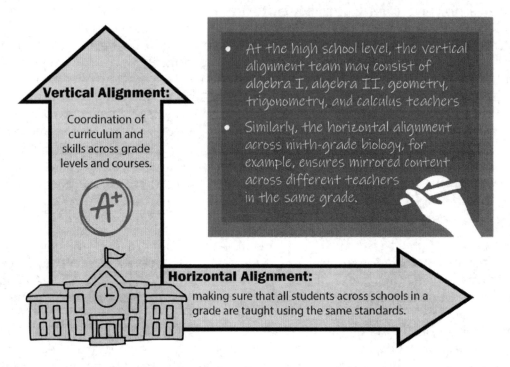

The school leader must monitor curricular programs to ensure that student needs are being met. If curricular programs do not meet student needs, students will not be successful and campus goals will not be met. The curricular program must meet the **academic and social needs** of students. For example, if a population of students on campus is consistently exceeding the performance standards on assessments, they need a curricular program that extends their learning and supports their academic growth. If the entire curricular program is centered on remediation, that group of students will not have their needs met. Campus leaders examine student needs and design the curricular program based on those needs. Such decisions may include which classes to offer, the uses of self-contained instruction or content-specific instruction, the offering of the arts and other ancillary instruction, the integration of tutorials and remediation into the school day, and many others.

Ensuring Content Standards Needs Are Met

The school leader must monitor curricular programs to ensure that they meet content standards. **Content standards** are determined by the state and are the basis for the design of **state testing**. Therefore, when curricular programs are not aligned to the content standards, students will not be prepared for state testing. If students are not prepared for state testing, they will not perform well and campus goals will not be met. Campus leaders must be mindful of how students will be assessed so that the curricular programs support instruction to adequately prepare students for those assessments. Additionally, ensuring that the campus curricular program meets content standards aids in **vertical and horizontal alignment** of instruction and curriculum both on campus and within the district. Vertical and horizontal alignment helps with collaborative planning among colleagues and ensures continuity of instruction for students, especially those with high mobility rates within the school district.

EFFECTIVELY MONITORING CURRICULAR PROGRAMS

Leaders can effectively monitor the curricular program by analyzing data, conducting observations, and soliciting feedback from stakeholders. If a curricular program is **appropriate**, student performance data in regard to content standards will be reflective of that. If students are not performing well, the campus leader may need to identify whether the curricular program has **deficits** or the programming is **mismatched** with student needs. Also, the leader can identify if the curricular program is working, based on **observations of instruction** on campus. For example, if the leader observes that students are demonstrating high levels of engagement in science courses, there may be an opportunity to expand the curricular program in science. Also, the leader can solicit **feedback** from stakeholders, such as teachers, students, and parents. These people may identify needs or strengths of the curricular program for the leader to address. For example, Language Arts teachers may identify a need to separate reading and writing instruction in the curricular program to provide students with more time for instruction in these areas.

Assessment and Accountability

EVALUATING THE QUALITY OF TEACHING ON CAMPUS

The quality of teaching on campus can be evaluated through observations and data. A school leader should spend time in the classrooms to **observe** teaching in action. A school leader will recognize effective and ineffective teaching practices. It is important to observe teaching to evaluate quality so that if corrections are necessary, these can be made in time to affect student performance. After teaching has been completed, the school leader can analyze **student performance data** to evaluate the quality of the teaching. If teaching is of good quality, the majority of students should be able to grasp the concepts and demonstrate mastery on assessments. If many students are unable to master these concepts and objectives, teaching efficacy needs to be evaluated. School leaders can use both formative and summative assessments as indicators of teaching quality.

EVALUATING THE QUALITY OF LEARNING ON CAMPUS

Student learning can be evaluated in a number of ways. A school leader can determine the quality of learning on campus through observations, feedback from students, and student performance data. When the school leader **observes classroom instruction**, he or she has the opportunity to observe students in the learning process. If students are excited about the content, are engaging significantly in the process, and are successful when checked for understanding, there is likely a high quality of learning. Also, a school leader may solicit **feedback from students** regarding their learning. This can be in the form of surveys, focus groups, or individual interviews. The students can be asked about the learning environment, the relevance of content, and the rigor of the instruction, among other quality indicators. Finally, a school leader needs to **analyze student performance data** to determine the quality of learning. If students are not meeting expectations on assessments, the quality of learning can likely be improved.

IMPROVING TEACHING ALREADY DEEMED EFFECTIVE

Even if teaching is deemed effective, there are still benefits to improving. Some school leaders focus solely on improving ineffective instruction, but that narrow focus results in a missed opportunity to develop and reinforce a **culture of high expectations** on campus. Effective instruction can become highly effective with additional support and strategies. When a school leader is committed to **improving all instruction** on campus, even instruction that is considered effective, all staff are encouraged to grow professionally for the benefit of students. This fosters an environment of **continuous improvement** and also helps teachers to seek changes in the instructional program and in student diversity. This environment also encourages innovation in the classroom to find new

and creative ways for instructing learners. Also, increasing the effectiveness of teaching can help high-performing students to grow and perform at even higher academic levels.

Addressing Ineffective Teaching

It is a school leader's responsibility to address ineffective teaching. First, the leader must **identify** ineffective teaching. This is done through observations of classroom instruction and review of student performance. Next, a leader must **communicate** to the teacher which aspects of the instruction are ineffective. A leader should be strategic in communicating areas of improvement to avoid discouraging the teacher and to focus the teacher's growth in the areas that will have the most impact on students. Then, the leader must provide the **resources and support** to improve the ineffective teaching. This can include professional development and instructional coaching. The leader should also continue to **monitor instruction** to determine if improvements are being made. In some instances, depending on the severity of the deficits in instruction, the school leader may decide to change staff's instructional assignments or even remove staff from their assignments. If staff is changed or removed, the school leader must adhere to district policies regarding staff changes.

Formative Assessments

Formative assessment is designed to **monitor student learning**. Formative assessment is useful in providing **feedback** to students so they will know which areas they need to improve and so teachers will also know areas in which to improve their teaching. The results of formative assessment may help teachers identify **instructional areas for re-teaching** or identify **students for interventions and tutorials**. Formative assessment may include checks for understanding within the classroom, classroom activities, and other guided and independent work. Formative assessments are usually activities that are low stakes, meaning that often no grade or point value is attached. For example, a teacher may ask students to represent their understanding of a concept using a graphic organizer. A teacher may also provide feedback on a pre-writing activity before a student writes an essay. Formative assessment may occur frequently and feedback should be timely in order to be relevant.

Summative Assessments

Summative assessment is used to evaluate student learning for **mastery**. Summative assessment usually occurs at the end of an instructional unit or a designated period of time such as a grading period or school year. These assessments are aligned to objectives or standards and are usually **high stakes**, which means they may count for a significant portion of the grade or may determine students' progress in their educational careers. A summative assessment may be a midterm or final exam, a research project, a unit test, or a standardized exam. The results of summative assessments may determine a student's grade promotion or earning of course credit. Results from summative assessment may also determine a school's performance according to accountability standards. Summative assessment results are often used by school leaders for **instructional planning** and **goal-setting** for the subsequent school year.

> **Review Video: Formative and Summative Assessments**
> Visit mometrix.com/academy and enter code: 804991
>
> **Review Video: Assessment Reliability and Validity**
> Visit mometrix.com/academy and enter code: 424680

Indicators of Effective Teaching

A leader can use several indicators to identify effective teaching on campus. With effective teaching, there is a clear **goal or objective** to be accomplished with the instruction. This objective is communicated to students and is evident throughout the lesson. Additionally, there is a clear **lesson cycle** throughout the instructional delivery, such as a gradual release teaching model in which students are supported throughout the learning process. When there is effective teaching, students are **engaged** in learning and demonstrate **retention** of the concepts through formative assessment. Effective instruction includes **diverse instructional strategies** to meet the needs of learners and is responsive to the results of the formative assessment conducted in the classroom. Also, effective teaching is evident in **student performance data**. Students who receive effective instruction are able to perform to standard on assessments.

Assessing Program Quality

A leader can assess program quality using data and feedback from stakeholders. **Data** that can inform a leader regarding program quality includes participation or attendance data, student performance data, and any other metrics that are collected, such as those specified by grants or state and national associations. If a program is good quality, parents and community members will **participate** in it, which is reflected in the participation and attendance data. Also, **student performance** will reflect whether a program is high quality. If student performance is below standard, this may be an indicator that the school's programming may be misaligned or below standard. Other metrics dictated by **outside agencies** may include the data relating to parent and community events, awards received, college acceptance, and others. A leader can also obtain feedback from **stakeholders**. Teachers, staff, students, and community members will generally be pleased with the implementation of a high-quality program. Low approval of the school's program may suggest that the leader needs to examine its appropriateness on campus or its implementation.

Alternative Assessment Methods

Traditional methods of assessment usually involve a standardized test with closed questions, which require students to select an answer from several choices. Educators are now trying to incorporate a greater variety of assessment methods so that students can demonstrate mastery of content and objectives in different ways. These **alternative methods** may include writing assessments, project assessments, and performance assessments. **Writing assessments** may include responding to open-ended questions or writing an essay or work of fiction. **Project assessments** typically require students to conduct extensive research and compile a final product with multiple parts or aspects. Project assessments have typically been used in science and social studies courses but are now being incorporated across the curriculum. **Performance assessments** require the student to perform in front of peers or the teacher. These may include a speech, skit, dance, or some other physical demonstration of their learning. Many of these alternative assessments are also facilitated using technology applications.

Communicating Progress Toward Goals

COMMUNICATING WITH STAFF

It is important for a school leader to communicate with staff about progress toward goals to maintain or increase **momentum**, as well as to celebrate **successes**. A leader can communicate with staff about progress toward goals through the **normal channels**: emails, employee newsletters, or staff meetings. Incorporating goal progress within these forms of communication helps the staff to view goal progress as something that is as important as the other topics that are being communicated. Also, it does not require staff to utilize a new or foreign form of communication to determine progress toward goals. However, a leader may want to publicize progress in more **public or visible ways**. These may include public announcements, posters or charts in hallways and meeting rooms, or special charts and graphs that can be shared with staff. Reaching goals or goal milestones can also be celebrated with awards, certificates, or other means.

COMMUNICATING WITH PARENTS AND COMMUNITY

A leader should communicate with parents and community about goal progress often and in a variety of ways. This can include **community meetings** in which stakeholders are invited to hear about school performance in a variety of areas, with a focus on goals. Additionally, the leader can provide a **newsletter or bulletin** to update the community on school performance, upcoming events, and ways to get involved with the school to help achieve the goals. Many schools feature phone systems that can **mass call** the homes of students, which can be used to communicate announcements regarding school goals and progress toward them. Similarly, school leaders can mail **letters** to parents with updates regarding the school goals. Progress toward school goals can also be communicated in other **meetings** that involve parents and community members, such as committee meetings, parent teacher organization meetings, and advisory board meetings.

COMMUNICATING WITH STUDENTS

Teachers can communicate with students about the school's goals and how their individual efforts and performance contribute toward achieving them. For goals that are related to student academic performance, teachers can help students take ownership of their own performance by setting **individual goals** and tracking their progress toward them. Students can be provided with **data trackers** to track their own progress toward their individual goals. Teachers can speak with students individually about the support they need to accomplish their goals. Teachers can also set **class goals** that align with campus goals and encourage students to reach them. For example, if the school has a goal of 90% proficiency in math performance, a math teacher can help students set individual goals in math. This ensures that students understand how their behaviors affect their class and school and demonstrates how they can contribute to the school's success while achieving their own success.

TWO-WAY COMMUNICATION

Two-way communication on progress toward goals is important because it provides stakeholders with the opportunity to convey to the leader why **goals** may or may not be achieved. When a leader facilitates two-way communication, he or she can receive **feedback** on the efficacy of existing strategies, ideas for additional strategies, or requests for additional resources or support. For example, if the campus has a goal to increase student proficiency in technology and the leader has purchased certain technology hardware to accomplish this goal, teachers may provide feedback that the chosen hardware has not been effective in exposing students to technology and that another type of hardware may be necessary. Additionally, two-way communication may reveal unexpected **barriers** to achieving goals. For example, a teacher may inform the leader that the technology goal may be difficult to achieve because the school technology infrastructure cannot support the increased internet usage on campus. A leader can benefit from two-way communication about progress toward goals by receiving additional information that can lead to **refining or revising goals**, or that assures the leader that the right actions have been **implemented**.

Professional Influence for Systemic Change

PROFESSIONAL EDUCATION ORGANIZATIONS AND ASSOCIATIONS

It is important for school leaders to participate in professional education organizations and associations. Many organizations have been created to **support educators** in various stages of their career. There are organizations primarily created for teachers in the classroom, even organizations specific to particular content areas. There are also organizations created specifically for **school administrators**. Additionally, school leaders may consider joining organizations related to the **field** in which they obtained their degree. These organizations provide training, information, and networking opportunities. Some offer legal help and protection as well. Most organizations charge a fee for membership, and members have access to a website, newsletters, training opportunities, job postings and leads, networking events, and much more. The information provided through these organizations can also help school leaders stay **current** on trends in education, changing laws and policies, and politics that affect the field of education. Additionally, **networking** within these professional organizations can provide opportunities for growth, advancement, and partnerships.

IMPACT OF PROFESSIONAL INFLUENCE ON THE SCHOOL

The school leader often has influence in the community due to the position of leadership. This **influence** comes from the connection to others who are in a position to support the school's vision and goals. Additionally, the size and diversity of a school leader's **network and contacts** can increase the power of that influence. The school leader's professional influence can be used to bring **positive attention and resources** to the school. For example, a school leader may know professional athletes, musicians, or actors within the community and can invite them to speak to or mentor the students on campus. Having such people on campus can inspire the youth and encourage them to succeed academically. The school leader can also use his or her influence to secure **opportunities for students** from businesses and organizations in the community, such as field trips, internships, or other educational opportunities. Finally, the school leader's professional influence can be used to **promote social justice** within the school and the community. For example, the school leader may advocate for a public library within the community.

SPHERE OF INFLUENCE

A sphere of influence refers to a leader's power to affect others, even without formal authority. School leaders have **authority** over staff and students. Staff can be reprimanded or terminated and students can be disciplined. Staff and students conform their behavior to the expectations of the leader because of the leader's authority over them. In contrast, the leader does not have authority over **parents, community members, district personnel, and other stakeholders**. However, the leader has the ability to **influence** these people through speech and other communication, as well as behavior. For example, a school leader cannot mandate that a neighborhood organization offer childcare services on campus after school because the school leader has no authority over that neighborhood organization. Instead, the school leader could use his or her influence to **encourage or persuade** the neighborhood organization to provide childcare services in partnership with the school. A school leader must recognize that when operating within the sphere of influence, skills such as understanding, compromise, persuasion, and clear communication are necessary to reach desired outcomes. This skillset differs from the skills used with those under the school leader's authority.

Educating Community Stakeholders About Local Education Processes

The purpose of educating community stakeholders about local education processes is to help them understand the reason for **local policies and procedures** and to help them engage in the **local education processes**. Community stakeholders who are uninformed or misinformed on local education processes may mistakenly assign responsibility or culpability to the school and school leader. Stakeholders should be aware of the **decision-makers** within the school district, the **processes** for decision-making, and how they can **participate** in those processes. This can help stakeholders to be effective in **enacting change** for decisions and processes that they do not agree with. For example, the school's dance program may be eliminated. Stakeholders may mistakenly believe that this was the school leader's decision when, in reality, the school district eliminated funding for these types of programs district-wide. Stakeholders should be educated regarding the **budgeting process** and how they can participate in the decision-making for district and school budgets.

State and Federal Education Processes

The purpose of educating community stakeholders about state and federal education processes is to help them understand the reason for the **laws and policies** that govern the education system and to help them engage in the **state and federal processes**. Many school policies and procedures are developed in response to state and federal laws. When community stakeholders are aware of the laws that impact their children, they are more likely to engage in the processes to **effect change**. For example, a community may believe that their students should not be subject to standardized testing. Those community members would need to be informed of the accountability laws that require assessment of students. Then the community members would be able to participate in the processes that could affect those laws in the future, such as voting.

Identifying Areas in Need of Improvement

Feedback from Students

Students can help the school leader identify areas of the school in need of improvement from the **student perspective**. This perspective is invaluable when evaluating **school programming** and **school culture**. For example, the school leader may have instituted an art program for students based on the perception that students wanted more arts on campus. Students can inform the school leader how well that art program meets their needs. They may explain that the student body was interested in digital arts rather than classical arts, therefore making the school leader's art program ineffective. Students have to abide by the **rules and policies** that school leaders design and can often provide feedback on how effective those rules and policies are. Students can inform the school leader of aspects of the school that do not enhance school safety, are deemed unfair or inequitable, or are simply ineffective. Students are also helpful in providing solutions for areas of improvement on campus.

Feedback from Teachers

Teachers can help the school leader identify areas of the school in need of **improvement** from their perspective. Teachers are responsible for **implementing** the school program the leader designs. As a result, they are often aware of needed areas of improvement that the school leader cannot see. When a school leader facilitates discussions on school improvement with teachers, they are in a position to **gather information** that they may not have discovered otherwise. For example, the teachers may point out a misalignment in the curriculum's scope and sequence and the assessment calendar, which causes the performance data to be skewed. This information can help the leader analyze data that has already been collected and devise a plan for revising the assessment calendar.

Additionally, including teachers in this discussion increases buy-in. This process allows them to voice their concerns and to identify areas of the school program that need improvement for them to do their job more easily and effectively.

Feedback from Community Stakeholders

Community stakeholders can provide the school leader with the **community perspective** of school areas in need of improvement. The school is an integral part of the community and plays a significant role in **meeting the needs of community families**. Community stakeholders can inform the school leader of areas in which the school is not meeting those needs. For example, community members may inform the school leader that school dismissal procedures are inadequate and that the school is creating disruptive traffic congestion in the community at dismissal time. The school leader can work with community members to develop a plan that is appropriate for the school and respectful of the surrounding community. Engaging community stakeholders in discussions relating to the efficacy of the school program also creates **buy-in of the school vision and goals**, as well as building relationships between the school and the community.

Feedback from District Personnel

Feedback from district personnel regarding areas of campus improvement is valuable. **District personnel** offer a unique perspective because they are able to view the school as it relates to the entire district's curricular program, mission, and goals. As a result, their perspective can help the school leader remain in alignment with **district expectations**. District personnel can also provide feedback based on how the school **compares** to other schools in the district. School leaders do not often have the opportunity to visit all the other schools within the district to gather ideas and best practices, but other district personnel can provide this perspective. Additionally, district personnel are often the people responsible for **evaluating** the school leader's performance. Addressing weak areas identified by district personnel can ensure that the leader is meeting the district's performance expectations.

Root Cause Analysis

Conducting a root cause analysis involves identifying the root cause or underlying source of a problem. A **root cause analysis** begins with identifying the problem, then systematically identifying the source of that problem with the understanding that a sequence of events or chain of causes and effects may have led to the problem's manifestation. Conducting a root cause analysis is valuable because the **main source of the problem** can be addressed rather than just the symptoms. For example, the school leader may notice that math scores are below expectations. A further analysis of the data may indicate that the majority of the low performing students have their math class in the morning. A further analysis may indicate that a significant number of students arrive late to school every day and are missing the math instruction needed to perform well on the assessments. The school leader may conclude that addressing the tardiness may help to improve math scores. Root cause analysis helps the school leader to address the right problem in order to improve outcomes.

SWOT Analysis

A SWOT analysis is a method of identifying the strengths and weaknesses of an organization in order to develop an **improvement plan**. SWOT stands for Strengths, Weaknesses, Opportunities, and Threats. The **strengths** of an organization are what provide the school with a competitive advantage over other schools. A school may be technology-rich, which is a strength. **Weaknesses** describe areas of disadvantage relative to other schools. A school may have a poor attendance rate in comparison to other schools. **Opportunities** are areas the school may be able to use by leveraging strengths to address weaknesses. The school may identify that the technology can be used to provide students with instruction at home when absent or to provide accelerated instruction when they return to school. **Threats** are aspects of the environment that the school has little or no control over but may negatively affect the school. The school may identify that the closure of a chemical plant has resulted in the layoff of many students' parents. Conducting a SWOT analysis is helpful in identifying areas of potential improvement, even for schools that are already high-performing.

AREAS TO BE EVALUATED FOR WEAKNESS

All areas of school programming should be evaluated for weaknesses. **Academic performance** is most often evaluated because this is the basis for school accountability measures. A school leader should examine the alignment of curriculum to assessments, the quality of the instruction that is delivered, and the rigor at which it is delivered. However, other aspects should also be evaluated. These include school safety, school culture, parental and family engagement, and much more. For example, a school leader should determine if school safety procedures are up-to-date and should also assess the performance of students and staff during safety drills. **School culture** can be evaluated based on student and staff perceptions as well as by the experiences and feedback of visitors on campus. Also, the school leader can identify whether the school is achieving **family engagement** on campus, if it is in the desired areas, and if it is producing the desired outcomes. There are always aspects of the school program that can be improved, so the school leader should have a mindset of continuous improvement.

USING DATA TO IDENTIFY AREAS OF WEAKNESS

Data is essential in the identification of weaknesses in the school program. Differences and changes in the data, identifying potential **areas of improvement**, may be observed. The school leader may identify **disparities** in the data between the school and others in the district. For example, the school leader may note that on a district benchmark assessment, his or her school had the lowest overall performance. Based on that data, the leader could develop a plan for improvement. Data may also reveal a disparity in performance on campus from one school year to the next, or between various groups of students. Other data that can be used to identify areas of needed improvement include student attendance data, discipline data, compliance in data reporting, staff performance or evaluation data, and more. All data collected on campus has the potential to indicate **needed improvements** in the school program. The school leader should analyze the data in comparison to other data as well as changes, trends, and gaps in the data.

Advocating for Change

PROMOTING AWARENESS AND ACTIVISM

The school leader has the influence to encourage stakeholders to lobby and use political activism to bring about change, especially in regard to social justice. The primary way that the leader can encourage engagement is by **educating** the community on present issues. The leader often has several opportunities to speak to community families en masse. These opportunities can be used to educate families about education trends and politics that will ultimately affect their community, school, and families. By **promoting awareness**, the leader can empower parents and community members to become active. The second way the school leader can encourage engagement is by showing community stakeholders how they can become **involved**. The school leader can invite community stakeholders to be active in bringing about change by writing letters, sending emails, making phone calls, or engaging with political leaders.

CAUTION FOR POLITICAL ACTIVISM

In the school leader's efforts to advocate for students and for social justice, the school leader must engage carefully. Most school districts have **guidelines** for how a school leader can represent him or herself in the community while representing the school district. These guidelines usually apply in regard to supporting specific political parties or candidates, persuading others how to vote in elections, and various other activities. A school leader must identify what actions they are allowed or not allowed to take while in the position of leader. Outside of school hours, the leader may have additional freedom to engage in such activities, but must still be aware of how his or her **influence and authority** are used in such activities. The school leader should consult with the school district or the leadership of their professional organizations regarding the implications of **political engagement** prior to doing so.

Trends in Education

TECHNOLOGY

ONE-TO-ONE TECHNOLOGY MODEL

The one-to-one technology model is the practice of providing a **device or access to technology** to each student on campus. As technology use has increased in schools, access to technology has been a focal point to aid in student performance and growth. In many instances, school leaders calculate the **ratio** of computers or devices to students. For example, the school may purchase enough computers to ensure that there is one computer for every 10 students. When there are not enough devices on campus for every student, computer and internet access may be limited due to the need to share technology on campus. This may be done by equipping classrooms with a limited number of computers, making laptop carts available, or creating computer labs, all of which must be shared by teachers and students. With the one-to-one technology model, the ratio of technology to students is **one device for each student**. This allows **maximum access to technology** on campus. These devices are usually personal laptop computers or tablets. In some instances, the students are entrusted with the technology and are permitted to take the devices home for technology access outside of school hours.

BRING-YOUR-OWN-DEVICE TECHNOLOGY MODEL

The bring-your-own-device technology model describes the practice of allowing students to bring their own **technology devices** to school for use in classroom instruction. Many families provide their children with computers, tablets, and phones that can access the internet. When this model is implemented, students can bring these devices to school and use them to participate in computer-based or web-based activities. The bring-your-own-device model is **beneficial** because it saves schools from purchasing the number of devices necessary for every student to have access. The **downside** of this model is that the school is not responsible for the care or repair of students' devices, not all students have a device, and there is often difficulty in designing lessons compatible with various types of technology. For example, there are different specifications for playing videos on tablets, laptops, and phones, which can be challenging to a teacher attempting to incorporate videos into the lesson. Also, this model has **limited efficacy** in impoverished communities, in which the majority of students do not have access to these devices.

VIRTUAL SCHOOL MODEL

The virtual school model is the practice of providing **online courses** to students, using a web-based platform or other computer-based program rather than physically attending a class. A student has access to instructional content online and participates in activities and tests to assess learning. In some virtual school models, students have **virtual access to a teacher**. In other models, the computer program is **automated** and student progress may be self-paced. Virtual school has been used in all grade levels as a supplement to traditional instruction or as a replacement. Virtual school can also be utilized for students who are home schooled. When used as a supplement to traditional classes, students may use virtual school to make up failed courses, participate in tutorials or interventions, or to access courses that are not offered on campus. The virtual school model requires that students have access to a technology device and internet service. Many **businesses** also develop platforms and coursework for virtual schools. Most commonly, courses focus on the core content areas of reading, math, social studies, and science, but many learning platforms offer electives and tutorial programs.

BLENDED LEARNING

Blended learning is the process of incorporating **technology use** into **traditional classroom instruction**. In the blended learning model, teachers identify places in the lesson that can be **supplemented** with technology or in which technology can be used to drive the lesson. In this model, the teacher may use the technology in the lesson, but the focus is on students utilizing technology in the classroom. For example, a teacher may deliver content on a topic and then assess students' understanding with an online assessment tool. In the blended learning model, technology can be used to deliver content, such as accessing information through reading and videos or by creating slideshows or other presentations. Technology can be used to **assess** student learning as well. Blended learning models are often paired with **project-based learning models**. This allows students the freedom and opportunity to use the technology with limited guidance by the teacher to meet lesson objectives. In the blended learning model, technology use is **flexible**, so it may vary by content area or lesson as teachers still implement traditional instructional strategies.

> **Review Video: Benefits of Technology in the Classroom**
> Visit mometrix.com/academy and enter code: 536375

SCHOOL DISCIPLINE
ROLE OF MEDITATION IN SCHOOLS

Meditation is the act of engaging in quiet and silent thought or reflection. This practice has been used in schools as a strategy for **redirecting poor student behavior**. When a student breaks a school rule or disrupts class, rather than discipline with in-school suspension, out-of-school suspension, or other traditional consequences, the student is instructed to **meditate**. When students are given the opportunity to meditate, they are placed in a quiet environment where they can focus on calming down, breathing, and thinking about appropriate behaviors to display. Schools that have implemented meditation as a discipline strategy have seen a decrease in suspension rates and fewer discipline referrals from teachers. The practice of meditation is thought to alleviate **emotional issues** such as anxiety, anger, depression, and frustration, which could be sources of student misbehavior.

CHALLENGES OF PROMOTING SCHOOL SAFETY

It is a school leader's primary responsibility to keep students safe while at school. This responsibility can be challenging for a variety of reasons. Recent acts of school violence have caused educators and government officials to revisit laws, policies, and procedures relating to school safety. In some schools, **metal detectors** are used to promote school safety, but some deem that practice to be controversial. As schools are built or remodeled, **school designs** include limited entrances and exits to the school building and compartmentalized front office areas that can prevent unauthorized people from gaining entrance into the school. Other strategies include staffing **uniformed police officers** on campus during school hours, implementing **standardized dress**, and limiting **backpacks and other large bags** on campuses. Additionally, many schools practice **drills** for emergencies, such as having an intruder on campus. Promoting school safety is challenging because even the best preventative measures cannot guarantee that nothing will threaten the safety of students and staff.

Curricular Programming
Accelerated Learning

Accelerated learning is the practice of delivering content to students at an **accelerated pace**. For example, a traditional high school course that is delivered during an 18-week semester may be condensed into six or nine weeks. The purpose of accelerated learning is to provide students with **additional learning opportunities**. For example, if a student is already proficient in math, it can be reasoned that he or she should not have to sit through an 18-week course. Accelerated learning is also useful for students who have previously taken a course but were unsuccessful. These accelerated classes may be offered during summer breaks or built into the school's instructional program. Accelerated programs are often facilitated with **technology-based programs**, which can personalize and deliver content based on a student's needs. For example, a student enrolled in an accelerated course may take a pre-assessment online and then be assigned coursework based on assessment performance. A student would not have to complete coursework in areas of the course in which mastery is demonstrated.

School-Within-a-School Model

A school-within-a-school model describes the creation of a specialized school program to be operated on the **same campus** as the traditional school program. The students participating in the specialized program are still students of the school, but may have limited or no interaction with the rest of the student body. For example, a high school may implement an engineering-based program on campus to which students must apply and be accepted. Students participating in this program will attend school on campus, but their classes, course pathways, and other activities are **separate** from the remainder of the student body. A school may have several schools within the school or just one. Each of these schools may be designated with its own budget, programming, and administration. In most models, the schools are still identified as one school for state and federal accountability purposes. However, some schools and school districts have extended the model and created an entirely separate school housed on the same campus. In these instances, the school programs are separate and only share the use of the school facilities.

Project-Based Learning

Project-based learning is the instructional practice of assigning projects to students as a means of driving instruction. In **project-based learning**, students are presented with a problem that must be solved. They are usually assigned to **groups or teams** for completion of the project. To solve this problem, students have to learn content, usually from more than one content area, and demonstrate **mastery of a variety of objectives and skills**. The teacher who has assigned the project delivers certain content to students and often provides access to designated resources. Students are responsible for extending their learning and conducting research, using the available resources and the internet. The project is generally complex and can take as little as a few days to complete, or an entire school semester. With more complex project assignments, teachers expect students to demonstrate mastery of a greater number of learning objectives. Therefore, there may be multiple performance expectations for the project, such as papers, presentations, and more. Some schools integrate project-based learning into the curriculum, while other schools have designed their entire curriculum around project-based learning.

Flipped Classroom Model

A flipped classroom model describes the instructional practice of changing the **delivery** of instructional content and the opportunities for **guided practice** within the lesson cycle. In a traditional classroom, a teacher delivers the content and may provide limited guided practice on an in-class assignment. The student may be assigned extended practice independently within the class or in the form of homework. In a flipped classroom model, the student is provided with the instructional content **electronically**, typically in the form of a recorded lecture or presentation video to watch outside of the classroom. In the classroom, the time that would have been dedicated to delivering content is used to support the student in **guided practice**. This allows the students more time and access to the teacher during the aspect of the lesson in which they are likely to need the teacher's guidance the most. This practice is considered a flipped classroom because in essence the lesson is done at home and the homework is done at school. Many schools have incorporated flipped lessons into their curriculum sparingly, while other schools have transformed their entire curricular program using the flipped classroom.

CHARTER SCHOOLS

A charter school is a specialized public school that operates according to a **charter** with a local or national organization. The charter may dictate how the school operates and whom it serves. Charter schools are **publicly funded**, which means they have to meet state and/or federal accountability standards. However, unlike traditional public schools, charter schools do not obtain funding from **local taxes**. Attending a charter school is free to students and their parents, but there may be an application or entrance requirements. Charter schools provide communities with additional options for educating their children. Some charter schools specialize in serving at-risk youth, a particular gender, certain career paths, or other niche areas. Proponents of charter schools view these schools as an additional option for students, especially if the community schools are not meeting their needs. However, opponents of charter schools believe that these schools take funding, enrollment, and support away from neighborhood schools.

MIDDLE COLLEGES

Middle colleges are **alternative high school programs** that are operated on community campuses. The purpose of a middle college is to provide an alternative environment for high school students and facilitate **independent student learning**. Students who attend middle colleges are given freedoms and liberty similar to college students and may even have a shorter school day or flexible school schedule. The school is operated by school district staff and students take their traditional high school courses, but they are also given the opportunity to take **college-level courses** taught by **community college professors**. Middle colleges often appeal to students who do not fit in with the environment or culture at their traditional school or who seek to earn college course credits while still in high school. Some middle colleges are designed and funded as charter schools while others are developed and operated as part of the traditional public-school system.

PERSONALIZED LEARNING

Personalized learning is the instructional strategy of tailoring academic content and instruction to students based on their individual needs. **Personalization** can be achieved based on a student's learning styles, personality, interests, career goals, and academic progress. Providing personalized learning can be complex, so much is implemented with **computer programs**. Before personalization can occur, a student must be **assessed** on content relative to the type of personalization. For example, if learning will be personalized based on a student's learning style, he or she may take a learning style inventory. Based on the inventory results, a personal learning plan will be developed. The purpose of personalized learning is to address the **individual needs** of the student, with the goal of helping him or her achieve **academic growth and success**. Instruction may be differentiated based on the content the student receives, how the content is delivered, how the student is expected to engage with the content, the pace of progress through the content, and how students demonstrate mastery of the content. Personalized learning often accompanies **technology implementation models** such as one-to-one technology.

FLEXIBLE SCHOOL DAY

In a traditional school day, students report to school at a certain time in the morning, remain at school for nearly seven hours, and are then dismissed in the afternoon. A **flexible school day** modifies this traditional schedule to **accommodate** students and their families. There are many variations of the flexible school day, which may include attending a four-hour block of school at some scheduled time throughout the day, attending school in the evenings, or attending school at unscheduled times and accumulating hours over the course of a school week. A flexible school day is especially beneficial to students who are at risk of dropping out or have dropped out of school in the past. These students may have personal obligations that make it difficult to attend school on a traditional schedule, such as working full-time or caring for a child. Implementing a flexible school day is beneficial to the school and to students because students can attend school in a way that meets their individual needs and the school can help students complete their academic expectations for accountability purposes.

COLLEGE AND CAREER READINESS
DUAL-CREDIT ENROLLMENT

Dual-credit enrollment is a curricular program designed to give students the opportunity to earn **college credits** while they are still in high school. The program is called **dual-credit** because students enroll in high school and college at the same time. To participate, students must meet entry requirements for the **local community college**. This usually involves earning a specific score on an exam for math and reading. Once admitted to the college program, students take core courses that earn high school and college credits **simultaneously**. For example, a student may take a Freshman English 1301 course at the college level, which will also earn credit for the high school English year four requirement. The number of college credits that students may earn depends on the school-college partnership and availability of courses, but many schools offer the opportunity to earn an **associate's degree** while students are still in high school. This saves students and their families money in college tuition and also increases the likelihood that students will persist in college and earn degrees. These college classes can be taught on the high school campus by a qualified teacher or a visiting professor, or the students may travel to the local community college for part of the school day.

ADVANCE PLACEMENT COURSES

Advanced placement courses are college-level courses that are taught to high school students. **Advanced placement (AP) courses** contain the content of college-level courses and are taught with college-level rigor by teachers who meet certain qualifications. These courses are usually core content courses such as reading, math, science, or social studies. Students remain on the high school campus to take these courses and receive **high school credit** for successful course completion. However, students also have an opportunity to take an exam at the end of each course that can qualify them to earn **college credit**. If the student achieves an acceptable test score, he or she will earn college credit for that course, which is transferrable to most colleges or universities. Students may participate in a combination of AP and dual-credit courses to increase the number of college credits they can earn while still in high school. This saves students and their families money in college tuition and also increases the likelihood that they will persist in college and earn degrees.

INTERNATIONAL BACCALAUREATE PROGRAMS

An **International Baccalaureate (IB) program** is a rigorous school curricular program that has been implemented in schools across the world. In order to participate in this program and to be recognized as an IB school, schools must meet certain program requirements and be monitored and evaluated regularly. The authorization process can take two to three years. As an IB school, schools receive **professional development** and participate in the **international network** of IB schools.

Additionally, students who attend IB schools often demonstrate higher levels of academic success when compared to schools without IB programs. This is due to the **specialized curriculum** offered as well as the **higher level of rigor** in IB schools. Students also have the opportunity to become more culturally aware and sensitive due to their acquisition of a **second language** as part of the program and their exposure to other students around the world.

ROLE OF CAREER PATHWAYS IN SCHOOLS

Career pathways are specific tracks that students can participate in to prepare them for specific career fields or jobs. These tracks or pathways include **coursework** that is relevant to a student's chosen field. For example, if a student is interested in a career pathway for law and public office, his or her pathway may include more reading, writing, and social studies courses than students in other career pathways, as well as more elective courses related to the skills necessary to be successful in that career. **All school levels** can implement career pathways. In elementary schools, the delineation between the various pathways may not be as defined as in high schools, but it can lay the foundation for future studies. For example, a student in a fine arts career pathway from elementary school to high school would likely have an advantage over students who did not participate in a career pathway but are interested in fine arts due to the general exposure to and participation in fine arts related coursework. Some state accountability systems require high school students to identify career pathways as part of **graduation requirements**.

ACCOUNTABILITY

STUDENT GROWTH

Student growth has become a focus in school accountability. In years past, **student performance** has been the sole focus. As a result, educators primarily focused on students who were likely to perform well on high-stakes tests. As a result, students who were not likely to pass these tests were **underserved**, along with students who would likely pass the test regardless of teacher intervention and support. In contrast, a focus on **student growth** and accountability for such growth means that educators must serve all students. Even if a student does not pass a state-mandated test, growth in performance must be demonstrated. This growth is often measured against a prediction of how the student is expected to perform, based on assessment data from previous years. To ensure that schools are adequately educating all students, **accountability standards** incorporate measures of student growth in addition to measuring student performance.

STUDENT PERFORMANCE

Student performance in school accountability describes how students perform on **state-mandated assessments**. A certain percentage of students must pass these tests for a school to be deemed acceptable. This performance is evaluated in each **core content area**, depending on the accountability system, but most frequently in reading and math. The performance standards and content areas evaluated can vary based on grade level and can also change with federal or state legislature. A school that performs well in one subject and not in another is still a failing school. Additionally, to ensure that all students are performing well and not just certain groups of students, school performance is evaluated for particular **subgroups** of students, based on demographics. These demographics may include race or ethnicity, socioeconomic status, special education status, limited English proficiency status, and more.

CURRENT FEDERAL LEGISLATION

The most recent legislation related to public school accountability is the **Every Student Succeeds Act (ESSA)**, which was enacted in 2015 during President Obama's administration. This legislation replaced the **No Child Left Behind (NCLB) Act** of 2002, enacted during President Bush's administration. ESSA provides more flexibility to states by allowing individual states to provide plans for addressing **key educational goals** such as closing the achievement gap, ensuring and increasing equity in schools, improving the quality of instruction in schools, and improving growth and performance outcomes for all students. However, the basis of the law remains the same as that of NCLB. All students should have **full educational opportunity**. Consequently, there is a remaining focus on serving low-income students, students with special needs, and other students who have traditionally been marginalized in the public school system.

Failure to Meet Accountability Standards

Schools that do not meet accountability standards may be subject to local, state, or federal **sanctions**. For a first-time failure, consequences may not be severe. The school will likely have to provide **notice** to parents and the community that accountability standards were not met. The school may then have to develop a **formal plan** that outlines changes to help meet accountability standards the following year. Many school districts have strategies and supports in place for schools that do not meet accountability standards. Additionally, the state and federal government provide **resources** for these schools. The goal is not to punish school staff but to provide the resources and supports necessary to increase the likelihood of student success. This may include training and professional development, consulting staff, curriculum, and more. However, schools that **consistently fail to meet accountability standards** may experience more severe consequences. These may include changing or removing staff, changing the school leader, implementing specialized or stringent school programming, or even closing the school.

Decreasing Student Dropout Rates

A school's dropout rate is measured for school accountability. Additionally, dropouts miss their educational opportunity. Consequently, many school leaders are developing creative ways to **decrease dropout rates**. To encourage students to remain in school, leaders are implementing more engaging **curricular programs** and featuring **career pathways** and opportunities to earn **college credit**. Other strategies include providing mentoring programs, offering a variety of extracurricular activities besides sports, and providing counseling and other mental health services. Also, some schools offer **accelerated school programming** to potential or recovered dropouts in an effort to help them to graduate more quickly. To encourage dropouts to return to school, schools are providing assistance, support, and resources to **families**. This type of support often requires partnership with other **organizations** within the community. School leaders and other school staff often visit homes in the community to persuade students who have dropped out to return to school.

Chapter Quiz

Ready to see how well you retained what you just read? Scan the QR code to go directly to the chapter quiz interface for this study guide. If you're using a computer, simply visit the bonus page at **mometrix.com/bonus948/nystcescbl109110** and click the Chapter Quizzes link.

School Culture and Learning Environment to Promote Excellence, Equity, and Social Justice

Transform passive reading into active learning! After immersing yourself in this chapter, put your comprehension to the test by taking a quiz. The insights you gained will stay with you longer this way. Scan the QR code to go directly to the chapter quiz interface for this study guide. If you're using a computer, simply visit the bonus page at **mometrix.com/bonus948/nystcescbl109110** and click the Chapter Quizzes link.

Culture of Learning

A culture of learning is an environment with an emphasis on learning and a high expectation for academic achievement. It involves intellectual stimulation for students, staff, and leadership. Evidence of a **culture of learning** includes implementing effective classroom instructional strategies for student learning, implementing processes of continuous improvement to increase student learning and academic performance, participating in professional development for teachers and staff collectively and individually, and the acquiring and sharing of knowledge by leadership. When a culture of learning is present, school leaders seek ways to support the learning needs of all students so all can be **academically successful**. School leaders also seek ways to support the learning needs of **teachers and staff** to assist them in their professional growth.

FUNDAMENTAL ELEMENTS OF A CULTURE OF LEARNING

It is the leader's goal to develop a culture of learning on campus. The leader must incorporate this goal into the school vision and goals. As a result, when there is **evidence of a culture of learning** on campus, this is also evidence that the leader's vision and goals are being implemented. In a culture of learning, both adults and students work toward **learning goals** and are self-motivated to achieve these goals. They also have access to the necessary **resources** to support and drive engagement in the learning process. Evidence of the culture of learning includes **students and staff** who are goal-oriented and self-motivated to learn and engage in the learning process, who have motivation to perform at the highest levels academically, and who perform skilled use of available resources to engage in the learning process. When these are present, it will be evident that the vision and goals can be accomplished.

DEVELOPING A CULTURE OF LEARNING

To develop a culture of learning on campus, a school leader must consider this culture in all decision-making. First, the school should be **designed** in a way that facilitates a culture of learning. This means that there are sufficient **learning spaces** to accommodate a variety of learning strategies, along with furniture and resources that support those learning spaces. For example, there should be a library resource center with appropriate shelving, books, and technology resources. A school leader must also hire and train **staff** in a way that supports a culture of learning. Candidates for hire that do not support a culture of learning should not be selected. The leader must also communicate **expectations** for a culture of learning to staff, students, parents, and community stakeholders to ensure that everyone is aware of the expectations. When possible, the leader can support the school's culture by encouraging **families** to develop their own culture of learning and providing the resources and support for them to do so. For example, the leader may give books to families to encourage reading in the home.

School Vision and Goals

SCHOOL VISION

The school vision serves as a guide and a foundation for all strategic planning and communicates the **purpose** and **focus** of the school to all stakeholders. One of the goals of a school leader is to create a culture of learning on campus. Including this concept in the school vision can help to communicate the importance of cultivating a culture of learning to all stakeholders. Also, the school vision will help to guide the creation of **goals** that lead to the development of this culture. A school vision that includes this focus will ensure that school goals are aligned with a culture of learning and will help to establish and maintain the culture. When the school vision clearly incorporates a culture of learning, it will be apparent to all stakeholders that this is a key part of the school's purpose and focus.

SCHOOL GOALS

School goals help to determine where to devote energy and resources. When leaders set goals, they identify the necessary **resources** for achieving them. Goals must be aligned with the **characteristics** and **outcomes** of a culture of learning to ensure that the available resources, such as staff, funds, and time, are used to develop and maintain this culture. Rather than diverting resources to various competing goals, this will maximize the use of resources and effort. When a leader uses school goals to support a culture of learning, the culture will be strengthened as school goals are attained. The various aspects of a culture of learning can be incorporated into the school goals. For example, school goals can include high expectations for academic performance, goals related to college and career readiness for students, and implementation of student-centered instructional strategies for teachers.

STUDENT-CENTERED SCHOOL GOALS

A leader can employ several strategies to ensure that school goals are student-centered. First, goals should be designed with **student outcomes** as a focus. These can include any outcome that is measured in terms of student-related data, such as academic performance or attendance. For example, a school leader may develop a school goal of increasing the campus attendance rate to 99% for the school year. This goal is directly related to a student outcome and the strategies that would be implemented to achieve this goal would directly benefit students. Second, all school goals should directly **impact students**. When developing goals, it is appropriate to ask how accomplishing the goal would impact students, as well as how students would be affected if the goal were not accomplished. If there is no impact to students, the goal is likely not student-centered. Third, goals should be developed with the purpose of **benefitting all students**. Student-centered goals do not marginalize or omit groups of students but benefit all students. For example, a school leader might set a school goal to increase test performance in reading for all students, not just those who have demonstrated deficiencies in prior performance.

Student Centered Goals
1. Focus on Student Outcomes
   - academic
   - attendance
2. Directly impact
3. Benefit all students

PURPOSE OF A SCHOOL VISION

The purpose of a school vision is to convey the **direction** of the school to all stakeholders. A vision is a message or statement that describes how a leader envisions the school in the future. Through the school vision, the school's **focus** and **priorities** can be conveyed to all stakeholders, including staff, students, and the community. The school vision should inspire and motivate teachers and staff to pursue the school's goals. The school vision also provides direction for the teachers and staff in decision-making processes. All **strategic planning** should be guided by the school vision so that all goals and plans are designed with the purpose of achieving this vision. An example of a school vision is as follows: Our vision at XYZ Middle School is to equip and prepare students to be college and career ready, life-long learners, and responsible global citizens who are exemplary examples of the core values of respect, integrity, and perseverance.

Data-Informed Goals and Vision

TYPES OF DATA USED TO DEVELOP A SCHOOL VISION

The majority of data that an education leader will have access to and be expected to analyze is **quantitative data**. This includes student academic performance data, attendance data, demographics, and many other key data points. Quantitative data can be analyzed using mathematical processes and can be represented in numerical form. For example, a school leader may calculate that the campus attendance rate is 96.8% annually or that 1 out of every 10 students receives special education services. Quantitative data can provide answers to "what" or "who" questions, but it cannot provide answers regarding "why" or "how." To understand why the data appears as it does, it is important for leaders to gather **qualitative data** from students, staff, and stakeholders. Qualitative data reflects opinions, perceptions, feelings, and assumptions. For example, a school leader may receive student concern about bullying on campus, or parents and community members may communicate to the school leader that the staff do not seem friendly. Quantitative and qualitative data should be used together to develop the vision for the school.

Sources of Data

There are many sources of quantitative and qualitative data that a leader can use to develop a school vision. Sources of **quantitative data** include student academic performance data, attendance data, demographics, and other key data points. **Student academic performance data** is frequently used in developing a vision. Leaders can obtain this data from historical standardized test performance data, beginning-of-the year assessments in a variety of academic areas, teacher-assigned grades for classroom performance, and benchmark assessments. **Qualitative data** can be obtained from observations of teachers and students, feedback from teachers and students, focus groups, anonymous surveys, and other information from stakeholders. This type of information tells the education leader about school culture, values, attitudes, and beliefs. It should be used as a frame for understanding the quantitative data in order to gain a complete picture of the school's status.

Aligning School Goals with School Vision

The school vision describes how the leadership envisions the school in the future, and the school goals are the ways that the school will accomplish that vision. Each **school goal** should clearly demonstrate that by accomplishing the goal, the campus will be closer to realizing its **vision**. For example, a school may state in its vision that it will be a premier STEM (Science, Technology, Engineering, and Math) school. School leaders should work toward that vision by setting ambitious goals in the areas of science, technology, engineering, and math. **Aligned goals** could include the academic performance of students in these subject areas, increasing STEM course offerings, recruiting students for the STEM program, or earning awards and recognition in STEM competitions. An **unaligned goal** could be expanding the fine arts program. Aligning school goals with the school vision will ensure that all resources and energies are devoted to realizing the vision.

Using Data from Multiple Sources

It is important to use data from multiple sources to develop the school vision and goals because one source may portray a **limited** or **skewed** picture of the school. Using multiple sources can confirm the **validity** of data and provide a more complete picture of the complex dynamics of a school campus. For example, a school leader may obtain past academic data showing that fifth grade students have consistently performed at an advanced level. However, additional data may demonstrate that these students were already performing at an advanced level prior to fifth grade and were not growing academically. Additionally, using multiple sources of data can help a leader identify specific areas for **improvement** so that goals are targeted. For example, a leader of a high school may find that incoming ninth-grade students are consistently performing below standard in math. However, investigating which middle schools these students attended may reveal that the struggling students all attended the same middle school. Instead of assuming that math was an area of deficit for the ninth-grade class, this additional data could lead to a more specific goal in which resources are targeted.

Involving Stakeholders in Developing Vision

TYPES OF STAKEHOLDERS

Stakeholders include anyone who has an interest in or is vested in the school. The **primary stakeholders** in schools are the **children** because they are most directly impacted by the decisions made regarding the school, so they should be engaged in the development of the school vision. Another significant group of stakeholders includes the school's **faculty and staff** because they are also directly impacted by the decisions. Other stakeholders include parents, district personnel, school board members, community members, and community business partners. A leader can involve these stakeholders in the development of the school vision by soliciting their **opinions and feedback**. This can be done through one-on-one interviews, focus groups, and community meetings, among other methods, to obtain their perspectives. Stakeholders can be motivated to engage in the development of the school vision when the school leader communicates a desire for their involvement and demonstrates respect for their input and opinions. This requires the school leader to devote time and opportunity to meet with various stakeholders and to engage in conversation regarding the school vision.

USING A VARIETY OF PERSPECTIVES

It is important to involve stakeholders in the development of the school vision to incorporate a variety of perspectives and to increase buy-in for the vision. Often, school leaders who are in the process of developing a vision for the school are new to the position, so they cannot be expected to know every aspect of the school dynamics or all the nuances of the campus. It is important to involve stakeholders in the process of developing the vision so that the leader can have as much information as possible. Also, including stakeholders in the process creates **buy-in**. If stakeholders believe that their feelings and opinions have been disregarded in the creation of the vision, they may disengage from the goals aligned to that vision or even oppose it. A leader wants all stakeholders to be **advocates** of the school vision, so stakeholders must be included in the development of the school vision.

REACHING CONSENSUS AMONG STAKEHOLDERS

When engaging stakeholders in the development of the school vision and goals, it can be a challenge to reach **consensus**, especially when viewpoints seem to conflict. It is important for a school leader to clearly communicate how consensus will be fairly achieved. Stakeholders who are aware of the process for providing input before participating will know what to expect and are more likely to be receptive to **compromise** in the event of dissension. Additionally, the leader must be **respectful** of all input and must acknowledge opinions and perspectives, even if they are not aligned with his or her own or the majority. Incorporating **voting processes**, such as an anonymous ballot or online survey, can facilitate the use of the majority's viewpoints without identifying dissenters. Finally, the school leader must convey that, although the stakeholders' input is valued and will be considered, he or she still retains the ultimate **responsibility** for decision-making.

Goals that Meet Diverse Needs

ADDRESSING EQUITY ISSUES

When developing the school vision and goals, a school leader must ensure that all students—regardless of race, religion, academic background, or education access—will be **successful**. When collecting data to inform the development of the school vision and goals, a school leader should determine whether any groups of students have been **disenfranchised** in the past and, if so, how the school vision and goals can be designed to prevent that disenfranchisement from happening in the future. For example, a school leader may find that historically students who are of limited English proficiency (LEP) have not performed as well as their peers in math on standardized tests. This may necessitate the design of additional goals to support the improvement of LEP students in math. Equity does not mean equality. **Equity** means that some groups of students may need additional resources and support in order for them to meet performance standards. The school vision and goals must take into account the strengths and needs of all students so that all can receive an equitable education and be successful.

IDENTIFYING THE DIVERSE NEEDS OF STUDENTS

Students have diverse needs, and not all of these needs can be predicted based on the students' demographic groups. For example, not all students in poverty have the same needs, nor do all students who speak limited English. The school leader should make an effort to **identify student needs** so they can be addressed in the development of the school's vision and goals. A leader can identify these needs by speaking directly to **students**. This gives students the opportunity to articulate their own needs. Also, the leader can speak with **families** to identify additional student needs. This is particularly helpful when students are young and cannot accurately identify their own needs. Finally, the school leader can observe students in the school and identify **deficit areas** of the school program. For example, the school leader may notice that many students arrive late to school and are tired and hungry when they arrive. The school leader can then use observational data to inform the development of the school goals and vision.

Implementing Vision and Goals

DEVELOPING AN IMPLEMENTATION PLAN

To achieve a school vision and goals, a plan must be in place. A well-constructed plan serves as a **guide** for how the goals will be accomplished. Having a plan conveys to stakeholders that the vision and goals are feasible and instills confidence in the campus administration. A plan also serves as a **framework** for directing the actions of a leadership team and campus faculty and staff. Additionally, a leader cannot be everywhere all the time, so having a plan in place ensures that **progress** can be made, even in the leader's absence. Finally, having a plan helps to keep the efforts of leadership and staff **focused**. Many aspects of a school campus can become distractions to the primary goals, and these distractions can cause leaders to divert resources and efforts to the wrong areas. A plan keeps efforts and resources focused and purposeful, which increases the plan's chance of being effective.

COMPONENTS OF AN EFFECTIVE PLAN

An effective plan should include action steps, people responsible, time frames, milestones, resources needed, and evidence of implementation. The **action steps** in a plan should clearly outline what needs to be done to accomplish the plan. These steps should be broken down so that someone who did not participate in developing the plan can understand what needs to be done. An effective plan also identifies the **people responsible** for each aspect of the plan. If no one is held accountable for the actions to accomplish the plan, they likely will not get done. The plan should also be **time bound**. This will help to identify whether the plan is on track for completion. **Milestones** serve as checkpoints that also help to determine the progress of the plan. The plan will include the **resources needed** to accomplish it so that these resources are planned for and obtained. This will prevent delay in accomplishing the plan. Finally, the **evidence of implementation** should be included in the plan so that ongoing monitoring can take place. Evidence of implementation could include documents, visible indicators, or regular meetings, depending on the aspect of the plan.

POTENTIAL BARRIERS TO IMPLEMENTING VISION AND GOALS

Both expected and unexpected barriers may arise when implementing the vision and goals. It can be **expected** that stakeholders who did not wholeheartedly agree with the creation of the vision and goals may be reluctant to implement the plan to achieve them. This can be a barrier because a lack of support for or direct opposition to the vision and goals can delay progress. Many **unexpected barriers** may also arise. These may include changes in district policy and procedure, changes in state law, shortfalls in school budgets, and staff changes, among others. For example, standardized test performance expectations or adoption of a new test can affect goals. Additionally, the loss of a teacher or the promotion of a leadership team member could also affect the successful implementation of the vision and goals. Some school districts have experienced unexpected loss of instructional time due to inclement weather conditions, creating a barrier to accomplishing school goals.

TYPES OF BARRIERS TO IMPLEMENTING VISION AND GOALS

When planning the implementation of the school vision and goals, the school leader may encounter barriers that will slow the planning process. One barrier is attempting to **analyze too much data**. Data is valuable to the planning process, but an abundance of data can become overwhelming and delay progress. The school leader must identify what data is needed and what can be put aside. Another barrier is the **lack of consensus** from other stakeholders who are providing input to the development of the plan. Stakeholders such as community members, parents, and staff may have conflicting ideas and suggestions related to the development of the vision and goals. The leader must determine which feedback to incorporate in the plan, as not all ideas are sound or can be prioritized. Finally, a barrier that can be difficult to overcome is **garnering support** for the implementation of change on campus. In most instances, a school leader will be appointed in the place of a predecessor who already had a school vision and goals in place. Stakeholders may be resistant to drastic changes in the school vision and goals, so the school leader must overcome these objections to do what is best for the students.

OVERCOMING POTENTIAL BARRIERS

A leader can employ various strategies to overcome potential barriers to implementing the vision and goals effectively. To **overcome a lack of support** for the vision and goals, the leader can include as many stakeholders as possible in their development. This will increase buy-in and communicate the vision and goals often so that stakeholders are reminded of the school's focus. A leader can also include **strategies** in the action plan to address potential barriers, such as loss of staff. For example, a leader can designate teams, rather than individuals, to work on components of the plan. Therefore, if a staff member is lost, other team members can continue implementation of a goal. The leader can also consider **actions or contingency plans** to enact if barriers arise. For example, if a goal requires a designated number of new computers, a leader may consider what to do if a budget shortfall allows for the purchase of only half of the computers.

LEADING BY EXAMPLE

Leading by example can support the implementation of the school vision and goals by inspiring others, conveying priorities, and garnering support from stakeholders. When a leader sets an **example of expected behavior**, staff and students will be inspired to participate and to follow the leader's example, **implementing** the vision and goals in the same way as their leader. This increases the effort devoted to accomplishing the vision and goals. When the leader engages in behaviors that implement the vision and goals, this conveys to stakeholders that the vision and goals are **priorities** because this is where the leader chooses to devote time. When a leader's priorities are clear to stakeholders, it is easier for the leader to encourage them to participate in those prioritized activities and to implement action plans related to those priorities. For example, if a leader makes it evident through his or her own actions that reading instruction is a priority for the campus, then stakeholders will expect and support further initiatives relating to reading instruction. In contrast, when a leader's actions do not match the goals and vision, this results in a mixed message to stakeholders.

ALIGNING HUMAN, FISCAL, AND MATERIAL RESOURCES

The strategies and initiatives for implementing the school vision and goals require **resources**, so a leader must ensure that all human, fiscal, and material resources are aligned to the vision and goals. **Aligning resources to the vision and goals** will ensure fewer barriers to implementation. In contrast, when resources are not aligned to the vision and goals, not only will leaders find it difficult to implement the mission and vision, they will also find that their efforts are diverted to the other areas that the resources have been devoted to. This results in a less significant **impact** of those resources for the benefit of students and the campus as a whole. For example, if the vision for the school is to have state-of-the-art technology for classroom instruction, the leader must ensure that there are qualified staff members who are able to utilize the technology, funds for the purchase of technology hardware and software, and additional resources such as storage and server space for the additional technology. If any aspect of the resources is **misaligned**, there is a possibility that the goal or vision will not be obtained.

DELEGATING

A leader cannot do an effective job without support. In order to balance the duties and responsibilities of being a campus leader, an effective leader must identify tasks and activities that can be **delegated** to other leadership team members or administrative staff. If a leader does not delegate tasks and responsibilities, he or she may be overwhelmed and unable to meet all of the demands necessary to implement the mission and vision. When a leader designs an **action plan** for accomplishing the vision and goals, he or she must also identify the **staff members** who can complete those actions. For example, another member of the leadership team can be assigned a specific project, such as hosting the quarterly community literacy nights for the school year. Also, a clerical staff person can assist the leader in designing and formatting documents related to a project. The role of the leader is to lead and manage a team that can implement the vision, not to implement the vision independently and individually. Delegation is also important when the leader is not on campus or available. This ensures that the work of accomplishing the vision and goals will continue even in the leader's absence.

Measurable Expectations and Goals

USING DATA TO SUPPORT MEASURABLE EXPECTATIONS

Data can support the setting and tracking of measurable expectations. When a leader uses data to communicate **expectations** to faculty and staff, it increases the staff's ability to meet those expectations and helps staff to determine if they are meeting expectations. For example, a leader can set the expectation that teachers and staff maintain a 98% attendance rate at work. Setting this measurable expectation makes it easier for staff to self-regulate and also helps leaders to address failure to meet expectations. By using data, a leader can determine if expectations are being met, which can help determine whether the school is on track to **meet or exceed goals**. For example, a leader may expect 90% of students to meet performance standards in reading. If 93% of students meet performance standards, the leader will know that the expectation is being exceeded and it is likely that the school will meet their goal. In contrast, when data is not used to support expectations, it can be difficult to determine progress toward meeting expectations, identify potential areas of weakness, or address failures to meet expectations.

IDENTIFYING TRENDS AND PATTERNS

The identification of trends and patterns in school performance can be valuable in forming action plans so that decision-making can be targeted and strategic. When expectations are measurable, the data that is collected and analyzed can reveal **patterns and trends**. For example, if a leader were to review student reading progress, using data from the last three assessments, it may be revealed that a particular demographic group is consistently underperforming. This trend can help the leader provide **targeted resources and interventions** to meet the reading performance expectation. Similarly, an analysis of student attendance data may reveal a pattern of poor attendance on rainy days. Identifying this pattern can help the leader to **address the barriers** that rainy days create for student attendance so that students can meet attendance expectations.

MONITORING PROGRESS TOWARD GOALS

A leader must monitor progress toward goals to increase the likelihood of meeting those goals. Leaders should check the **progress** of goals in regular intervals throughout the school year based on these measurable expectations. This allows the leader to determine if the school is **on track** to meet a goal and, if not, allows time to make changes to the action plan. For example, a leader may set an annual goal for 90% of students to meet academic performance expectations in math on standardized tests. This goal could be broken down into measurable expectations, such as performance on particular math standards, which are reviewed at regular intervals, like every three weeks. If a leader were to determine that at least 90% of students were not successful on a particular math standard, this could indicate a danger of not meeting the annual goal. However, because this data was obtained before the administration of the standardized test, the leader has time to develop and implement **interventions** such as math tutorials, increasing the likelihood of meeting the goal.

SUPPORTING HIGH PERFORMANCE EXPECTATIONS

Measurable expectations support high expectations because they clearly define the expectations for students and staff, as well as the standard used to measure the expectation. A measurable expectation can lead to **higher expectations of performance** because it is clear and facilitates monitoring. When expectations are not measurable, the result is ambiguity or confusion. It can be difficult for a person to know if he or she is meeting expectations, and this ambiguity can convey that they will not be monitored. In contrast, when expectations are measurable, a leader can clearly convey how students and staff can meet those expectations and how they will be **monitored**. For example, if a leader sets a general expectation for high student performance in math, teachers may be confused about the performance indicators and subsequently have varying expectations for math performance and how students can demonstrate that performance, such as classwork, homework, and exams. In contrast, a leader could set an expectation that all students will maintain a passing grade in math classes and pass all math exams. The leader can then monitor the expectation by reviewing class and exam grades so that those who are not meeting expectations can be addressed.

MEASURABLE VS. NON-MEASURABLE GOALS

Measurable goals can be **quantified** and non-measurable goals **cannot be quantified**. An example of a measurable goal is: 95% of 8th grade students will earn a score of 70% or above on the math benchmark exam. This goal is **measurable** because it can be determined whether or not it was met by calculating the percentage of students who demonstrated the defined proficiency on the exam. It also identifies what **performance** is expected of the students in order to reach the goal. When goals are measurable, it is easy to determine whether or not they have been met. In contrast, a non-measurable goal may be ambiguous, and it may be difficult to determine whether or not it has been met. An example of a **non-measurable goal** is: 8th grade students will be successful on the math benchmark exam. This goal is not measurable because it does not state how students demonstrate success on the benchmark exam, nor how many students must be successful to meet the goal.

CONVERTING NON-MEASURABLE GOALS INTO MEASURABLE GOALS

Non-measurable goals can be converted into measurable goals by making them **quantifiable**. To make goals quantifiable, the leader must determine how **success** is measured for each behavior identified in the goal and how to know that success has been achieved. When a goal involves a **performance standard or assessment**, it should be clearly identified. For example, rather than using the phrase "demonstrate proficiency" in a goal, the leader should identify what constitutes proficiency, such as earning a particular score. Some goals involve behaviors that are not easily quantifiable, such as goals related to culture or attitudes. In these instances, a leader must determine how these behaviors will be measured, such as by **observations or surveys**. For example, a leader may wish all staff to be perceived as courteous. The leader can survey students and parents regarding the courtesy of staff and set a goal of an average rating of 4 out of 5 or greater in the area of courtesy. Alternatively, the leader may use observations to measure the goal, such as requiring front office personal to greet all visitors immediately upon entry 100% of the time.

INEFFECTIVENESS OF NON-MEASURABLE GOALS

Non-measurable goals can often be ineffective because they do not clearly convey how to **achieve the goal** or how one knows when the goal has been achieved. When there is no measure of what constitutes **success**, then those working toward the goal will identify their own perception of success, which may not be in line with the leader's expectations. For example, if the goal is for all 5th grade students to be successful on a test, a leader may expect students to earn scores of 90% or greater and the teacher may expect scores of 70% or greater. In order to ensure clarity of goals and to help develop strategies to reach those goals, the goals must be **measurable**. This ensures that all know the exact target that they are trying to reach and can determine if and when they have reached that target.

Local, State, and Federal Policy

RELATIONSHIP BETWEEN FEDERAL, STATE, AND LOCAL EDUCATIONAL LAWS, POLICIES, AND PRACTICES

Almost all aspects of the education process are governed by laws, policies, and practices. **Laws** governing the education process are established at the national and state level and supersede district and campus policies. **Federal laws** take precedence over state laws. **State laws** supplement and complement the federal laws. Local education agencies (LEAs) then interpret federal and state laws to create **policies** for their school districts that help schools to adhere to those laws or to clarify areas that the laws do not explicitly address. Individual campuses create **procedures** to address areas not explicitly outlined by district policy. For example, federal law states that students must be assessed by a standardized exam for grade promotion and graduation. State law dictates which tests the students take and when they are tested. School districts determine the policies for administering those tests, within the guidelines set by the state. Campuses implement district policy and may incorporate their own practices such as cell phone policies, dress code polices, or other school day aspects that are impacted by testing. Whenever there is a conflict between law and policy, law takes precedence.

AREAS OF THE EDUCATION PROCESS IMPACTED BY LAWS

Federal and state laws impact almost every aspect of the education process. Often these laws require additional policies and procedures to ensure adherence to the laws. However, there are specific areas of the education process that are highly **impacted by federal and state law**. These include educating students with disabilities, educating English language learners, standardized testing, student confidentiality, school liability, school performance expectations, technology use, school finance, and many more. School leaders must understand the laws and how these laws can influence the development and implementation of their **vision and goals**. While many school districts develop policies and practices that aid school leaders in adhering to the law, it is the school leader's responsibility to remain current on school law at both the state and federal levels.

IMPACT OF LAWS AND POLICIES ON PROFESSIONAL ETHICS

Federal and state laws dictate the requirements that educators must meet to be certified. As part of these requirements, educators must adhere to ethical codes and standards of behavior. The **ethical codes** address areas such as general conduct, conduct toward colleagues, and conduct toward students. Educators are expected to adhere to these standards of behavior; otherwise, sanctions may be placed on their educator licenses or their licenses and certifications may even be revoked. On any given school day, an education leader may make a number of decisions and must be fully aware of the legal and ethical ramifications of each one. Additionally, school leaders must understand that ethical decision-making is not only a result of personal morals and values but also of **codes and standards of behavior** that are set forth by federal and state government. The code of ethics requires that educators abide by all laws, but some decisions address "gray areas" in which there are no explicit laws, policies, or procedures. In these instances, school leaders must ensure that their decisions align with the educator code of ethics.

DEVELOPMENT OF POLICIES

Schools and school districts often develop policies as a **safeguard** for staff and students. Laws enacted at the federal and/or state level are often broad and subject to interpretation. As a result, policies are developed to **define** specific actions and behaviors that adhere to those laws, with the purpose of trying to ensure that people abide by the law by adhering to policies. Policies are meant to be a **protection** to those who adhere to them. For example, a law may broadly state that schools must administer a confidentially secure assessment of student performance in Math and Reading. The school district may then develop policies to ensure that tests are administered to students in a confidential and secure manner. A person who violates a policy does not necessarily violate a law, but this is possible. School leaders and school staff should abide by local policies as a protection, ensuring that they are adhering to state and federal laws.

Relationship Between Vision and Goals with Legal Responsibilities

ALIGNING VISION AND GOALS TO SCHOOL, LOCAL, STATE, AND FEDERAL POLICIES

The school vision and goals must be **aligned** to school, local, state, and federal policies so that they can be legally and ethically accomplished. If the school vision and goals are not aligned to these laws and policies, it is possible that working toward these goals would constitute breaking the law or violating policy. Because laws and policies supersede campus initiatives, it is important to align goals to these so that **resources** can be used efficiently. Even if the misalignment of the goal to the laws and policies does not constitute a violation of the law or policy, it could cause resources and efforts to be diverted, resulting in **loss of efficiency and impact**. For example, students with disabilities may require additional academic services, as dictated in special education law and policy. The campus leader must provide the resources necessary to meet these students' needs, so it would be efficient to align the school's other goals and resources to this requirement.

COMMUNICATING SCHOOL LAWS AND POLICIES

It is important to communicate school laws and policies to the community so that they can be **informed** of the requirements and constraints that govern the school leader's actions, decision-making, and goal-setting. The community should be aware of the laws and policies that helped to shape the school leader's vision for the school. The community may be **unaware of laws and policies** that can influence the operations of the school and how these laws and policies may affect the feasibility of their ideas and suggestions. For example, the community may wish to do away with a particular extracurricular sport because of low participation and lack of performance by the athletes, but they may be unaware that certain sports must be offered on campus due to compliance to Title IX of education law. A principal could explain that the current education law requires that the particular sport be offered so that there is no perceived discrimination in sport offerings at the school.

IMPACT OF LAWS, REGULATIONS, POLICIES, AND PROCEDURES ON VISION AND GOALS

Laws, regulations, policies, and procedures should be reviewed and considered during the development and implementation of campus vision and goals. Adherence to these laws and regulations supersede campus initiatives, so it is efficient and effective to align these with the vision and goals to prevent conflict or inefficiency in use of resources. A leader can evaluate these first, and then determine how the vision and goals can be designed in a way to help the school meet or exceed these regulations. For example, if accountability standards require that schools have a passing rate of 90% or above for the state exam in reading, then the school leader should set a goal to meet or exceed that requirement. If the school leader were to set the school goal at 85%, then meeting the school goal would still cause the school to fail according to state accountability standards. In order to be strategic, a school leader should determine what is **expected** of the school according to law and policy, and then determine how their vision and goals can **align** with those laws and policies.

Communicating and Implementing Vision and Goals

IMPORTANCE OF THE CLEAR COMMUNICATION OF THE VISION AND GOALS

It is important to communicate the campus vision and goals clearly so that stakeholders can **understand and support** them. If the vision and goals are unclear, stakeholders may have difficulty determining if they support the vision and goals or may be unsure of what to expect on the campus when the vision and goals are implemented. To communicate clearly, a leader should avoid **technical terms and jargon** that may not be easily understood by stakeholders. For example, a leader can communicate to stakeholders that the campus goal is to increase reading performance, rather than referring to a specific reading program or strategy that may not be familiar to them. Clear communication of campus vision and goals helps to garner **support from stakeholders** for campus initiatives. When communication is clear, the vision and goals can be easily aligned with outside support and resources from the district, community, and state and federal programs.

SUPPORTING A CULTURE OF LEARNING BY COMMUNICATING THE VISION AND GOALS TO STAKEHOLDERS

When the vision and goals are communicated effectively to stakeholders, they can in turn support the culture of learning. When stakeholders know and understand the vision, they can identify how to **support** it and help to **develop the culture of learning**. For example, if a business stakeholder in the community becomes aware of the school's vision to implement technology in the classroom to develop a culture of learning, he or she may decide to donate computers for a computer lab. Had the stakeholder not known that the school could benefit from the donation, he or she may not have taken that action. All stakeholders may not be in a position to give to the school, but they can support the culture of learning through their **participation** in school and community events and by **advocating** for the school and its needs to school and government representatives. Communicating the vision and goals to stakeholders increases the number of people who can offer their support in implementation.

ENSURING CLEAR COMMUNICATION

A leader will know if the communication of vision and goals to stakeholders is clear and effective by observing the **stakeholders' behavior**. When the vision and goals are clear, stakeholders are more likely to **buy in** to the leader's vision and assist in achieving it. Stakeholders who understand the vision and goals can articulate them in their own words. They will be able to **communicate** the vision and goals to other stakeholders and to the leader. Their behavior will be **aligned** to the vision and goals as well. Also, stakeholders who understand the vision will propose ideas and actions that are aligned to the vision, avoiding those that are opposed or a distraction to the vision. When communication of the vision and goals is clear and effective, all stakeholders will **understand** the vision and goals and how they can participate in achieving them.

HIERARCHICAL COMMUNICATION

Hierarchical communication refers to communicating up and down the chain of command. Leaders **communicate up** by communicating with superiors, such as district office staff or the superintendent. Leaders **communicate down** by communicating with faculty and staff. Communicating with various members of the hierarchy often takes different communication skills. For example, communicating with a supervisor may involve responding to specific requests or demands or demonstrating alignment of campus vision and goals with the school district's vision and initiatives. Communicating up may occur via emails and memorandums, meetings, or visits on campus. In contrast, communicating with faculty and staff requires communicating in a way that inspires them to perform as a team in order to achieve the campus vision and goals. This type of communication also involves holding campus team members accountable for their performance. This communication may occur via emails or memorandums, faculty meetings, or in professional learning communities. Leaders must **recognize their audience** when communicating so that they can use the most effective communication strategy.

COMMUNICATING IMPLEMENTATION OF THE VISION AND GOALS

A leader must ensure that stakeholders are aware of how the various campus initiatives and actions align to the school vision and goals. A leader can do this by frequently and clearly **identifying this alignment**. This can be communicated in writing or verbally. Campus plans for the implementation of the vision and goals should **identify** the planned initiatives and activities. For example, if the school's vision is to achieve excellence in literacy, the leader could indicate in the campus plan that the school will host a literacy night. At the literacy night, the leader should clearly explain to participants that it is a strategy for achieving the goal of excellence in literacy. The leader could also include the school's vision statement on the agenda for the literacy night. A leader cannot assume that all stakeholders understand the connection between the day-to-day campus activities and the vision and goals. Therefore, the leader needs to **verbally explain the connection** at every opportunity.

COMMUNICATING THE VISION AND GOALS THROUGH OTHERS

A school leader can utilize other people to help communicate the vision and goals. Members of the leadership team can help. Often, these **other school leaders** come into contact with staff and parents more frequently than the principal and therefore have more opportunities to convey the vision and goals. Additionally, parents can be instrumental. **Parent leaders**, such as those who lead parent organizations or are influential in the community, can help to spread the word about the school vision and goals. Also, in diverse communities, **staff members** who speak multiple languages may be utilized to communicate the school vision and goals to parents and community members of a variety of backgrounds. When **stakeholders** hear the vision and goals from people other than the leader, they will perceive that the vision and goals are supported and are more likely to support them as well. In order for this type of communication to be effective, the school leader must ensure that all have a sound understanding of the school vision and goals before sharing them with others.

Verbal and Nonverbal Communication

Leaders can clearly communicate the campus vision and goals to stakeholders using verbal, written, and nonverbal communication. Leaders can **communicate verbally** by formally hosting meetings and events that help to share the vision and goals for the campus. Leaders can host community meetings and invite parents, community members, and other stakeholders to attend. These meetings are opportunities for the leader to clarify and elaborate on the vision and goals. Leaders can also hold staff meetings and student assemblies with those on campus. Additionally, the vision and goals should be verbalized at every opportunity. A leader can use **written communication** to communicate the vision and goals, such as in formal reports, emails, and memorandums. For example, some leaders incorporate the school's vision in the footer of formal written documents so that it is always visible. All written communication should align to the vision and reinforce the goals for the campus. Finally, the leader's behavior can serve as **nonverbal communication** of the vision and goals. For example, if the vision of the school is to cultivate students who are life-long learners, then the leader can model this behavior by reading, participating in training, and taking classes.

Aspects of Clear Communication

Timely Communication

Timely communication requires proper planning. The **calendar of events** for the school year should be outlined in advance. The leader needs to identify the types of communication to share at various **periods** throughout the year, such as the beginning of the school year, school holidays, testing periods, and others. A leader must also provide **advance notice** so that staff and families can properly prepare and plan for school events and activities. Leaders can provide this advance notice using calendars, announcements, flyers, and phone calls. Communicating in **multiple ways** ensures that the communication is received in a timely manner. There can be an abundance of information about events, activities, and other aspects of the school that needs to be shared with staff, families, and students, so the leader should delegate the aggregation and dissemination of this information to other staff as necessary. The leader can set expectations for how these staff members communicate to families and students. For example, if a school department hosts an event, the event should be placed on the school calendar, and parents should be informed with sufficient time to prepare for and support the event.

Two-Way Communication

The act of communication involves a sender and a receiver. If communication is sent but not received, it is not effective. A leader can increase the possibility of effective communication by using a **variety of mediums**. These may include phone calls, meetings, emails, memorandums, and formal letters or documents. Additionally, a leader can survey stakeholders to determine the **preferred mode of communication**. For communication to be deemed effective, leaders must confirm that it has been received. Leaders can request a response or feedback on the communication so that it is acknowledged and the leader can be sure that the message was received in the intended way. Effective communication also means that the leader can be the **receiver** of communication, not just the sender. Leaders should be open to taking phone calls, responding to emails, or participating in meetings that allow others to communicate with them. When the leader acts as the receiver, he or she should acknowledge that the message was received so the sender is aware that the communication was effective.

Handling Miscommunication

If the leader becomes aware of a miscommunication, he or she should act immediately to correct it. Failing to correct a miscommunication can lead to confusion, conflict, and lack of engagement in and support of the school program. First, the leader should **identify the miscommunication**. Then the leader should make an effort to **correct** it by acknowledging that the message was not sent

properly and providing the correct message. For example, a school leader could notify parents that the school's art program would not be part of the vision for the upcoming school year, and the parents might infer that the art program would be eliminated. The school leader should inform parents that the art program will not be eliminated and then explain how it would be affected in the upcoming school year. The school leader should also assume **responsibility** for the initial ineffective communication.

Leadership Models and Styles

IMPACT OF A LEADER'S PERSONAL VALUES AND BELIEFS ON THE EFFECTIVENESS OF LEADERSHIP

A leader's personal values and beliefs shape his or her behavior, as well as expectations from staff and students. One's personal beliefs will dictate what is **prioritized** as a leader and as a campus team. If the leader's values and beliefs reflect positive attributes, these can have a positive impact on the effectiveness of leadership. In contrast, beliefs and values that are contrary to district and community norms can make it difficult to lead effectively. Additionally, if **staff members** have values and beliefs that are contrary to the leader's, they may find it difficult to follow the leader. For example, if the leader values reading and believes that everyone should be an avid reader, he or she would likely emphasize and prioritize reading initiatives and be effective in promoting reading on campus. On the other hand, if a leader did not personally value a characteristic such as punctuality in staff and students, that leader may have difficult effectively enforcing promptness among staff and students on campus. The leader's values and beliefs are often demonstrated in the school mission and vision, as well as through the leader's words and actions.

ACTING AS A ROLE MODEL

People observe the leader's behavior for **alignment** between his or her words and actions. This alignment is necessary for a leader to be viewed as genuine and authentic. The leader serves as a **role model** for both staff and students. For **staff**, the leader should exemplify the mission and vision of the school through behavior and words. The leader should also set the example in adhering to campus and district policy, like those described in the employee handbook. Additionally, the leader should set the example for **campus culture**, such as how staff members treat one another and students. For **students**, the leader is a role model in dress, conduct, speech, and other areas. Many people in the community may look up to the leader as well as an example to follow. As a role model, the leader's behavior can influence the behavior of others as he or she comes into contact with them.

SERVANT LEADER

A servant leader is a person who leads by **serving others first**. A servant leader identifies the team's needs by assessing the team or listening to team members and then meets those needs. Meeting the team's needs helps to equip them to get their job done effectively and efficiently. A servant leader shares power through **empowering** others to be effective and by providing them with the tools and resources to be effective. This is in contrast to a leader who exerts authority over others in a "top-down" approach. A servant leader is often found **participating** in the work with the team, both to support the team and to experience the team members' jobs. A faculty with a servant leader is more likely to feel more confident in their ability to do their job because their leader has empowered and equipped them and does not micromanage their work. Servant leaders are often described as caring, compassionate, thoughtful, and humble.

Transactional and Transformational Leadership Styles

Transactional and transformational leadership styles are very different and produce different results from team members. **Transactional leaders** are most concerned about how to effectively implement and perform under the current rules, policies, and procedures, whereas transformational leaders are focused on change and improvement. Transactional leaders emphasize compliance and monitor progress toward goals using systems of rewards and punishment. These leaders can be task-oriented or focused on results only. These types of leaders can become micromanagers. In contrast, **transformational leaders** focus on the staff behaviors that lead to success. They focus on organizational values and implementation of the mission and vision in order to meet goals. These types of leaders focus on growing staff members in order to meet goals and solicit staff buy-in in the decision-making process. There are pros and cons of each leadership style and many leaders alternate between these leadership styles or blend them together in order to lead effectively.

Shared Leadership

Shared leadership is the **delegation** of authority and responsibility to other team members. This type of leadership is the opposite of **authoritarian leadership** or micromanaging. Instead, a leader will appoint people with particular leadership responsibilities and grant them the authority to fulfill those responsibilities. For example, the school leader may ask a skilled teacher to lead a curriculum revision process and supervise a group of other teachers on the task. When sharing leadership, responsibility can be delegated to any staff persons who are capable of fulfilling the role. It is not dependent on job titles. Shared leadership also involves including team members in the leader's **decision-making processes**. This means that the school leader may solicit opinions, ideas, and feedback from staff members before making a decision. This can be accomplished through focus groups, appointing advisors, or taking votes during meetings.

Distributing Responsibility through Roles and Delegation

Roles That Can Help Accomplish the Vision

Many roles are performed on campus to ensure that day-to-day activities are carried out. Each of these roles can contribute to accomplishing the **school vision**. Some of the roles include the administrative team, school counselors, teacher leaders, and support staff. The **administrative team** is essential in accomplishing the vision because projects and assignments that directly impact the vision and school goals can be delegated to them. These administrators have the authority and training to support the leader in leading the campus to success. **School counselors** can help accomplish the vision by supporting the psychosocial needs of students so that they can be their best, academically and socially. School counselors are often part of the team that handles student scheduling and post-graduation plans, so they can help students meet the expectations associated with campus goals. **Teacher leaders** can also help to accomplish the vision by leading, encouraging, and supporting their fellow teachers. Finally, **support staff** can help accomplish the vision by ensuring that plan logistics are appropriate, communication is timely and effective, and staff and stakeholders feel supported and equipped to implement the vision.

Distributing Responsibility and the Role of Shared Vision
Goal Implementation with a Shared Vision

A vision can be shared in two ways. In the **development** of a vision, the leader can solicit the **opinions and feedback** of stakeholders so that a variety of perspectives, opinions, and beliefs can be incorporated into the vision. When the vision is developed in this manner, participants can see their contribution to the vision by the way that it is articulated and implemented. A vision is also shared when a leader effectively **communicates** the vision, the rationale for the vision, and the plans for implementing the vision to stakeholders. When a vision is shared, this can assist with **goal implementation** because of buy-in from stakeholders. People are more willing to agree with and participate in plans that they helped to develop. Additionally, having a shared vision means that stakeholders will understand it well enough to work toward goal implementation, even without direct supervision from the leader. They will be able to take action to advance toward the campus goals.

Delegating Tasks and Responsibilities

Leading a campus is a great responsibility that cannot be done alone. To lead effectively, a leader must **delegate** tasks and responsibilities. Delegation is important because a leader does not have the time or resources to perform all responsibilities alone. Most initiatives require a **team** of people to get the job done in a timely and efficient manner. Delegation is also important because a leader will not have all of the **skills** necessary to perform every task. For example, a project may require computer networking expertise, which the leader may not have. In order for projects to be completely effective, tasks and responsibilities should be delegated according to **skillsets**. Delegation is also important because there are tasks and responsibilities that only the leader can perform, so his or her time should **prioritize** these types of activities. Other activities that can be accomplished by other team members should be delegated whenever possible. Delegation also ensures that the campus will run efficiently in the **absence** of the leader, such as during a meeting or other event.

Delegation and Accountability

For delegation to be effective, a leader must hold team members **accountable**. A leader cannot delegate tasks and responsibilities without checking on the progress, or he or she may discover too late that the job was not done or did not meet expectations. Instead, a leader can incorporate accountability into delegation. This can be done by setting regular **check-in dates** with team members to meet about task progress, providing the leader with an opportunity to give feedback. The leader can also set certain **milestones** that must be accomplished to demonstrate progress. The leader should emphasize to the team member that **completion** of the project is his or her responsibility and that completion is a reflection of job performance. When a leader includes accountability through regular check-ins, pre-established milestones, and communication of responsibility, the team member will be clear about expectations and able to perform the delegated task, and the leader will be reassured that the job is being completed to satisfaction.

Delegation and Authority

For effective delegation of tasks and responsibilities, those responsible must have the appropriate **authority** to accomplish the tasks. Often, the projects that need to be delegated are not ones that can be done independently. They require the **coordination** of other people and resources. It may be necessary for the school leader to expressly communicate to the person to whom the task is delegated as well as those assisting that the project leader has the authority to implement the project. This will help those leading the project to have **confidence** in their ability to get the job done. For example, if a project requires the scheduling of a community meeting, the project leader would need the authority to secure the venue, make purchases, and gather volunteers for the event. Providing team members with authority enables them to accomplish their delegated tasks with little to no dependence on the school leader. In contrast, when a project leader does not have the appropriate authority to get the project done, the project could be delayed or remain incomplete, waiting on assistance from the school leader.

Monitoring and Communicating About Progress Toward the Goal

EFFECTIVELY MONITORING GOAL PROGRESS

A leader effectively monitors goal progress by implementing clear checkpoints and milestones in goal activities. Each goal should be broken down into smaller goals, or **milestones**, that can be reviewed in regular intervals. This allows the leader to analyze progress toward the goal in a timely manner so that, if progress is insufficient, there is time to intervene and make changes to the action steps. For example, if the campus goal is to achieve a 90% passing rate on reading assessments for third-grade students, the campus leader would want established milestones to monitor reading progress throughout the school year. The leader may review reading data every three weeks to determine if third-grade students are reaching and maintaining a 90% passing rate in reading. If not, the leader could implement additional strategies to increase the support for reading instruction. **Checkpoints** for goals are often aligned with grading periods, as identified on the school academic calendar.

EFFECTIVELY COMMUNICATING GOAL PROGRESS

Goal progress should be communicated effectively and in a timely manner, especially to those who are instrumental in achieving the goal. First, the school leader should **monitor goal progress** closely so that it can be communicated in a timely manner. Communicating goal progress is pointless if it is done with no time left to make adjustments. The school leader should **communicate progress consistently**, whether positive or negative. Communicating **positive goal progress** is encouraging to others and reassures them that their actions are appropriate. This can serve as positive reinforcement that may even increase staff performance. In contrast, communicating **negative goal progress** is necessary so that corrections can be made. When communicating goal progress, conducting **in-person** conversations or meetings is beneficial because it allows for two-way communication. During these conversations, the school leader may discover unexpected barriers and challenges that need to be addressed.

Adjusting and Revising Goals

ADJUSTING VISION, GOALS, IMPLEMENTATION, AND COMMUNICATION STRATEGIES

CONTINUOUS IMPROVEMENT

The process of continuous improvement is the ongoing act of assessing performance and adjusting efforts to improve that performance. With a process of **continuous improvement**, parts of the work process can be addressed before they begin to fail. Low-performing processes are improved as well as performance that is considered acceptable. All aspects of the work process are examined to determine where improvements can be made to reach **excellence**. To implement a process of continuous improvement, **procedures of evaluation** must be developed and implemented at regular checkpoints. Based on these evaluations, the leadership team can identify areas of improvement and initiate **interventions and actions** based on these areas. In schools, the regular evaluation of process toward the campus vision and goals can be developed into a process of continuous improvement. However, campus leaders must focus on both the strengths and weaknesses of the campus in this process. Deficient areas can be improved to perform to standard and areas performing at standard can be innovated for improvement.

EFFECTIVELY MONITORING PROGRESS

A leader can effectively monitor progress by planning regular checkpoints, analyzing data, and actively engaging in the work. The leader must plan in advance when to check progress on the projects and tasks that are being implemented on campus. This monitoring should include the projects that the leader is working on as well as those that have been delegated to others. These **checkpoints** should occur with enough frequency that adjustments can be made in a timely manner. The leader must also **analyze data** on a regular basis. All goals should have measurable metrics, which means that data points can demonstrate whether the goal is on track to be achieved. Therefore, a leader must be skilled at analyzing data and making decisions based on it. Finally, a leader can effectively monitor progress by viewing the work and **engaging** in it firsthand. For example, if a campus goal is to reduce the number of students who are tardy, the school leader may engage in morning duty to monitor the arrival and attendance tracking of students. This engagement can add context to the data and help the leader to identify areas of improvement.

FACILITATING SELF-DIRECTED CHANGE AND IMPROVEMENT ON CAMPUS

Self-directed change and improvement can help achieve the campus vision and goals. Staff members who can make changes and improvement to their practice on their own do not require as much **intervention** of campus leaders and coaches as other staff members, freeing those resources to be utilized in other areas. To succeed on their own, staff members must be fully aware of the **campus visions and goals** and the **expectations** placed on them in pursuit of those goals. A leader can facilitate self-directed change and improvement by providing **adequate staff resources**, such as instructional resources and professional development opportunities. The leader must also provide staff members with **access to data** for monitoring progress and performance. Finally, the leader must develop a **culture and climate of self-improvement** in which staff are comfortable revealing weaknesses and taking risks to improve their practice.

HELPING WITH ADJUSTMENT OF THE VISION AND GOALS BY SELF-REFLECTION

Self-reflection is the process of examining one's self in relation to a desired expectation of performance. This process can help with **adjusting the vision and goals** when it is completed by those responsible for carrying out tasks and projects related to the vision and goals. Self-reflection can help to determine whether the goals should be **revised** or if they or the people striving toward the goals need **improvement**. For example, if a campus goal is to improve reading instruction, reading teachers could engage in self-reflection to determine if they are implementing the action plan with fidelity and are teaching to their best ability. If not, the teachers would engage in **self-directed change** to meet the goal. In contrast, if the reading teachers were faithfully implementing the action plan and performing to the best of their ability, this could indicate that the goal itself and its associated strategies may require revision to meet the students' needs. When all staff members engage in self-reflection, it becomes easier for the campus as a whole to make changes and improve.

SYSTEMATICALLY REVIEWING AND REVISING GOALS

Goals are not concrete and should be reviewed and revised periodically. A leader can examine goals to determine whether a campus is likely to **achieve or exceed** them. A leader can also determine whether goals are in complete **alignment** with the vision of the schools. Just as a leader regularly monitors the activities implemented for the completion of the goal, the leader will need to examine the goals themselves. Since a goal is measurable, the leader can determine if the **current data** shows that the campus is on track for meeting it. The leader may observe unexpected **barriers** to achieving the goal that require a revision or the setting of an additional goal. For example, if the school sets a goal for reading performance, the leader may notice that students receiving special education services are not performing as well as students who do not receive these services, and that their reading performance is contributing to a low overall reading performance goal. The leader may then create a new goal that specifically addresses the needs of this student population with its own set of strategies and interventions.

Adjusting Communication Strategies

Communication of the vision and goals to all stakeholders is critical to the successful achievement of the vision and goals. The leader will know that communication strategies need to be adjusted if staff members have difficulty **articulating** or **implementing** the goals and vision. All staff members should be able to discuss the campus goals and vision among themselves and with other stakeholders. If they are unable to do this, it is possible that communication was not **effective** initially or that subsequent communication of changes and adjustments to the vision and goals was ineffective. Another indication that communication strategies need adjustment is difficulty for staff members in **implementing the action plans** related to the vision and goals. If they are unclear about what is expected of them or what steps they need to take to meet expectations, these aspects of the action plan may not have been conveyed clearly. Communicating effectively removes **barriers to implementation**.

Gathering Data and Identifying Strong and Weak Areas

Identifying Strengths and Weaknesses of Campus Performance

The school leader can use quantitative, anecdotal, and observational data to identify the strengths and weaknesses of campus performance. This involves regular reporting of **student performance data** and other data points related to key areas such as attendance and discipline. This data is usually analyzed in relation to goal setting and review, so leaders can actively identify the **strengths and weaknesses** of the campus when this data is reviewed. Also, other team members or district office personnel might convey areas of strength or weakness to the leaders based on their campus experiences. These people may share how a particular teacher or department is performing or provide feedback regarding a system or process on campus. Also, a leader may make **observations on campus** to help identify areas of strength or needed improvement. For example, a leader may participate in lunch duty in the cafeteria and observe processes that need to be improved. A leader should refer to **multiple sources of data and evidence** to develop a holistic view of the strengths and weaknesses of campus performance.

Addressing Identified Strengths

A leader should address identified strengths on campus by using them as opportunities for praise and reinforcement, as well as leverage for improvement. Effective leaders encourage staff by praising and celebrating **achievements** and recognizing **strengths**. This motivates staff members to continue the effective performance. For strengths to remain as strengths, a leader must recognize them and **reinforce** the actions and attitudes that led to their achievement. The leader can also use these strengths as **leverage** for making improvements. For example, if the third-grade reading teachers have consistently achieved high performance in reading, this can be recognized and praised. Then the strategies that these teachers implement in the third-grade classroom can be analyzed for application to the other grade levels. Reinforcing and praising strengths builds confidence in team members, helping them to address needed improvements on campus. Similarly, the skills that are effective in building the strengths can also be applied to areas of weakness.

Addressing Identified Weaknesses

Weaknesses identified on campus must be addressed to improve them. However, this should be done strategically to avoid demoralizing team members. If a leader identifies multiple weaknesses, they can be **prioritized** rather than attempting to address all of the weaknesses at once. Attempting to address all at one time can be overwhelming to team members. When developing plans to address weaknesses, the leader needs to identify how the **strengths** of the campus and the individual team members can be used to improve the areas of weakness. For example, a campus may be having difficulty with classroom management, but certain teachers may be effective classroom managers. These teachers can be used to develop a campus-wide strategy for addressing this area of weakness. Similarly, the campus may demonstrate weakness in math performance, but strength in reading performance. The campus leader can identify the strategies that make reading performance effective and implement them in math instruction.

DISTRICT ACCOUNTABILITY MEASURES

The purpose of school accountability measures is to ensure that all students are learning and performing according to predetermined standards. These **measures of accountability** are standardized, and the state and federal governments provide **assessments** of schools based on these accountability standards. School leaders can use these school reports to identify areas of strength and weakness in the school programming as measured by performance on state-mandated assessments. For example, the school leader may review the school's accountability ratings and find that the third-grade class did not perform according to expectations in reading. Based on that information, the leader can identify which teachers taught third-grade reading, what curriculum was used, and other factors that may have impacted students' scores. That information can then be used to determine what aspects of the third-grade reading program are strong and which are weak and need improvement. School accountability measures are a critical means of determining a school's strengths and weaknesses.

Implementing Changes

PROFESSIONAL DEVELOPMENT

To implement change, identifying areas for improvement is not enough. Staff members need to know what they can do to improve their practice. As a result, **professional development** can help a leader implement change. When leaders participate in professional development themselves, they can learn how to be better leaders and how to implement new or better instructional practices on campus. When teachers and other staff participate in professional development, they can also learn how to grow as professionals and implement **improved instructional strategies** in the classroom. Leaders should tailor professional development to meet the needs of the staff and to address campus weaknesses. Leaders should also offer opportunities for **staff members** to participate in individualized and group professional development, organized by content area, grade level, or shared strengths or weaknesses. Also, leaders should implement professional development in innovative ways, such as coaching, modeling, book talks, and other professional development strategies.

STUDYING RESEARCH-BASED AND PROVEN BEST PRACTICES

Areas of deficit or weakness on campus often result from a lack of knowledge rather than a lack of capability. Leaders and team members must continually learn about their practice and how they can improve and should search for successful strategies that can be implemented on their campus. To address weak areas, it is better to implement strategies that are backed by **research** and have been **proven** to obtain good results. This can save the campus the time, effort, and resources that could be wasted if untested, unproven strategies are implemented unsuccessfully. When a leader is looking for strategies to foster change on campus, using research-based, proven best practices is beneficial because there will be **clear direction** for successfully implementing the strategy as well as an idea of the expected results. When untested strategies are implemented, the outcome is less sure. Untested strategies also often take more research and a process of trial and error to implement, also known as a learning curve, both of which can delay the implementation of change.

ENLISTING SUPPORT

A leader cannot bring about campus change alone. To make changes happen, the leader must enlist support. Fostering change as a **change agent** requires leaders to be strategic in how they communicate the change and how they garner supporters for it. First, the leader needs to **communicate** the change effectively. Many people are unwilling to support changes because they fear the unknown. The leader should not only communicate what is to be changed, but also how it will affect the various staff members and how they are aligned to the vision and goals. Next, the leader needs to gather other leaders within the team and **persuade** them to support the change. Leaders on campus may carry official titles of leadership or simply have influence over other staff members. Enlisting the support of these people will positively affect the perceptions of the remaining staff. Lastly, the leader needs to be a constant **advocate** of change and **participate** in it. Staff members will watch the leader to see if the desire for change is authentic and long-lasting. They will be more likely to support it when they observe that the leader is serious about change.

ANTICIPATING AND PREPARING FOR WHEN TO IMPLEMENT CHANGE

When implementing change, a school leader should anticipate and prepare for **varying levels of support**, as well as direct **opposition** to the change. Some team members will be as **enthusiastic** about the change as the leader. The leader should be prepared to leverage these team members by encouraging them, providing them with resources necessary to implement the changes, and using them to influence the other team members. Some team members will be **indecisive** about the change and not quite ready to support it. The leader should be prepared to spend more time and resources on this group to help encourage them to support the change. This group may require additional communication strategies and support to bring them on board. The school leader should also anticipate a third group of staff members who are **opposed** to the change and may even be vocal in their opposition. The school leader should be prepared to defend the change and offer rebuttals to arguments against it, both publicly and privately. The majority of the leader's focus should be on the first two groups; however, the oppositional group can be detrimental to the progress of the first two groups if it is not addressed appropriately.

MODELING OPENNESS TO CHANGE

The leader is a model on campus and team members will imitate his or her attitudes. If a leader would like the staff to be open to proposed change, he or she must also be a **model of openness to change**. There are many ways to accomplish a goal, and just because something is working does not mean that it cannot be improved. Changes may be proposed by team members other than the leader, from the school district, or even from the state. In these instances, the leader should model openness to change. The leader can be **receptive** to the proposed change and **optimistic** as to how the change can positively affect the campus. The leader can also demonstrate a **positive attitude** during the change, should it be implemented. The leader can expect a similar response from staff if change is proposed on campus, so leadership should model the qualities and attitudes they desire from staff. In contrast, if the leader is not open to change, staff will likely imitate that attitude and be opposed to changes proposed by the leader.

Chapter Quiz

Ready to see how well you retained what you just read? Scan the QR code to go directly to the chapter quiz interface for this study guide. If you're using a computer, simply visit the bonus page at **mometrix.com/bonus948/nystcescbl109110** and click the Chapter Quizzes link.

Developing Human Capital to Improve Teacher and Staff Effectiveness and Student Achievement

Transform passive reading into active learning! After immersing yourself in this chapter, put your comprehension to the test by taking a quiz. The insights you gained will stay with you longer this way. Scan the QR code to go directly to the chapter quiz interface for this study guide. If you're using a computer, simply visit the bonus page at **mometrix.com/bonus948/nystcescbl109110** and click the Chapter Quizzes link.

Recruiting Staff Members

RECRUITING TEACHERS AND OTHER STAFF MEMBERS

A leader should be strategic in recruiting new teachers and staff members. To determine whether candidates will be a good fit on the campus, the leader should examine them in relation to the school culture, vision, and goals. A leader should first use the **school culture** as criteria for recruitment. For example, if the school culture is one of innovation and creativity, the leader will want to recruit candidates who have demonstrated creativity in the past and are comfortable taking the risks necessary to try new things. Also, the leader will want to recruit candidates with the necessary skills to aid in implementing the **school vision and goals**. For example, if the school vision is to become an exemplary campus in the integration of technology into the learning process, the leader should recruit candidates who are skilled with technology and are comfortable utilizing it. Using such criteria when recruiting teachers and other candidates will ensure that they will be a good fit on campus and contribute to the school's success.

INCLUDING OTHER TEAM MEMBERS IN THE RECRUITMENT PROCESS

Including other team members in the recruitment process is beneficial for several reasons. First, having more than one person participating in this process reduces the potential for demonstrating **bias** during the recruitment and hiring process. Other team members may notice aspects of potential candidates that the leader missed, which can help to provide a **well-rounded view** of each candidate. Also, other team members may have different perspectives regarding the **needs and dynamics of the campus**, which can help to determine whether potential candidates are a good fit for open positions. Lastly, **staff morale and campus culture** can benefit from allowing team members to participate in the process of selecting their future coworkers. Some schools allow students to participate in the recruitment and selection process of teaching candidates because they are the ones who will ultimately be affected.

Evaluating Staff Performance

EVALUATING STAFF MEMBERS

For a campus to reach its goals and achieve its vision, all staff members must perform to expectations. It is essential that staff members be **evaluated** to ensure that all are performing to expectations. Evaluations of staff members provide an opportunity for leaders to identify areas of **strength and weakness** among the staff and to provide constructive **feedback** to staff members so that they can grow professionally. Leaders can use these evaluations to determine what additional **support and resources** are needed to support or improve the staff member performance. For example, a leader may discover through evaluation that the science department demonstrates deficiencies in providing hands-on instruction to students. The leader can then identify professional development and coaching to assist the science teachers in improving this area. Evaluations are also used to determine whether staff members will have continued employment on campus. Staff members who consistently perform below expectations may have to be removed from their position and assigned to a different position or campus.

STANDARDIZED EVALUATION

State law requires that teachers be evaluated with a **standardized evaluation system**. The state may recommend a certain teacher evaluation system, but school districts can often choose which system to implement. Whether the school district adopts the recommended evaluation tool or develops its own, the standards for evaluation must meet or exceed the expectations outlined by the state. For teachers to be evaluated, the **evaluators** (usually campus administrators such as principals and assistant principals) must be trained in using the tool. Additionally, **teachers** must be trained on the tool that will be used to evaluate them. Evaluation often includes regular observations by the evaluator, collection of artifacts or data related to their practice, and conferences with the evaluator to discuss feedback. Teacher evaluation is usually based on **performance** in relation to the standards outlined in the evaluation tool, as well as **growth or progress**. Teacher performance standards are often related to instructional practice and strategies, professionalism, growth and professional development, and student performance. The evaluation process occurs throughout the school year and teachers receive a final evaluation rating at the conclusion of the school year.

OBSERVING STAFF PERFORMANCE

Leaders should use as many opportunities as possible to **observe staff performance** so they will have a well-rounded view of the performance. The opportunities may include various days of the week or times of day, as well as varied circumstances. Teachers can be observed while engaging in their instructional practice in the **classroom**. They can also be observed while they are engaged in collaboration as they participate in **professional learning communities**. Additionally, teachers can be observed while they are fulfilling **duty assignments** such as arrival, dismissal, cafeteria, or hall duty. Other staff members can also be observed at different times, whether performing normal duties or engaging in special events such as community events, student events, or district events. A leader should be intentional and deliberate about seeking out different opportunities to observe staff at a variety of times, in a variety of circumstances, to obtain a fair and holistic view of staff performance.

OBSERVING STAFF IN VARIED SCENARIOS

It is important to observe staff in a variety of scenarios and at different times to get an accurate impression of staff performance. If a leader observes a staff member infrequently or always at the same time, this may lead to an inaccurate perception of that person's performance. For teachers, **class dynamics** may vary throughout the day. When a leader does not vary the time of day for observing a teacher, he or she will not know how that teacher responds to varied classroom dynamics or how instruction is practiced in all of the assigned courses. For example, a teacher may have a small class in the afternoon with fewer challenges than other classes. If a leader observes the teacher only during that class, he or she may not see all of the **instructional and classroom management skills** that the teacher demonstrates throughout the school day. If a leader consistently observes a teacher at the same time, it can also lead to predictability. A staff person could prepare for observation, so that it is not an authentic reflection of that person's regular work performance.

IMPROVING STAFF PERFORMANCE

Conducting observations can help to improve staff performance by providing opportunity for **feedback and growth**. Observations allow a leader to see a staff member in action. When a leader observes a teacher or other staff member, he or she will note **strengths and weaknesses** in that employee's performance in relation to campus and district expectations. The leader can specifically reference what was observed as evidence of those strengths and weaknesses. This data will then help the leader to provide feedback regarding performance. The leader can also provide suggestions for improvement or give access to professional development and resources that will help the staff member to improve. Observations can also illustrate staff members' strengths so that they can build on them and continue to grow in those areas. Feedback and recommendations can also be used immediately to improve performance.

Professional Development and Staff Performance Standards

CALIBRATING STANDARDS

One campus may include multiple people who evaluate the performance of teachers and staff. The process of **calibration** is the training of all evaluators to maintain and look for the same **standards of performance**. When a team is not calibrated, different evaluators may have different perceptions of excellence, which can lead to confusion and inconsistency in staff performance. To calibrate staff evaluators, the team of evaluators should observe a staff person **together** at the same time. They each conduct an observation as if they were conducting it alone. After the observation is complete, the team of evaluators meets to discuss what they observed and how they would evaluate the staff person. The leader helps the team identify where their evaluations are **aligned or misaligned** in regard to the performance expectations. For example, a leader may believe that the observed teacher did a poor job implementing collaborative learning, while another evaluator believes that the teacher implemented collaborative learning in an acceptable manner. The leader would then refer to the performance standards and discuss the observed evidence to reach a consensus. This process would be repeated until all evaluators are able to assess staff members in like manner.

SUPPORTING TEACHERS' GROWTH WITH EVALUATIONS

Teacher evaluations support their growth because evaluations help to identify **areas of needed improvement** and hold teachers accountable for addressing those areas. Evaluations are based on a set of **performance standards** and will reveal if a teacher is not adequately meeting any of those standards. A teacher who needs to improve will know exactly where to focus improvement efforts, based on the evaluation results. The evaluation will also help the leader know how to best support the teacher in **growing professionally**. Additionally, evaluations hold teachers **accountable** for improving their practice. The accountability comes from the process of conducting evaluations, including timelines and deadlines, self-reflection, and conversations with the evaluator regarding areas of growth. When professional growth or efforts to achieve growth are not observed in the teacher, the teacher is at risk for receiving a negative evaluation at the end of the school year. A negative evaluation could result in outcomes such as probation or termination. The process of evaluating teachers ensures that they are growing professionally to become the best teachers they can be.

SELECTING PROFESSIONAL DEVELOPMENT FOR STAFF MEMBERS

A leader needs to be deliberate in selecting professional development for staff members so that it is purposeful in helping staff achieve the campus goals and vision. One strategy a leader can use includes analyzing how the professional development **aligns** with the campus vision and goals. For example, if the campus goal is to increase reading performance, then selecting a professional development session on implementing effective reading instructional practices would be appropriate. Another strategy that a leader can use to select professional development is to **identify weak areas** of staff based on observations and evaluations. A leader may observe that several teachers are having difficulty implementing effective classroom management strategies, so that leader may seek out professional development that addresses classroom management. Also, a leader must ensure that staff members participate in professional development that is **mandated by the district or the state**, such as something related to special populations of students or law and policy.

SUPPORTING TEACHERS' GROWTH WITH COACHING

A coach is a professional who helps a teacher to develop the skills necessary to work effectively. A coach is a staff person who does not supervise or evaluate the person being coached. This helps to foster a **relationship of trust** between the coach and the teacher. A coach will identify a teacher's areas of **strengths and weakness** based on a predetermined rubric or set of expectations. Then the coach will provide one-on-one support to help the teacher **improve targeted areas**. The coach may provide books and resources or recommend professional development sessions. The coach may also **model** effective teaching, **observe** the teacher in practice to provide real-time feedback, **assist** in the lesson planning process, and **guide** the teacher in self-reflection and critical analysis processes. A coach provides **individualized, targeted support** to teachers, which helps them to grow, usually in a shorter period of time than other forms of professional development support.

UTILIZING HIGH-PERFORMING TEACHERS TO SUPPORT THE GROWTH OF OTHERS

High-performing teachers on campus can support the growth of other teachers by becoming leaders, serving as models, and coaching. High-performing teachers may exceed performance expectations in many areas or only a few, but their strengths can be **leveraged** to benefit the other teachers on campus. A leader may utilize high-performing teachers as leaders on campus in several ways. These teachers may be promoted to **lead departments** or be tasked with **leading collaborative meetings**, such as professional learning communities. Leaders may also direct these teachers to lead **on-campus professional development sessions** relating to their areas of strength. These teachers can also serve as **models** to the other teachers. Teachers who need to improve in certain areas may be asked to observe a high-performing teacher to see how a particular skill or strategy is implemented in the classroom. A high-performing teacher can also have a coaching role for other teachers to provide one-one-one support in certain performance areas.

PRINCIPAL AS AN INSTRUCTIONAL LEADER

The principal should act as the instructional leader on campus. This is important because it helps the leader to focus on instruction on campus, helps to support teachers, and establishes credibility with the faculty. When a principal is an instructional leader, **instruction** is prioritized. This impacts all school operations, including scheduling, alignment of resources, and support. Also, instructional leaders are able to support teachers in improving their skills related to **teaching and learning**. A principal who is experienced in and familiar with instruction will be a better evaluator of instruction and can offer expertise in improving instructional practice. Also, acting as an instructional leader gives **validity** to the principal's feedback relating to instruction. Teachers will be more receptive to feedback and advice regarding their instructional practice if the leader has demonstrated that he or she prioritizes instruction and has knowledge and expertise in that area. The principal should be prepared and willing to take the lead instructionally on campus in a variety of forms, such as providing feedback, demonstrating or modeling expectations, and collaborating and problem-solving with teaching staff.

Principal Participation in Professional Development

A principal should participate in professional development for his or her own growth and development and to demonstrate solidarity with staff members. When possible, a leader should participate in **professional development** with the staff so that he or she can learn as well. Leader participation in professional development helps to identify the actions and behaviors he or she can expect from **staff** that also participate in the session. For example, if teachers participated in a professional development session regarding collaborative learning strategies, the leader would need to know what effective implementation of those strategies would look like in the classroom and how to support teachers as they implement them. Also, when the leader participates in professional development with staff, this demonstrates to the team that the leader values the opportunity for professional development and views it as a **priority**. This will increase **buy-in** from the staff and help them to be more receptive of the information and training that they receive at the professional development session.

Collaborative Teaching and Learning

Collaborative Teaching and Learning

Collaborative teaching involves two or more teachers engaging in instruction together. Collaborative teaching can take many forms, such as team teaching, co-teaching, and others. For example, one teacher may act as a **lead teacher** and present instruction to students while the other teacher acts as a **support**, helping to manage student behavior and reinforce concepts with struggling students. In another model, a teacher may present **new instruction** to students while another teacher in the room provides **remedial or intervention instruction** to a small group of students. Other team-teaching models involve students being divided into **groups** and receiving new instruction from a teacher within their groups. In a team-teaching model in which both teachers act as lead teachers, there are often **student rotations** or **instructional stations** involved. Collaborative teaching requires **co-planning** on the part of the team teachers and a good **working relationship** between them. Collaborative teaching allows for more flexibility within the classroom and exposes students to differentiated instruction and a variety of teaching styles.

Professional Learning Communities

Professional learning communities can be structured in a variety of ways to support collaboration among educators on campus. Most often, these **professional learning communities** are organized in a way that allows staff with shared roles or responsibilities to collaborate together under the leadership of one person who is designated to **lead** the community and is often trained to do so. For example, a professional learning community structured by **grade level** may consist of all eighth-grade teachers. In contrast, a community structured by **content area** may consist of all math teachers on campus. The campus leader may determine which structure best meets the needs of the teachers and students. Professional learning communities are usually **goal-driven**, which encourages participants to collaborate in order to achieve the established goals. Professional learning communities are often guided by the following questions: What do we want students to learn? How do we know if they learned it? What do we do if they did not learn it? What do we do if they did learn it? While participation in professional learning communities may be voluntary on some campuses, for many schools it is mandatory for teachers to participate.

PURPOSE OF PROFESSIONAL LEARNING COMMUNITIES

The purpose of professional learning communities, also referred to as **PLCs**, is to improve the educational performance and achievement of students through **educator collaboration**. PLCs are structured ways to facilitate **sharing knowledge** and **improving skills** among educators through data analysis, action research, exchange of expertise, and professional dialogue. In PLCs, teachers may discuss their practice and seek ways to improve. For example, teachers participating in a PLC may share lesson plans with committee members for feedback. Teachers may also share student work with committee members to calibrate grading practices or solicit ways to improve the quality of students' work. For example, a teacher may present a sample of student writing to committee members to get feedback on suggested focus areas for subsequent instruction. Teachers may also discuss student performance data in PLCs. This data may include summative assessment within the classroom or formative assessment, such as benchmark data or standardized testing data. Teachers may also use PLCs to discuss professional literature.

BENEFITS OF COLLABORATIVE TEACHING AND LEARNING

There are many benefits of collaborative teaching and learning. When teachers collaborate, they are able to **share ideas**. This fosters innovation and growth on campus. Collaboration also helps to **solve problems** more quickly. When a teacher has an issue, other teachers can provide resources, suggestions, or advice to help address the issue so the teacher does not have to research solutions independently and attempt to solve the problem through trial and error. For example, if a teacher has difficulty reaching a particular student, collaborating with other teachers who have that student in class and have been successful can help to identify ways that the teacher can reach the student. Also, collaboration among teachers builds **community** and fortifies the **school culture**. When teachers work and plan together, they build relationships with one another that can foster feelings of belonging and support. Teachers who are collaborative know that they can celebrate successes with their team members and that if they have a problem or challenge, they have a team of supporters. When teachers have these types of relationships and feel **supported**, it is easier to retain them in the classroom and encourage them to grow professionally.

SUPPORTING COLLABORATIVE TEACHING

A school leader is instrumental in ensuring that teachers are able to collaborate on campus. First, the school leader must plan a **school schedule** that allows for collaboration. This could mean that there are designated times for professional learning communities or that teachers who need to plan together have planning periods scheduled at the same time. For example, if the school leader expects all teachers in a certain grade level to collaborate, then the instructional schedule must accommodate a shared planning time for those teachers. The school leader also needs to **train staff** how to participate in a collaborative learning environment in line with the campus vision and goals. This requires the leader to set clear expectations for the operation and outcomes of collaborative planning, such as those outlined in professional learning communities. Also, the leader must designate teachers or leadership team members to **lead collaborative planning** so that there is organization and accountability. Finally, the leader can support collaborative teaching and learning by **participating** in collaborative meetings when possible and **modeling** collaboration in other areas.

COLLABORATIVE LEARNING

Collaborative learning is an instructional strategy in which students are organized into **groups** for learning. These learning groups allow students to support each other and dialogue about the instruction and content. Collaborative learning reinforces **listening and speaking skills** in addition to the presented content. Teachers may employ several different strategies to organize students into collaborative groups. These include ability grouping (or homogenous grouping), heterogeneous grouping, and flexible grouping. In **homogenous grouping**, a teacher may organize students into groups based on proficiency with a certain skill so that targeted support and activities can be provided to groups based on their collective need. In **heterogeneous grouping**, students with different strengths or skills may be grouped together to balance out the group's deficits. Students may remain in these designated groups for a certain period of time, such as a grading period. **Flexible groups** are dynamic and take on different forms based on the instructional goals set by the teacher. These groups may have different sizes and composition based on needs.

Resources for Effective Instruction

APPROPRIATE PHYSICAL RESOURCES

Effective instruction requires appropriate physical resources. The leader can support instruction on campus by providing adequate physical resources for instructional staff. **Physical resources** include all of the tangible items needed to deliver instruction, such as furniture, books, and supplies. For example, **classroom spaces** must be able to accommodate teachers and learners, so there must be an adequate number of desks or tables and chairs, as well as physical square footage of the instructional space. Also, teachers need access to **instructional supplies** and appropriate **technology** for instruction. Other physical resources include curriculum, textbooks, computer labs, and other instructional resources. Leaders can identify necessary physical resources based on the school's **vision and goals**. For example, if the campus is striving to excel in STEM instruction, the leader needs to equip the school with science materials, computers, and other physical resources required for effective STEM instruction. Also, the leader may seek feedback from instructional staff regarding the necessary resources to be effective in the classroom. For example, a teacher may need additional bookshelves to accommodate leveled books within the classroom.

APPROPRIATE HUMAN RESOURCES

Effective instruction requires the appropriate staff in place to deliver and support the instructional program. **Human resources** that are part of the instructional program include teachers, librarians, aides, and many others. A leader must ensure that the right number of people with the appropriate skills and qualifications are placed in the appropriate **instructional positions**. For example, it is the leader's responsibility to ensure that all classes are assigned a highly-qualified teacher for the start of the school year. This may mean that the leader actively recruits and screens teaching candidates to have a fully-staffed campus throughout the school year. Additionally, a leader must respond to needs for **additional staffing** or **changes in staffing** throughout the school year. For example, if students demonstrate deficits in math, the leader may identify math tutors to provide additional instruction. Also, a leader may notice that students with special needs require more support within the classroom and can implement a co-teaching model to support instruction. The leader can also seek **feedback** from staff to determine where additional instructional staff may be needed or where staff changes need to be made.

IMPORTANCE OF RESOURCES FOR EFFECTIVE INSTRUCTION

A leader must ensure that the appropriate resources are provided to instructional staff in order to support **effective instruction** on campus. A **lack of resources** on campus can make it difficult for teachers to teach and for students to learn. For example, if a teacher is assigned 22 students in her classroom, but there are only 20 desks, the teacher will have difficulty arranging her classroom in a way that is conducive to learning. Also, if a classroom does not have a highly-qualified teacher assigned to it, students will lose out on quality instructional time. In contrast, when teachers and other instructional staff are provided with the **physical and human resources** needed for effective instruction, both they and the students benefit. For example, if the school's vision is to cultivate reading skills in students, teachers would benefit from books, bookshelves, online reading programs, a library, and a librarian in order to achieve that vision. As a leader may not be able to provide all of the desired resources for instructional staff, he or she must decide which resources can be provided based on the school budget.

OVERCOMING BUDGETARY CHALLENGES

At times, the school budget will not be sufficient to provide the desired instructional resources for teachers. In these instances, a school leader may need to seek additional ways to provide these resources. One way to overcome this challenge is to seek **funding from outside the school**. This may mean applying for **grants** or seeking **donations** from various businesses and organizations. The funds acquired can be used to purchase the desired resources. An additional strategy is to ask the **manufacturers** to donate the resources to the school. The school may volunteer to be a pilot school for the implementation of new resources. Also, parent organizations can conduct **fundraisers** to supplement the school budget and secure the needed resources. For example, the PTO may conduct a fundraiser to purchase supplies for the art program. The school leader should also determine whether the next school year's budget should accommodate the resources for the subsequent school year.

TIME MANAGEMENT

USING PLANNING TIME TO SUPPORT EFFECTIVE INSTRUCTION

Teachers have planning time scheduled into their instructional day. This **planning time** is determined when the master class schedule is designed for the campus, so leaders must consider in advance how much time is allotted to teachers for planning. A leader should encourage teachers to use this time to **support effective instruction**. For example, teachers can assess the quality of student work, prepare feedback for students, and determine which skills or content may need to be retaught. Planning time can be used to examine **resources** and determine how they can be incorporated into instruction or to identify differentiated instructional strategies for reaching diverse learners. Teachers may also choose to **collaborate** with other teachers in the planning and delivery of lessons. Leaders should ensure that teachers have adequate planning time and access to resources to support their efforts during planning time. Additionally, leaders should be considerate of teachers' planning time by avoiding scheduling meetings, conferences, duty, or other assignments during this time whenever possible.

IMPACT OF TIME MANAGEMENT ON INSTRUCTION

Instruction on a school campus is delivered according to a strict **schedule**. Specific times are allotted for various aspects of the instructional program. A school leader's ability to **manage** his or her own time as well as to occupy the time of other **campus staff** can affect instruction. For example, the leader's timeliness in approving decisions relating to instruction can impact the timeline of projects. The timeframe in which the school leader obtains **resources** for the instructional program can also impact instruction. For example, if the campus would like to integrate technology into the curriculum, the leader's ability to secure computers for the students and teachers affects when instruction could begin. Additionally, the leader's daily decision-making regarding use of time can impact **instruction**, such as scheduling of meetings, school assemblies and activities, and conferences with staff. The leader must manage his or her time in planning, decision-making, and other duties throughout the school day to support the instructional program.

PRESERVING INSTRUCTIONAL TIME

Preserving instructional time means reducing the number of distractions and interruptions to the instructional program, specifically the time students spend in the classroom. **Interruptions** to instructional time may include announcements, school assemblies, meetings, or any other activities or events that distract from the instructional routine. For example, a campus leader may desire to host a school-wide event such as a pep rally during the school day. The leader would need to consider the impact on the instructional day from hosting such an event. He or she may decide to adjust the day's schedule by taking a few minutes from each class, rather than having students miss a large portion of instructional time from one class, to accommodate the event at the end of the day. A leader may also decide that a pep rally does not warrant the interruption of instructional time and instead may postpone the event. Leaders who **preserve instructional time** use school-wide public announcements sparingly, adjust schedules for school assemblies to reduce the impact on instructional time, and try to schedule other meetings and events outside of the instructional day when possible.

Chapter Quiz

Ready to see how well you retained what you just read? Scan the QR code to go directly to the chapter quiz interface for this study guide. If you're using a computer, simply visit the bonus page at **mometrix.com/bonus948/nystcescbl109110** and click the Chapter Quizzes link.

Family and Community Engagement

Transform passive reading into active learning! After immersing yourself in this chapter, put your comprehension to the test by taking a quiz. The insights you gained will stay with you longer this way. Scan the QR code to go directly to the chapter quiz interface for this study guide. If you're using a computer, simply visit the bonus page at **mometrix.com/bonus948/nystcescbl109110** and click the Chapter Quizzes link.

Using Community Resources

ENGAGING COMMUNITY STAKEHOLDERS

A school leader can take several steps to engage **community stakeholders** in order to utilize community resources and build partnerships. First, the leader should **communicate** effectively with stakeholders. Stakeholders are more likely to engage when they are aware of the activities happening at the school, the vision and goals for the school, and the accomplishments of the students and staff. When stakeholders are aware of these things, they are able to identify where they can support the school. Next, the school leader should invite stakeholders to **visit** the school and **participate** in school activities. This may include activities such as Career Day, awards assemblies, graduation, fairs, and more. Finally, the school leader should engage in **activities hosted by community stakeholders**. This will demonstrate that the school leader is supportive of their endeavors and is open to learning about the stakeholders' roles in the community. As the leader builds relationships with these stakeholders, he or she can identify individualized ways to further engage community stakeholders.

COMMUNITY RESOURCES

Almost all aspects of the school program can be supported with community resources. **Local community organizations** can prove to be valuable in a broad range of areas that benefit the school, its staff, and the students. These may include transportation, training, academic support, extracurricular activities, fundraising, clubs, sponsorships, internships for students, physical resources such as equipment, services, and much more. For example, community volunteers help to **maintain school safety** with services such as greeting visitors, monitoring halls, or assisting with arrival and dismissal. Some community organizations may be able to provide **school supplies** for students or classroom supplies for teachers, which can support the instructional program. Other organizations may have access to men and women who can serve as **mentors** to at-risk youth on campus. It is up to the school leader to identify community resources near the school and determine if and how those resources can benefit the school community.

COMMUNITY PARTNERSHIPS

Community partnerships are beneficial to the school and the community. Establishing **community partnerships** is a way of providing **resources** to students and their families, usually at little or no cost to them. This can be invaluable to low-income families who otherwise would not be able to afford the services. Additionally, establishing community partnerships creates **sustainability and stability** within the community. When the school and its families patronize the organizations in the community and utilize their services, this helps to ensure that the organization will remain operable in the community. Frequently, services disappear from communities because they are underutilized, especially in impoverished communities. Finally, community partnerships established by the school leader help to **align** the school vision and goals with those of the community to garner more support and resources to accomplish the vision and goals.

SERVICES FOR STUDENTS

Many community resources used to support schools are targeted toward students in need. Some community resources target **academic needs**. These include providing tutorial services, free or low-cost school supplies, free books, internships, training programs, and more. Other community resources target **physical health needs**. These resources may include free or low-cost immunizations, free or low-cost dental services, free or low-cost medical checkups, and more. These types of resources may also address other physical needs of students, such as food, clothing, toiletries, or haircuts and grooming. Additionally, some community resources cater to the **psychosocial needs** of students. These resources may include mentoring, counseling, therapy, peer mediation, and many others. Some organizations provide specific services while others offer a variety of services. School leaders need to coordinate access to and delivery of these services to best meet students' needs.

SERVICES FOR STAFF

Even though staff members of the school do not necessarily reside in the community associated with the school, some community organizations extend benefits and resources to **staff** because of their service to the community. These resources may include **memberships or discounts** to local businesses for purchasing food or supplies for the classroom, access to free **training or resources** that can aid in their professional development, or **partnerships** with local businesses to supplement instruction in the classroom. Many organizations in the community are willing to donate time, money, or resources and supplies for special events or activities hosted at the school. Consequently, the school leader and staff members should keep community stakeholders informed about school events to help determine how these community partners can support the school.

SERVICES FOR PARENTS

As residents of the community, parents often have access to certain resources. At times, these resources can be delivered through the school to increase the likelihood of **parental engagement** in these resources. These services may include English as a Second Language (ESL) classes for non-native English speakers, GED or adult high school programs, technology courses, individual and family counseling, and much more. Additionally, some community services assist adults with acquiring housing or meeting household expenses such as rent, utilities, and food. Other services may include childcare, parenting classes, and other supports for the adults and their families. For many of these community organizations, the rationale for providing support to parents is that the children will benefit, which in turn **positively affects their school life** in areas such as attendance and academic performance.

PARTNERING WITH COMMUNITY AND RECREATIONAL CENTERS

Partnering with community and recreational centers is often an opportunity to provide students and their families with **resources** they may not normally have access to or take advantage of. Often, community members are unaware of services that these organizations provide at little to no cost, such as childcare, use of gym facilities, access to technology, and more. Similarly, these organizations can help to **expand the school program**. For example, an organization may partner with the school to provide childcare on campus for students whose parents cannot pick them up at school dismissal time. Similarly, a community center may provide GED preparation to adults and can offer these services on the school campus to parents. These partnerships are **mutually beneficial** and often involve sharing services and facilities.

COLLABORATION TO BENEFIT BOTH SCHOOL AND COMMUNITY
MEMORANDUM OF UNDERSTANDING

A memorandum of understanding is a contract between two parties, outlining the details of an agreement in which no money is exchanged. It is an agreement of **services to be provided**. For example, an organization may offer to provide tutorial services for students in reading and math after school on campus at no cost to the school. The school and the organization would draft a **memorandum of understanding** that outlines the tutorial services to be provided and the school leader's promise to provide a location on campus for the services. Both parties would sign the document and receive an original copy. The verbiage of the memorandum of understanding can be the same as in a traditional contract, but often the language is simpler as the sole purpose of the document is to state the exchange of services with no monetary compensation. The purpose of the memorandum of understanding is to **document** the services that are to be provided. This type of documentation can be helpful for both parties in providing evidence that the services were agreed upon and delivered.

COLLABORATING WITH COMMUNITY MEMBERS

Collaborating with members of the community can have long-term benefits for the school and the surrounding community. When there is collaboration and partnership between the community and the school, there can be an **alignment of vision and goals**. This fosters long-term, mutually beneficial **partnerships**. For example, community organizations and the school may identify a need for increased technology education within the community. They can collaborate to add technology programs in the school, programs for adults within the community, and an increase in internet access for community members. Also, community programs can be integrated into the school program and even housed on the school campus. For example, a GED program may be based on a school campus to increase accessibility to parents and encourage parental engagement at the school. Community support can sustain or boost student enrollment in school and participation in special school programs.

CONNECTION BETWEEN THE SCHOOL AND LOCAL EMPLOYMENT TRENDS

The school provides education and training that make students **employable** in the community workforce. As a result, the school can supplement or adjust programming to respond to **community needs**, such as training students in particular fields that are experiencing an employment shortage within the community. For example, the school leader and community members may identify a need for more healthcare workers in their community. They can tailor a school program to offer healthcare courses and training that could lead to certifications and degrees in the healthcare field. These students could then enter the local workforce with the skills to fill the needs of local employers. Many schools, especially secondary schools, partner with **local community colleges and community organizations** to identify employment trends to support the local community as well as to increase the likelihood that graduates can obtain employment.

ALIGNING EDUCATION EXPECTATIONS WITH EMPLOYMENT GOALS

It is beneficial to the school community, the community at large, and postsecondary education institutions to **align education expectations** between public school and college. Schools and students benefit when there is communication between area colleges and the school for the purpose of understanding the local education trends and needs. For example, the local community college can communicate to school leaders that recently enrolled freshmen have significant deficits in math skills. This information can prompt a school leader to analyze and revise the current math program and make the needed adjustments to ensure that students are graduating with the knowledge and skills needed to be successful in college. Similarly, communication between postsecondary institutions and school leaders can help to identify the **soft skills** that students need to be successful in college, as well as **trends in degree programs and career paths**. This type of communication can also lead to the institution of **higher education programming** on school campuses, such as dual-credit enrollment or training and certification programs.

MAINTAINING A SAFE SCHOOL

The first priority of a school leader is maintaining school safety. This benefits not only the students and staff, but also the community as a whole. When issues and conflicts identified at the school are resolved promptly, this can prevent **escalation** of those issues outside the school, which can ultimately prevent violence or other altercations in the community. Also, a safe school in the community becomes **a safe haven or refuge** for unsafe communities and neighborhoods. Community members are willing to engage in school events when they know that the school is safe and organized. Additionally, community members and organizations are willing to support and invest in schools that are safe and well-run. In contrast, when a school is not safe, this can lead to decreased enrollment and a lack of parental and community support.

RELATIONSHIPS WITH COMMUNITY ORGANIZATIONS

A school leader can build relationships with various community organizations through effective communication and active participation in community events. First, the school leader should effectively **communicate** to community leaders that he or she desires to partner and build a relationship. This communication can involve sharing the school vision and goals and learning about the vision and goals of the community organizations. This can lead to a discussion of how the school and community organizations can organize **mutually beneficial plans and activities**. Collaborating will help to establish relationships. Then, the school leader should be an **active participant in community events** so that he or she will be visible and recognizable, as well as to show support for the community. This participation may include attending events at other schools in the community, attending church services in the community, or participating in other community-sponsored events. Supporting the activities of community organizations demonstrates investment in the community and helps to build relationships.

COMMUNITY DYNAMICS

It is important for a leader to understand the dynamics of the community to meet the community's needs and to establish productive relationships. These **dynamics** can be revealed in a variety of ways. Often, **community leaders and parents** in the community are willing to discuss the community's makeup and dynamics. The school leader can search for **publications**, such as community newspapers or bulletins, to stay up to date on community affairs. These newspapers often highlight community leaders, organizations, community needs, and upcoming community events. Additionally, the school leader can attend **community meetings** such as town hall meetings to learn about the concerns of the community. It is also important to learn who the **government officials** in the area are, as well as candidates running for office in upcoming elections.

Communication with Family and the Public

COMMUNICATING WITH FAMILIES AND THE PUBLIC

A school leader should take advantage of multiple ways of communicating with families and the public. Communication can be facilitated through **technology**. Methods include emails, electronic newsletters, websites, social media, mass automated phone calls, and other forms of technology that can be used to share messages with large groups of people. The school leader can also communicate in ways that require **little or no technology**. This includes making personal phone calls, hosting community meetings, making public announcements at community events, mailing letters, and other methods. When hosting community meetings, the leader should ensure that these meetings are held at a **variety of times** that are convenient for parents and the community, such as early morning, late evening, or weekends. A leader can use a variety of ways to communicate and must identify the **most preferred and effective means of communication** for the school community. Additionally, the school leader can use **multiple modes of communication** to share the same message and reach as many people as possible.

OVERCOMING LANGUAGE BARRIERS

In diverse communities, school leaders often encounter language barriers when attempting to communicate with parents of students or other community members. It is helpful when a leader is fluent in more than one language, but often a variety of languages are spoken in these communities. To **overcome language barriers**, a leader should be proactive in devising communication strategies. First, the leader should be **aware of all languages** that are spoken in the school community. Then, the leader should attempt to have school employees who are fluent in the languages spoken on campus so they can **translate** when needed. Additionally, **school communications** can be translated into a variety of languages. Translators or translation machines can be available at community meetings, including sign language when appropriate. Many businesses offer translation services for documents, as well as for meetings and conferences held in real time.

COMMUNICATING WITH THE MEDIA

There are times that the school leader will need to communicate effectively with the **media**, for both positive and negative reasons. The school leader should first follow the protocols and procedures outlined by the school district when communicating with the media, especially in situations in which the media attention is negative for the school or district. Some school districts **centralize media communication** and do not permit school leaders or other staff to communicate with the media without express approval. When communicating with the media, school leaders should speak truthfully, communicate in alignment with the school and district vision and goals, and communicate according to instructions from the school district staff. A school leader can utilize media outlets to **positively highlight the school**, such as broadcasting upcoming events or spotlighting student and staff accomplishments.

FORMAL AND INFORMAL COMMUNICATION

Formal communication is usually prepared in advance. The school leader knows what is to be communicated and how. **Formal communication** is typically **structured and controlled** and is delivered in a formal way, such as in a presentation to the community or a speech at an event. Formal communication also involves **prepared print communication** such as a letter, email, or bulletin to the public. In contrast, **informal communication** is often **impromptu**. This often involves conversation with an individual or group, an unexpected phone call, or a text message. In informal communication, the topic may be unexpected or vary within the course of communication. Informal communication can occur before or after a formal meeting or event, as a result of an

unexpected phone call, or in any variety of circumstances in which the school leader was not prepared for the communication or conversation.

Speaking Informally with Stakeholders

School leaders should take precautions when speaking informally with stakeholders to **protect** themselves, the school, and the school district. **Informal conversation** can be used negatively by people who do not have the best interest of the school or school leader in mind or who are seeking personal gain. As a result, a leader should take care to be professional even in informal speech and to speak in accordance with the school and district vision and goals. For example, a school leader may make a joke during an informal conversation after a parent meeting that the parent does not believe to be in good taste. That parent can then make a formal complaint to the school district regarding the leader's professionalism. Regardless of the leader's perception of his or her relationship with the stakeholder, it is imperative to remember one's position as school leader when engaging in informal conversation. The leader should view all communication, formal or informal, as a **reflection** of the position of school leader and of the school and school district.

Communicating Through Email

When communicating via email, a school leader should make sure that the email communicates the message in the **intended way**. In order to do this, the leader should maintain a **professional tone**. Humor and sarcasm are not often conveyed well via email and should be avoided. The school leader should also review the email for proper spelling, grammar, and word use, as errors can cause the message to be misunderstood. The leader should use features such as *Reply All* and *cc* with caution, only sending the email to those who need to be included in the conversation. Also, the school leader should confirm that any necessary attachments are included in the email, if applicable. It is also a good practice to confirm with the recipient that the email has been received. Emails with attachments or mass emails are sometimes redirected to the recipient's spam or junk mail folder and may not be received in a timely manner, if at all.

Scheduling Parent Meetings

When scheduling parent meetings for large groups of parents, the school leader should consider the time of day and day of the week that these meetings are to be held. The goal of these meetings is to effectively communicate with parents in a group setting, so the school leader needs to ensure that the scheduled day and time accommodate the majority of parents for **maximum attendance**. The ideal times for these events will vary based on the needs of parents in the community. In many communities, parents work during the day, so **evening meetings** are more favorable. In some communities, certain days of the week are dedicated to religious activities, sporting events, or other engagements, and this should be taken into consideration when scheduling a parent meeting. For example, a school leader would not want to schedule a parent meeting at the elementary school on the same evening as the high school football game, as this would put the two events in competition. The school leader can talk to parents and **survey families** to identify ideal times to host meetings and should be open to hosting meetings at a variety of times, such as early in the morning or on weekends.

Shared Decision-Making and Stakeholder Involvement

SHARED DECISION-MAKING COMMITTEE

The purpose of the Shared Decision-Making Committee (**SDMC**) in schools is to provide a structured process for the inclusion of **stakeholders** in the school decision-making process. This committee is made up of school leadership, school staff, parents, community members, and other key stakeholders that the school leader may choose to include. The committee meets regularly to discuss **key decisions** that the school leader will make. These decisions may involve school programming, fundraising, planning for school events, and other initiatives. In these meetings, participants are informed of **key details** that should be considered in making these decisions and are given the opportunity to **voice their opinions** on the decisions as well as to provide **recommendations**. The SDMC provides recommendations to the school leader but does not have authority to dictate decisions. However, the SDMC provides an opportunity for stakeholder participation in the school process and helps to build relationships between the school leader and stakeholders.

FAMILY INVOLVEMENT

SCHOOL DECISION MAKING

The school leader should provide as many opportunities as possible to **include families** in school decision-making. First, the leader should **inform families in advance** of decisions that will be made. For example, the leader may alert the parents that he or she is considering converting the school playground into a garden. This gives families an opportunity to provide feedback prior to the decision. The school leader can use surveys to gather input from families regarding the school, providing data that can be used in decision-making. Additionally, the school leader can communicate with **parent organizations** on campus or form a **parent focus group** to gather feedback and opinions on decisions to be made at the school. Also, there should always be at least one parent representative on the **Shared Decision-Making Committee**.

DECISIONS MADE ABOUT THEIR CHILD'S EDUCATION

Each family should have the opportunity to be involved in decisions made about their individual child's education. These decisions may include course selection or school programming pathways, extracurricular activities like clubs and sports, opportunities for tutorials and extended learning, and many others. First, the school should provide clear and effective **communication** to the families, indicating areas of the school program in which they can help make decisions for their children. Then, the school leader can provide ways for parents to offer their **opinions**, such as through frequent parent meetings or holding one-on-one conferences. Also, phone calls and emails can be very effective in including parents in the decision-making process. Many schools send **informative letters or bulletins** home to parents to include them in the process. Some campuses have opted to staff a **parent liaison** who specializes in communicating with parents and encouraging their participation in the school decision-making process.

BENEFITS OF INVOLVING FAMILIES IN DECISION-MAKING

Involving families in decision-making is beneficial to both the families and the school. Involving families increases **buy-in** for the decisions that are made, which can lead to increased **support for school initiatives**. For example, if families help to decide which tutoring program to implement after school, they will be more likely to have their child participate in the tutorials. Involving families in decision-making also strengthens the **relationship between the school and families** and stimulates **parental engagement**. Also, when families are involved, they often share information and a **perspective** that can inform the school leader's decisions. This can help the leader make decisions that better address the needs of students and their families.

Two-Way Communication

Two-way communication is the process of sending and receiving messages. In two-way communication, a person who receives a message has an opportunity to **respond** or send a message back to the sender. When collaborating with stakeholders and families, it is important for the school leader to provide opportunities for **two-way communication**, in contrast to only sending **one-way messages**. Two-way communication helps the leader to confirm that the message or communication was received as intended. Sometimes a message can be unclear or misinterpreted, and this confusion can be identified in two-way communication. Additionally, two-way communication allows the school leader to learn more about the opinions, needs, and concerns of key stakeholders. Finally, two-way communication promotes involvement and engagement of the stakeholders, which can foster relationships between them and the school and increase buy-in from the stakeholders in regard to the school leader's vision and goals.

Ensuring Two-Way Communication

A leader can ensure two-way communication by providing many **opportunities** for stakeholders to communicate with him or her. For example, a school leader may host a community meeting and provide a time during the program for stakeholders to ask questions or voice their opinions. School leaders can also make themselves **accessible** to those seeking to communicate with them. This can be done in several ways, such as holding frequent meetings with stakeholders or choosing certain office hours with an "open-door policy." Other ways of promoting communication include sending out **surveys**, creating a **comment or feedback box** on campus, and being open to **phone calls and emails**. A school leader should be visible during parent and community events and display a willingness to engage in conversation with stakeholders, demonstrating **receptiveness** to two-way communication.

Chapter Quiz

Ready to see how well you retained what you just read? Scan the QR code to go directly to the chapter quiz interface for this study guide. If you're using a computer, simply visit the bonus page at **mometrix.com/bonus948/nystcescbl109110** and click the Chapter Quizzes link.

Operational Systems, Data Systems, and Legal Guidelines to Support Achievement of School Goals

Transform passive reading into active learning! After immersing yourself in this chapter, put your comprehension to the test by taking a quiz. The insights you gained will stay with you longer this way. Scan the QR code to go directly to the chapter quiz interface for this study guide. If you're using a computer, simply visit the bonus page at **mometrix.com/bonus948/nystcescbl109110** and click the Chapter Quizzes link.

Managing Operational Systems

ORGANIZATIONAL SYSTEMS

A school organizational system refers to how a school is organized in relation to resources, personnel, time, and space to achieve student learning and success. Examples of **school organizational models** include departmental models, project-based learning models, academy models, integrative models, small community models, and the school-within-a school model, among others. The organizational system dictates the **structure** of the school and its systems, how personnel are allocated and what personnel are needed, what resources are needed, and how the physical space of the school is designed and utilized. Consequently, the organizational system in a school dictates how **instruction** is delivered and how **student learning** is achieved.

TYPES OF SCHOOL ORGANIZATIONAL SYSTEMS

The different types of school organizational systems affect how instruction is delivered on campus. In the **departmental model**, the different subject or content areas are separated and distinct. Each of the subject-area departments have leaders or chairs who report to administration. In an **integrative model**, disciplines are combined or grouped together such as in the pairing of math and science classes or English and history classes. **Project-based learning models** facilitate interdisciplinary learning through student completion of large, extended projects. In **academy models**, a school may group students and classes based on college or career pathways. **Small community models** and **school-within-a-school models** are similar in that students are grouped into cohorts and remain within a small community for their instruction. Each community operates like a small school. In the school-within-a-school model, the small communities often have their own administrators. Other types of school organizational systems have developed as **technology** has become more accessible in schools, such as virtual schools and flipped classrooms.

DETERMINING THE BEST ORGANIZATIONAL SYSTEM

To determine the best organizational system for a school, a leader should first examine the school vision and goals. The organizational system should support the **school vision** and facilitate achievement of the **school goals**. For example, if the school is focused on reading performance and instruction, the leader may select a block scheduling structure to provide students with more instructional time in reading. A leader may also determine that, in order to provide socio-emotional support to students, dividing a large school into teams or houses would best facilitate relationship building and cultivate a small-school feel. A leader can also analyze the **school's culture** and identify the appropriate organizational system to support the ideal culture. For example, if the school vision is to create independent, life-long learners, the school organization system may involve giving students autonomy in their learning when possible. For example, the school could offer self-paced instructional programming, student course selection, and other exploratory opportunities for students.

AREAS OF ORGANIZATIONAL SYSTEMS NOT DIRECTLY RELATED TO CLASSROOM INSTRUCTION

Many organizational systems are part of the campus system but are not directly related to **instruction**. For example, the **cafeteria** represents a large system within the school. The process of feeding breakfast, lunch, and even dinner to students can be a complex organizational system. It involves providing the food, serving it, and maintaining the facilities in which it is served. This particular system may be regulated by state and federal regulations, which add additional complexities. Another organizational system is **behavior management and discipline**. There are processes in place to promote positive student behavior and deter negative behavior. This system may include the development and distribution of handbooks, training and communication regarding behavioral expectations, and imposing consequences for infractions. Other systems include student arrival and dismissal, extracurricular programming, counseling, and others. Even though these systems are not directly related to classroom instruction, they often **support** effective classroom instruction.

SYSTEMS THINKING

Systems thinking involves understanding how a system or an organization is constructed. It is an understanding of the many **parts** that make a system work, how those parts **interact** with one another, and how those parts relate to the larger context of the system. For example, the system of providing food to students in the cafeteria is one part of the larger campus system. A leader who understands systems thinking understands that how the cafeteria functions can directly or indirectly affect the way another system functions, such as the classroom. If the cafeteria is unable to serve breakfast efficiently in the morning, students may be delayed in getting to class, which in turn impacts instruction. Therefore, systems thinking helps in understanding how the organization or system as a whole can best function by improving the function of the **smaller systems** that make up the whole.

EFFECTIVE DATA SYSTEMS

Effective data systems are important for managing the **organizational systems** on campus. Data systems relating to student and staff population data are essential to the effective planning and management of the organizational system. For example, **staffing** is often determined by the number of students enrolled in the school and the allocation of those enrollment numbers to various aspects of the instructional program, such as grade levels, special populations, magnet programming, and more. Leaders must have **accurate data** for student enrollment in order to allocate staff to the various programs on campus. This type of data also impacts class sizes and student to teacher ratios. Additionally, areas of the campus have **capacity maximums** as dictated by fire code, and these limitations must be taken into consideration when planning lunch schedules, school assemblies, and other uses of school facilities. Effective data systems are also necessary to make decisions related to **funding** and **resource acquisition and allocation**, in addition to **instructional decision-making**.

Improving Organizational Systems

SHORT-TERM IMPROVEMENT

A leader should evaluate the school's organizational system for continuous, short-term improvements. Factors to consider include functionality, training, and resources. The organizational system should function smoothly and efficiently. This is indicated by **student and staff transitions** throughout the day as well as **flow of information and resources**. For example, if the school's organizational system is made up of small learning communities, it would be effective to place resources such as supplies and copiers near the learning communities. Also, the leader should ensure that staff has the appropriate **training** to support the organizational system. For example, if the organizational system is based on a project-based learning environment, staff will need appropriate, ongoing training to support this type of system. Finally, the leader should ensure that the school has the appropriate **resources**, both physical and human, to support the organizational system. This may include reassigning certain resources from one area of the school to another.

LONG-TERM IMPROVEMENT

For long-term improvement of a school's organizational system, the leader should consider **alignment** to vision and goals, availability and allocation of resources, and spatial designs. First, the organizational system should support the **school's vision**. For example, a virtual school environment may not be appropriately aligned to a school vision that prioritizes building social and collaborative skills in students, due to its focus on individual, computerized work. Consequently, the leader needs to determine if the school's **organizational system** needs to be changed to reflect the changing needs of the students and community that the school serves. Next, the leader needs to determine the availability of both **physical and human resources** and how those are allocated to support the school's organizational system. This may require hiring additional staff, replacing or redesigning staff positions, or acquiring new resources such as technology devices. Finally, the leader needs to consider whether the layout and organization of the **physical space** in the school is conducive to the school's organizational system. To implement a school-within-a-school model, for example, the leader may need to redesign or relocate certain classrooms and offices.

Physical Plant Safety and Compliance

Failure to ensure the physical safety of the **school plant** and comply with building regulations can negatively affect the instructional program. If students and staff are in danger of being injured or hurt due to aspects of the plant that are in disrepair or do not meet codes and standards, this can **interrupt** the school day and cause the school and school district to be **liable**. For example, if the school has an elevator in use that is not up to code, there is danger of a student or staff person becoming trapped in the elevator due to malfunction. This is dangerous to the person in the elevator and would necessitate emergency personnel, causing a disruption to the instructional program. Additionally, malfunctioning equipment such as leaks, loud machinery or A/C equipment, or pest infestations are distracting to the instructional environment and may cause damage to instructional resources such as books and technology equipment. **Compliance** with regulations, such as ADA codes, is important to ensure access for all students and staff, especially those with disabilities, to all areas of the campus.

MONITORING SAFETY AND COMPLIANCE

A leader can monitor the physical plant for safety and compliance in several ways. First, a leader should have a **plant operator** who is responsible for ensuring the plant's safety and compliance. The leader should meet with the plant operator regularly to address any concerns that may arise.

Second, the leader should conduct **regular walks** of the plant to inspect it for safety and compliance. During these walks, the leader should take note of plant aspects that may need repair or maintenance. Also, the leader may receive formal or informal **feedback** regarding needed repairs and maintenance from instructional staff. Finally, city or county officials will conduct regular **inspections** and provide **reports**. These reports will detail aspects of the campus that are in compliance, out of compliance, or in danger of being out of compliance with regulations. The school leader can use these reports to ensure the plant's safety and compliance.

BOND REFERENDUM

A bond referendum is a proposal to borrow funds long-term to fund **major capital improvements**. Since these capital improvements are costly, the bond allows the expenses to be spread over time so that the costs are covered by current and future taxpayers. The bond must be approved by **voters** because of the obligation that taxpayers will have in paying for the expenses incurred by the capital improvements. Funds secured through a bond referendum can be used for **construction** of new schools or district facilities, **renovation** of existing schools or district facilities, and other **updates** related to the physical aspects of the plant. Bond funds can be used to help schools update their buildings to new city or county building codes, ADA requirements, and technology requirements. Construction due to capital improvements may cause the **displacement** of students and staff from certain areas of the school plant where construction occurs or, in more substantial projects, **relocation** to another setting until construction is completed.

Acquisition and Maintenance of Equipment and Technology

DETERMINING EQUIPMENT TO ACQUIRE

A leader must decide if new equipment is necessary for the effective operation of the physical plant as well as the implementation of the instructional program. A leader should be aware of the **life expectancy** of the various equipment that is already on campus so that he or she can determine when new equipment may be needed. This helps in the planning of maintenance, repair, and replacement cycles. Also, the leader must determine if equipment is **mandatory** or **optional**. Equipment that must be present on campus for its operation is prioritized over equipment that can be acquired or repaired at a later date. For example, a leader may need to postpone the acquisition of new science lab equipment in order to repair air conditioning units. **School finances** must also be considered when contemplating the acquisition of new equipment. A leader may need to postpone the purchase of major equipment until a new fiscal year due to budget constraints. The school leader should also consider the **impact** of the new equipment. If the purchase of new equipment will impact the majority of the students or staff, it can be placed higher on the priority list than equipment that may impact a small group of students, such as a student organization or specialized instructional program.

ROLE OF TECHNOLOGY ON CAMPUS

Technology on campus impacts campus safety, communication, and instruction. Technology hardware and software are vital to the school. Technology can be used to assist with **campus safety**. For example, cameras are placed on campus to monitor activity. These cameras and the associated software necessary for monitoring and recording the camera feeds are important to school safety. Other technology used for safety includes intercom systems for screening of visitors, software to conduct background checks of visitors and volunteers, and automated door locking systems. Technology also aids in **effective communication** on campus. Emails, intercoms and radios, PA systems, marquees, and other forms of technology are used to communicate to staff and students. Also, technology is very useful for **instruction**. Computers, projectors, printers, and many other technological devices enhance the quality of instruction that is provided to students. Both staff and students may use these devices as part of the instructional routine.

Allocating Resources and Budgeting

CALCULATING FUNDING

School funding comes from a variety of sources. The **federal government** provides some funding, but this is usually not substantial and may fluctuate due to changing budget decisions at the federal level. The **state governments** also provide funding to schools based on income and/or sales taxes. The majority of school funding in most states comes from property taxes within the school district. Both residences and commercial properties are taxed and a portion of those taxes are allocated to school districts. Some states, such as California, allocate school funding differently and may use income taxes instead of property taxes as the primary funding source. Schools generally receive an allotment of funds on a **per-pupil basis**. The per-pupil allotment differs by school district but may average about $10,000 per pupil. However, certain programs warrant extra funds on top of this allotment, such as special education programs and technology programs. Schools and school districts often seek grants and donations from **foundations** to supplement their budget.

CENTRALIZED BUDGETING AND DECENTRALIZED BUDGETING

Centralized and decentralized budgeting refers to the locus of control for budgeting decisions within a school district. In a **centralized school district**, all budgetary decision-making is conducted by **district leaders** within the district office. Principals and the campuses they lead have little to no budgetary authority in a centralized district. When a district is centralized, principals must follow strict guidelines as to what can be purchased and when. The benefit of a centralized budgeting process is that budgeting decisions are controlled and quality and efficiency can be easily monitored. However, this type of system can prevent staff buy-in and cause school leaders to feel they do not have the authority to make the changes necessary for their school to be successful. In contrast, in a **decentralized district**, **principals** have the authority to make budgetary and purchasing decisions. This allows principals to determine which resources meet the needs of each individual campus and gives them the latitude and flexibility to address campus needs. The benefit of a decentralized budgeting process is the flexibility and increased buy-in of leaders. However, this type of system can be more difficult to monitor and cause more instances of mismanagement of funds.

ALLOCATING FUNDS

A leader should consider multiple factors when allocating funds. First, the leader should refer to the school's **vision**. The allocation of funds should align with that vision. Similarly, the leader should align the allocation of funds to the school's **goals**. It is likely that the goals that are set for the school require funds and resources to accomplish them, so these funds should be allocated first. A leader should also consider whether funds are **recurring or one-time funds**. When a school receives funds that will not be renewed, a school leader must ensure that whatever is completed with those funds is sustainable for the future once those funds are gone. The school leader must also evaluate the **school program** and **organizational structure** to ensure that sufficient funds are allocated to the successful and efficient operation of the school program.

FACTORS AFFECTING A DISTRICT'S BUDGET

A school's budget is not fixed but can vary from year to year based on a variety of factors. Funding from the federal and state government can fluctuate and impact campus budgeting. In some years, the government provides **one-time funding** that cannot be expected in subsequent years, which causes fluctuations. Additionally, the government can **change allocations** of funding for specific programs. For example, allocation of funding for Career and Technology Education may be altered, so even though the number of students participating in the program does not change, the received funds do. **Local property taxes** may change in a school district, affecting the money allocated to schools. Additional factors include changes in student enrollment, changes in school programming, and other factors. Each year, a school leader must evaluate the proposed budget for the school year and make decisions based on each year's **budgetary allocations**.

SEEKING ADDITIONAL RESOURCES

A school leader may seek additional resources for accomplishing goals because there may not be sufficient school funding to accomplish everything that needs to be accomplished. When planning school budgets, leaders have to determine how to **allocate funds**. Often budgets have **shortfalls**, especially for initiatives that are lower on the priority list. As a result, a leader may have to seek funding and resources from **outside of school** to accomplish these goals. These additional resources may be in the form of grants, donations, volunteers, etc. For example, if a school leader wanted to establish a garden on campus, rather than using school funds for the gardening supplies and staff to tend the garden, the leader may solicit donations of gardening tools and volunteers to work in the garden. These types of resources can be very beneficial to the instructional program and alleviate some of the constraints of the school budget.

THE LEADER'S ROLE IN ADVOCATING FOR RESOURCES

The leader has the primary role in ensuring that **sufficient resources** are available to accomplish the set goals. First, the leader should properly allocate the funds and resources allotted by the **school district** to meet goals. If there is a shortfall in resources, the leader is responsible for advocating on behalf of the school to solicit **additional resources**. This may include petitioning for additional resources from the school district or seeking resources from community organizations and businesses. A leader may apply for grants to support the school program; seek donations of funds, resources, or equipment; or gather volunteers for staffing support. For example, if the school cannot afford to purchase new computers, a leader may ask a business organization to donate used computers to the school. The leader should take initiative in securing the resources necessary to accomplish the goals that he or she set for the school.

COMMUNITY-BASED RESOURCES

There are many community-based resources that are likely available to schools. For many communities, **local churches** offer a variety of resources that can support the school, such as volunteers, food and clothing for students and families in need, and much more. Also, many cities have **local community programs** to support the physical and mental health needs of the community and to provide nutritional support to families in need. There may be programs related to local transportation, arts, sciences, sports, clubs, and others that are available in the community. A school leader should be aware of all of the **organizations** in the surrounding community and communicate with these organizations to determine how they can partner to support students and their families. Often, these community-based resources can support students' **non-instructional needs** so that they can participate in the school program. These needs may include counseling, health-related needs, food and housing needs, and others.

Recruiting Highly Qualified Personnel

HIGHLY QUALIFIED PERSONNEL

The term "highly qualified" is used to describe the **minimum qualifications** of a teacher according to the No Child Left Behind Act, enacted in 2001. To meet staffing expectations, a leader has the responsibility of ensuring that teachers are highly qualified. This means that the teacher must hold a **bachelor's degree** and either have full **state licensure/certification** or **demonstrate knowledge of the subject** that he or she will teach. Based on this definition, states have enacted various procedures that enable teachers to demonstrate their content area knowledge, such as testing. A teacher may be highly qualified in one subject area and not in another. For example, a teacher may be deemed highly qualified to teach chemistry due to holding a bachelor's degree in science and being state certified in chemistry, but that same teacher would not be highly qualified to teach biology. Having highly qualified staff on campus ensures that teachers are knowledgeable in their assigned content areas and capable of teaching the content to students.

RECRUITMENT STRATEGIES

Leaders can employ several strategies to recruit highly qualified personnel. Leaders can participate in **recruitment fairs**. These are often hosted by the school district or by community organizations. Leaders can follow up with people from the event for interviews or may even conduct screening interviews at these fairs. Also, leaders can contact **teacher preparation programs** for referrals of recently certified teachers. These entities have lists of recent graduates along with their areas of specialization. However, these lists include people with limited or no teaching experience. It can also be helpful to post advertisements on **traditional recruitment sites**. Some sites specialize in recruiting for education. Finally, leaders can use **word of mouth advertising** to recruit highly qualified personnel. Teachers and staff on campus may have colleagues in other locations who would like to work at a new school. For example, a person may want to work at a school that is closer to home or teach a different grade level.

IMPORTANCE OF BEING FULLY STAFFED

If a school leader has numerous teaching vacancies, it can be difficult to have all staff in place at the outset of the school year. However, the **beginning of the school year** is a critical time that can impact the success of the entire school year, so a leader should strive to have 100% of staff in place before school starts. First, important **training and professional development** occur prior to the start of school. A teacher who is hired later will miss these. Additionally, teaching staff begin to **bond and unite** as a team prior to the start of the year and a teacher would miss this opportunity if hired late. Also, students learn **procedures and expectations** for behavior and learning at the beginning of the school year. A teacher who is hired late may have to reset expectations for students, which could cause a difficult start for both the teacher and the students.

TEMPORARY STAFFING

At times it is necessary to have temporary staff to support the instructional program. If there is a teaching vacancy or if a teacher is absent for an extended period of time, a leader may have to obtain **temporary personnel** until a permanent solution is found. Often, however, temporary staff persons are **not highly qualified** and do not have the same **training and experience** that permanent staff members do. As a result, the quality of instruction may be reduced when temporary staff persons are in the classroom. Additionally, with temporary staff persons, there may be a need for increased monitoring and support from other permanent staff persons, such as clerks and administrators, to ensure the effective and efficient progress of the instructional program. This can produce further strain on staff and the instructional program. To ensure that the instructional program is excelling and that students are receiving high quality instruction, the school leader should minimize the need for temporary staff.

RECRUITMENT CONSIDERATIONS
IMPACT OF SCHOOL CULTURE

School culture is determined by the leader and the staff of the campus. The school culture can create a welcoming environment for new teachers or it can repel them. When the school culture is **positive**, focused on students, and driven by excellence, teachers will want to be part of that culture. They will be motivated by the positive culture and will recruit others to join the team. Additionally, when the culture is positive, students thrive, which can make the teacher's job easier and more enjoyable. On the other hand, if the school culture is **negative**, teachers and staff will likely have negative attitudes as well. Teachers will seek a way out of that school environment rather than encouraging others to join the team. This negative culture can negatively affect student academic performance and behavior. If a potential teacher candidate observes a negative school culture, he or she may be unwilling to work at that campus.

IMPACT OF LEADERSHIP STYLE

The leadership style of the school leader and other leaders on campus can positively or negatively impact **teacher recruitment**. A leadership style that is perceived as **negative** can deter teachers from wanting to work at that leader's campus. During the recruitment process, a candidate may observe how the school leader speaks to him or her, the way the leader treats staff and students, and other indicators of leadership style. For example, if a leader is perceived as being overly demanding, negative, or micromanaging, a teaching candidate will not want to work for him or her. In contrast, if a leader is **fair, supportive, and warm**, a teaching candidate will be attracted to the position. Effective leaders attract effective teachers. Teachers will seek to work on campuses where they will thrive and grow, and the school leader is an indication of whether the campus will meet a teacher's professional needs.

Safe Environments

PHYSICALLY SAFE ENVIRONMENTS

A physically safe environment is free from seen and unseen dangers that would pose a threat to the physical safety of anyone exposed to the environment. A **physically safe environment** is in good repair, accessible to all, and accommodating to its designated purpose. For example, a physically safe classroom would be free from damaged walls, ceilings, or floors; broken or damaged furniture; leaky pipes or plumbing; and electrical hazards. Additionally, a physically safe environment includes **well-controlled people** so that no one is physically harmed by the presence of others. This includes adhering to **capacity limitations** and monitoring the **conduct** of those present in the environment. For example, a school cafeteria should not exceed the posted maximum capacity of people, even for special events, and people should be able to move safely and freely in the cafeteria in accordance with its purpose.

EMOTIONALLY SAFE ENVIRONMENTS

An emotionally safe environment is an environment in which all people are able to **learn**. This type of environment is free from all obstacles, emotions, and conflicts due to **preventative strategies** and **quick resolutions**. When an environment is not emotionally safe, children can feel fear, anxiety, and a host of other emotions. In an **emotionally safe environment**, both adults and children feel comfortable participating in the learning environment and interacting with one another. There is an absence of peer-to-peer and peer-to-adult conflict as well as bullying.

Procedures and systems, such as counseling, mentoring, and other interventions, are in place to ensure the emotional safety of students on campus. There is an emphasis on **communicating** one's needs to foster active participation and engagement in the learning process. Additionally, the **physical arrangement** of the environment is designed to contribute to emotional safety, such as including windows and natural lighting, inspirational and positive posters and bulletin boards, and aesthetically pleasing furniture and decoration.

SAFE, EFFICIENT, AND EFFECTIVE OPERATION OF PHYSICAL PLANTS, EQUIPMENT, AND SUPPORT SYSTEMS

A leader must ensure that the school's physical plant, equipment, and support systems operate safely, efficiently, and effectively. The first step is to identify the appropriate staff to **manage** the physical plant. This person has the primary responsibility to ensure the safe functioning of everything on campus, so the leader must have the right person in place and must monitor his or her performance. Also, the leader must provide the plant manager with **competent staff** to support plant maintenance. In partnership with the manager, the leader can develop systems of **monitoring and inspection** to ensure that all aspects of the plant are running efficiently and safely. The school leader should also solicit **feedback** from other staff members who use certain aspects of the school plant. For example, if the school has a swimming pool, the leader should get feedback from the swimming coach or athletic director regarding the pool facilities. This feedback can help to identify areas of improvement, repair, or replacement needs.

LAWS AND POLICIES REGARDING MAINTAINING A SAFE ENVIRONMENT

Local, state, and federal laws and policies help school leaders maintain a safe environment for students and staff. These regulations and policies, when adhered to, create a minimum level of safety. For example, **federal laws** regarding aspects of school safety such as asbestos management, ADA compliance, internet safety, and others are interpreted into school policies. **School districts** may have additional safety requirements, such as the presence of police officers on campus, campus visitor policies, volunteer policies, and others. **Local laws and policies** may include fire codes and occupation limits, as well as other mandates for building safety that are not particular to schools but are implemented in all public places in the area. Each of these regulations and policies is meant to **enhance the safety** of the school, so the school leader should prioritize adherence to these regulations and policies. Failure to comply with local, state, and federal laws and policies can result in sanctions, fines, or other repercussions.

MAINTAINING A PHYSICALLY SAFE ENVIRONMENT FOR STUDENTS

A leader should take proactive steps to maintain a physically safe environment for students. First, the school leader should conduct regular **inspection and maintenance** of all parts of the building to ensure that no aspects of the physical building pose hazards to students. Next, the school leader should **monitor flows of traffic** within the school building to maintain safety. For example, a leader may notice that a school banner obstructs visibility in a hallway, causing students to bump into one another during transitions between classes. To promote safety, the leader should relocate the banner to a different area of the school. The leader should also ensure that common assembly areas such as hallways, courtyards, auditoriums, and others are monitored by school staff to prevent or identify **conflict between students** that could lead to physical harm.

MAINTAINING AN EMOTIONALLY SAFE ENVIRONMENT FOR STAFF

Like the students, staff members need an emotionally safe environment. A leader can establish and maintain an **emotionally safe environment** through leadership style, communication, awareness, and support. When a leader has a **caring and empathetic demeanor**, employees will feel emotionally safe. In contrast, **high-strung, micromanaging leaders** can create fear and anxiety in staff. Also, leaders need to maintain **open lines of communication** with staff members. This allows them to communicate their needs so the leader can address them when possible. A leader should be able to recognize and be aware of aspects of the environment that **endanger emotional safety** for staff and should be able to address those concerns. For example, a lax discipline policy can create a challenging environment for teachers and staff. A leader can take steps to remedy this and create a safer environment. Finally, a leader should provide **avenues of emotional support** for staff. This may include staff counseling, referrals, or other accommodations and support that can help staff members feel emotionally safe.

Disciplinary Expectations and Behavior Management

BEHAVIORAL EXPECTATIONS FOR STAFF AND STUDENTS

SAFE STUDENT BEHAVIOR

Student behavior must be regulated and controlled for a safe school environment. Students who are unsupervised or do not adhere to established rules and procedures pose a **threat** to the safety of the school and to themselves. As a result, **student behavior management** is necessary to maintain a safe environment. School staff and ultimately the school leader are responsible for the safety of students the entire time they are at school. Unsupervised students may lead to an unsafe environment since they are less prone to follow rules when supervision is absent. All students should be accounted for at all times and actively monitored. Additionally, students who misbehave can cause disruption, conflict, destruction of property, and a host of other actions that threaten the safety of the school environment. As a result, negative student behavior must be addressed quickly and effectively to maintain a safe environment.

> **Review Video: Promoting Appropriate Behavior**
> Visit mometrix.com/academy and enter code: 321015

BEHAVIOR MANAGEMENT AND DISCIPLINE STRATEGIES

A leader may use a variety of behavior management and discipline strategies, as well as instructing staff to use them, to properly manage student behavior. These different techniques and strategies almost all have certain characteristics in common. Effective **behavior management** requires active **supervision**. It is not enough for adults to be present wherever students are. They must survey students, anticipate student behaviors, and be prepared to intervene when necessary. Also, most strategies require that adults set clear **expectations** for student behavior. This can be done through establishing rules, behavior contracts, or other ways to articulate expectations. Finally, there must be clear **consequences**, applied fairly and equitably, for behavioral infractions. Many behavior management strategies encourage building relationships and rapport with students, incorporating positive consequences for appropriate student behavior, and addressing student behaviors without overly emotional responses such as yelling, sarcasm, or unprofessional language.

STUDENT BEHAVIOR MANAGEMENT AND STUDENT SUCCESS

Student behavior management and student success are related because poor student behavior detracts from the learning environment. If a student is behaving in a disruptive or disengaged way in the classroom, he or she cannot **learn effectively**. If the poorly-behaved student misses the instructional content, he or she will be less likely to succeed academically in that class. Poor student behavior can also negatively impact the **academic success of other students** in the room. For example, speaking out of turn, interrupting, and bothering others detracts from the learning environment. Finally, some behavioral consequences require the misbehaving student to be **removed** from the classroom. In these instances, the student often loses out on instructional opportunities, which can negatively impact academic success. Consequently, when student behavior is appropriately managed, the learning environment is preserved and all students have an opportunity to learn in a safe environment.

> **Review Video: Student Behavior Management Approaches**
> Visit mometrix.com/academy and enter code: 843846

FAIRNESS AND EQUITY

Student behavior management strategies and discipline must be applied in a fair and equitable manner to be effective and maintain a positive school environment. **Fairness** involves **communicating expectations** prior to applying discipline. If expectations are unknown or unclear, students can be frustrated and deem it unfair to be held responsible. Fairness also means that the adults **adhere** to the expectations and consequences that have been communicated to students and parents. For example, a behavior strategy may be to give a student a warning before applying consequences. A teacher may give students multiple warnings on one day and never give consequences for a particular behavior, but on another day, the teacher may immediately give a consequence for the same behavior without a warning. This type of inconsistent behavior from the teacher would be deemed unfair. Also, staff must practice **equity** in discipline. Adherence to written policies and procedures can ensure that all students are disciplined in an equitable manner, regardless of race, gender, or academic and behavioral history.

Emergency Preparedness and Response

PLANNING FOR CRISES

Even though crises are unpredictable, a leader can plan in advance to ensure that the school is as prepared as possible. First, the leader should have **emergency plans** in place for events such as natural disasters, fire, medical emergencies, intruders on campus, etc. These plans should be written and key emergency staff should be trained on how to implement the plans in time of crisis. Additionally, the leader can implement **drills** to practice the crisis plans. The leader can evaluate staff and student performance during these drills and provide feedback to participants or revise the emergency plans based on the performance. The leader should also be familiar with **district policies** regarding emergency plans, drills, and reporting. A leader should make contact with **local emergency services** in the community to establish a relationship and ascertain important information and contacts to help in the event of an emergency or crisis.

PROCEDURES IN EMERGENCY SITUATIONS

Procedures are necessary in emergency situations to ensure the safety of everyone affected. In emergency situations, emotions can cloud thinking and judgment. Additionally, people who are not familiar with a particular emergency situation may not know what to do in these instances. Having a **procedure** in place ensures that the right actions are taken in the event of an emergency, regardless of the emotional state or expertise of those involved. For example, if a person has a health emergency on campus, procedures should be in place for addressing the situation, including calling an ambulance, providing emergency aid, and maintaining the safety and order of the staff and students not immediately involved in the situation. These procedures should be taught to all **staff** on campus and be available in **written form** so they are accessible in the event of emergency. Having written procedures in place and abiding by them in the event of an emergency can also serve as legal protection for the school leader and staff.

KEY EMERGENCY SUPPORT PERSONNEL

The school leader should identify key emergency support personnel **on campus** to prepare them for emergencies. These key staff members should know their **roles** in each emergency instance and be trained on how to fulfill those roles in the event of an emergency. These staff members may include the school nurse, counselor, police officer or security personnel, administrators or other school leaders, clerks, and others, depending on the nature of the emergency. For example, a different team of personnel may be needed to respond to a health emergency than a natural disaster emergency. Emergency support personnel **outside of the school** may include key district staff members and personnel at various emergency response organizations, such as the fire department.

EMERGENCY PREPAREDNESS

Emergency preparedness means that the school leader and staff have identified **potential types of emergencies** and planned the **procedures, staff, and resources** needed to address each type. Emergencies may include health emergencies, fire, natural disaster, intruders on campus, and many others. For each of these potential emergencies, a **written plan of procedures** should be created, detailing how everyone on campus should behave in the event of such an emergency. **Key personnel** with specific roles and responsibilities should be identified in the written plan. Everyone should be trained prior to the emergency to follow the written procedures. For many emergencies, **practice drills** can be conducted, such as fire drills or school lockdowns. Also, **resources** should be acquired, stored in designated locations, and inspected periodically. These resources may include printed copies of emergency procedures, fire extinguishers, automatic defibrillators, first aid kits, and other resources.

INCIDENT COMMAND SYSTEM (ICS)

The **Incident Command System (ICS)** is a framework designed to enhance the coordination and management of emergency responses. In the context of school emergency response teams, ICS serves as a comprehensive structure that delineates clear roles, responsibilities, and communication channels during crises. One of the primary functions of ICS is to establish a unified command structure, ensuring that all involved parties—from school administrators to first responders—operate under a centralized leadership. This organizational clarity promotes efficient resource utilization and aids in effective decision-making, contributing directly to the competency of maximizing a safe and effective learning environment. By implementing ICS, school emergency response teams can optimize their use of resources, both human and material, to respond swiftly and appropriately to emergencies. The system allows for a strategic and coordinated approach that reflects effective fiscal management while prioritizing the safety and well-being of students and staff. Through standardized procedures and clear lines of communication, ICS minimizes potential chaos, enabling schools to navigate emergencies with precision. This not only aligns with the objective of maintaining a safe learning environment but also underscores the significance of judicious resource allocation in achieving this goal.

Promoting the Welfare of Staff and Students

KEY STAFF THAT CAN PROMOTE THE WELFARE OF STAFF AND STUDENTS

The key staff member responsible for promoting the welfare of staff and students is the **school leader**. The school leader creates a **school culture** in which students and staff feel safe, as well as **structures and systems** to provide support and intervention for students and staff in need. The school leader also sets the **example** for treatment of students and staff, such as displaying understanding, empathy, and compassion. The school leader should also identify other key staff who can promote the welfare of staff and students. Each member of the **leadership team**, such as assistant principals or deans, should take the lead in promoting the welfare of all and lead by example. The school leader should also enlist the support of counselors, nurses, and others who can be proactive in identifying and responding to the needs of students and staff. Additionally, teachers play a key role in identifying the needs of students and promoting their welfare within the classroom.

PROMOTING COUNSELING AND WELLNESS

A leader should promote counseling and wellness to encourage staff and students to take advantage of these supports for their own welfare. A leader can do this by making **counseling and wellness programs** visible to all. This may mean having signs and displays around the school that promote these programs. Also, the leader can communicate the **availability of these resources** using common means of communication, such as emails, news bulletins, school public announcements, and announcements in staff meetings. The staff members who lead counseling and wellness programs can be included in other school projects and programs, such as in behavior intervention meetings or academic interventions, so that they are viewed as an **integral part of the campus team**. A school leader can also consider hosting **mental health and wellness fairs** for school members and the community to raise awareness about potential health concerns and to promote available services.

STAFF HEALTH AND EMOTIONAL SUPPORT

A leader can watch for several indicators to determine that staff members may need a recommendation to **counseling and health services**. Teachers and staff who need help may be **frequently absent** without a reasonable excuse. These absences may be jokingly referred to as "mental health days" but are often indicators that a staff person is stressed or overwhelmed. Another indicator of a need for counseling and health services are **overly emotional responses** to everyday stimuli. These responses may include yelling, crying, or bursts of anger. The school leader can also look for **changes in staff behavior**. For example, if a staff member who is usually outgoing, energetic, and talkative becomes withdrawn and disengaged, this may indicate a need for additional support. Staff who are unable to do their jobs satisfactorily, especially if they have a history of satisfactory performance, may need support from counseling and health services. The school leader should keep communication open so that staff are comfortable communicating that they need help.

STUDENT HEALTH AND EMOTIONAL SUPPORT

A leader can watch for several indicators to determine that students may need a recommendation to **counseling and health services**. A student may begin to act out and display **negative behaviors** in the classroom with other students or with adults on campus. This can be an indicator if the student does not usually display poor behavior at school. Additionally, a student who is usually engaged in classroom activities and with peers but becomes **withdrawn and disengaged** may also need help. These indicators can also lead to poor academic performance, indicated by falling grades. Students in need of support may also demonstrate **emotional responses** in school such as angry outbursts, crying, yelling, or even physical altercations with other students. In some instances, a **parent** may communicate with a staff member that the child is having difficulty at home as well. A school leader should ensure that **systems** are in place on campus to allow students to express their needs so that they can be referred for services. This may include having walk-in counseling hours or open-door policies with key staff members.

AVAILABLE TYPES OF MENTAL HEALTH SERVICES WITHIN A PUBLIC-SCHOOL SETTING

School counselors are trained to work with students, teachers, and families to identify and address issues that may affect students' well-being and academic performance. Through **individual or group counseling** sessions, students can develop coping strategies, interpersonal skills, and emotional resilience, all of which helps foster an environment where they can thrive academically. Schools often implement **Social and Emotional Learning (SEL) programs** to promote the development of crucial life skills. These programs aim to enhance students' self-awareness, emotional regulation, and interpersonal skills, thus creating a positive and inclusive school culture. **Partnerships** with external mental health organizations allow schools to provide specialized services such as therapy and interventions for students with more complex mental health needs. Such partnerships allow students to receive the appropriate level of intervention based on their unique needs. Monitoring the impact of mental health services involves regular assessments of students' emotional well-being and the overall school climate. This can be achieved through surveys, behavioral observations, and academic performance data.

SEL PROGRAMS

Social and Emotional Learning (SEL) programs aim to equip students with essential life skills by promoting self-awareness, social awareness, responsible decision-making, and relationship-building. These programs typically involve structured curricula, classroom activities, and resources designed to enhance students' emotional intelligence and interpersonal skills, contributing to their overall well-being and academic success.

SPBS PROGRAMS

The **School-wide Positive Behavior Support (SPBS)** program focuses on establishing a positive school climate through proactive strategies. SPBS emphasizes clear expectations for behavior, consistent reinforcement of positive actions, and the use of data-driven approaches to address behavioral challenges. By creating a school-wide framework that reinforces positive behaviors and teaches appropriate alternatives, SPBS contributes to a culture where students feel supported and motivated to engage actively in their learning.

CASEL

The **Collaborative for Academic, Social, and Emotional Learning (CASEL)** is an organization dedicated to advancing the integration of social and emotional learning into education. CASEL provides resources, research, and frameworks to support educators in implementing evidence-based SEL practices. This collaborative approach ensures that schools have access to the latest research and effective strategies, facilitating the development of comprehensive programs that address the academic, social, and emotional needs of students.

MAKING REPORTS TO CHILD PROTECTIVE SERVICES

Child Protective Services is a service provided by state agencies to protect the welfare of children. This agency investigates allegations of **child abuse or neglect** and provides services to children should such allegations be proven valid. There will be instances in which the school leader or a school staff member has reason to believe that a child is being neglected or abused. Whenever there is suspicion of abuse or neglect, it is each staff person's responsibility, including the school leader's, to submit a **formal report** to Child Protective Services for investigation. For example, if a teacher reports to the school leader that one of her students has confided that his mother is hitting him with various objects and shows the teacher bruises, both the teacher and the leader should file a report. There can be legal ramifications for staff members who fail to report suspected child abuse or neglect.

Being proactive in promoting the wellness of staff and students means that the leader is actively looking for ways to **maintain the wellness** of all before problems arise. This is important because **prevention** is often more effective and less costly than trying to address a problem after it has already occurred. For example, taking steps to prevent teen suicide is a better course of action than addressing a grieving student body after a teen has committed suicide. Similarly, it is more effective to help an unwell teacher obtain needed help than to lose the teacher for the remainder of the school year due to a health crisis. The school leader should **proactively** promote wellness and identify potential wellness needs among students and staff so that mental health crises can be prevented or at least detected early in an effort to prevent tragedies that directly affect the student body and staff. Being proactive demonstrates to all that the leader is concerned about the wellness of staff and students and is willing to take the needed steps to address their health concerns.

Helping Staff and Students Deal with Grief on Campus

At times the student body and staff members will experience the loss of a peer or colleague. In these instances, the school leader will need to implement strategies to address the **grief** that students and staff experience. The first step that the leader must take is to **acknowledge** the loss. The leader should not operate with a "business-as-usual" attitude. Many schools have access to grief counselors who can be present on campus to assist students or staff who need assistance in dealing with their emotions. The school leader should also demonstrate **understanding and compassion** during this time and recognize that grief may cause students or staff to behave out of character, such as missing school, expressing outbursts of emotion like sadness or anger in school, or being disengaged from academic activities. It is important to **listen** to the needs of the students and staff during this time. The leader may provide opportunities for students and staff to express their feelings or to honor the one who has died.

Preventing Teen Suicide

The school leader can take steps to aid in the prevention of teen suicide or self-harm. Although many factors and influences outside of the school can lead a young person to commit suicide, the school and its staff can serve as a resource and support to students who experience suicidal thoughts. First, the leader should create a **school culture** in which students feel comfortable turning to teachers and staff for support. When this type of culture is present, a student is more likely to share thoughts of self-harm with a staff member, which can aid in prevention. The school should also have **counseling staff and resources** available for students who are experiencing emotional issues. Many schools discuss this topic with the student body and provide telephone hotline numbers for support 24 hours a day. Also, if an adult becomes aware that a student is contemplating suicide or self-harm, he or she has a duty to report it to the proper authorities.

Role Social Media Plays in Student Wellness and Mental Health

Social media has a large influence on students' wellness and mental health. Students who engage in social media often experience **negative emotions** as a result. Some students develop feelings of **inadequacy or low self-esteem** when they compare themselves to others online. This is the result of unrealistic beauty expectations and exaggerated portrayals of others' lives. Additionally, students may be exposed to **cyberbullying** via social media. This type of bullying can involve name-calling, threats, shaming, spreading rumors, and other negative behaviors that can negatively impact a student's well-being. Cyberbullying can lead to bullying and other conflict on campus as well. Finally, engaging in social media can be addictive for some youth. They may spend excessive amounts of time on social media or engage in risky behaviors in an attempt to gain social media attention. For example, a student may post provocative pictures of him or herself in an effort to attract attention. This can have negative consequences for the student's mental health and overall wellness.

DISTRICT LEADER AND PHYSICAL AND MENTAL WELLNESS

In addition to ensuring the wellness of students and staff, the school leader should take steps to ensure his or her own **physical and mental wellness**. A leader cannot fulfill job responsibilities properly if he or she is not well. Also, the school leader should set an **example** for staff and students by prioritizing personal health needs. This is primarily accomplished by being proactive instead of waiting until a health problem arises to address it. First, the leader should **delegate responsibilities** and **accept assistance** whenever possible to keep stress levels low. The leader should also get regular **checkups** to quickly identify potential health problems. **Eating and sleeping** properly are also key components of maintaining physical and emotional health. Finally, the school leader should take advantage of the **resources and supports** that are offered on campus and through the school district. These may include counseling, use of workout facilities, support groups, nurse hotlines, and many other resources designed to support the physical and mental health of staff.

UTILIZING COMMUNITY SERVICES TO PROMOTE WELLNESS

It is important for a school leader to utilize community services for staff and student welfare because school funds and resources are often insufficient to provide abundant resources for staff and students. Even if a school has sufficient budgetary resources, there is no need to spend funds on resources that may be available as a **free community service**. Also, utilizing community services may expand the number and type of resources that are available, which means more support and help for members of the school community. Most school services only provide services directly to students, whereas community services often have programs, resources, and support for the **entire family**, which can be more impactful to students and their families in many instances. Finally, utilizing community services builds **partnerships and relationships** between the school and the community, which can have long-range benefits for both parties. For example, schools and community organizations can partner in community events, student recruitment, and applications for grant funding.

IDENTIFYING COMMUNITY RESOURCES FOR PROMOTING WELLNESS

A leader can identify community resources for promoting wellness in a variety of ways. Often, these organizations desire to partner with the school and will visit or call the school to inform campus leadership of their services and identify ways that they can serve the school community. Sometimes school district offices maintain **directories** of community organizations and programs that support students and their families within the school district. The school leader can also do a basic internet search to identify nearby resources. **Local resources** include branches of city, county, or state organizations and are easily identified online. Finally, the school leader can make an effort to venture into the community and make **connections** with the leaders of area organizations to determine how the school and the organizations can collaborate.

Disciplinary Policy

DISCIPLINE POLICY AND CONFLICT RESOLUTION

DISCIPLINE

Discipline is training students to abide by a specific **code of behavior**. When discipline is present, **rules** are typically stated and taught, and **expectations for behavior** are defined in a variety of contexts and situations. In addition to the rules that are outlined as part of the discipline policy, there are **consequences** associated with failing to abide by the stated rules and expectations for behavior. Many people associate discipline with administering consequences for failing to follow rules. However, the essence of discipline is the practice of **training or teaching behavior**. In schools, rules are often set by the school district and written in a student code of conduct for district-wide discipline. Schools may also have campus-wide expectations for behavior as part of their discipline, as well as sets of rules for individual classrooms. When discipline is effective, students are fully aware of behavior expectations and the consequences associated with not meeting those expectations.

PROMOTING CONFLICT RESOLUTION

Conflict resolution is the practice of resolving conflicts or disagreements, such as verbal or physical altercations, between students to prevent further disruption. To promote conflict resolution, staff members must be vigilant in **identifying potential conflicts** among the student body. **Early intervention** is essential in resolving conflicts effectively. Staff members also want to **build relationships** with students and create an environment in which students feel comfortable reporting conflicts to adults. Both people experiencing the conflict should feel that there is an adult on campus who is willing and able to help them resolve the conflict. There should be **structures or systems** in place to practice conflict resolution, which can include identifying mediators, locating neutral spaces for conversations between the conflicted parties, including parents and guardians, and support services to meet students' mental health needs. Additionally, the campus culture should utilize and promote **conflict resolution**, rather than simply administering consequences. This can be done by promoting conversations between students and adults and among peers regarding various aspects of their school experiences.

APPLYING DISCIPLINARY POLICY

The school discipline policy must be applied to students in a fair and equitable manner. Many studies have shown that male students, especially minority males, are disciplined more often and more severely than their peers. **Unfair discipline** can lead to increased misbehavior from students who receive the discipline at a higher rate than others, as well as by students who witness the inequitable discipline. The student who is disciplined more frequently may believe that he or she will receive consequences regardless of behavior, so he or she may choose to misbehave and earn the consequences. Students who witness this may believe they will not be punished for their behavior, so they can behave however they like. Rules should be enforced **consistently**. For example, if a school rule states that students should not chew gum, this rule should be enforced at all times and with all students, not just when it is convenient for the teacher or other staff member. Additionally, applying discipline in an unfair or inequitable manner can **damage relationships** with students and parents and can negatively influence the school culture.

COMMUNICATING THE DISCIPLINE POLICY

The school's discipline policy should be communicated to students, staff, and parents. Students must understand **behavioral expectations** if they are to meet them. It cannot be assumed that all students and their families hold the same expectations for behavior. As a result, the school's discipline policy must be **clearly communicated**. This can be done with a printed **handbook** for student behavior, as well as through **verbal communication**. When the discipline policy is not communicated clearly, this can lead to confusion and anger when consequences are administered. Emotional reactions from students and their parents or guardians can be expected when consequences are administered, especially for severe consequences. Ambiguity around rules and consequences makes it difficult to administer discipline and can lead to the nullification of warranted consequences due to ineffective communication of the discipline policy.

BULLYING

Bullying occurs when one uses strength or other means of influence to **intimidate** another person. Bullying can be verbal, social, or physical and involves an imbalance of power. To prevent bullying, a school leader must employ several strategies. First, students and staff must be aware of what bullying is and is not. This will help to **identify** bullying quickly if it occurs. Also, the leader should create an environment in which bullying is **not acceptable or tolerated**. This will encourage those who are being bullied and those who observe bullying to report it so that it can be stopped. The school leader and the staff should also **model healthy, respectful relationships** with one another. The leader should not be a bully to staff, nor should staff bully students, as this would set an inappropriate model for students on campus. Additionally, acts of bullying should be addressed **swiftly and effectively**. This may include disciplinary consequences or other interventions such as peer mediation, counseling, or other strategies.

COMMON DISCIPLINARY PROBLEMS

Many disciplinary issues among students are common and can be prepared for with effective **classroom management strategies**. One category of common discipline problems is **disengagement**. Students who disengage are not usually disruptive of others in the instructional setting but are not receiving instruction. These students may put their heads down and sleep or participate in off-task activities such as drawing, reading, writing, or daydreaming. Another category of discipline problems is **disruptive**. These behaviors indicate that the misbehaving student is not participating in instruction and is also preventing others from participating. These behaviors include excessive talking, standing or walking around at inappropriate times, calling out, touching or hitting others, making disruptive noises, and many others. These types of behavior are often addressed by the teacher when they occur and do not require serious disciplinary consequences unless the behaviors are repeated and the student does not respond to redirection.

USING RESTORATIVE JUSTICE IN SCHOOLS

Restorative justice is a practice in which students who have harmed their school community or an individual through their misbehavior are required to **repair the harm**. The first step is to facilitate a **conversation** regarding the offender's behavior. This is usually led by an adult in the school. The offender has the opportunity to provide his or her side of the story and give input on the consequences. Traditional consequences usually include detention, suspension, and expulsion, among others, whereas restorative justice provides an opportunity for a holistic approach to **correcting the misbehavior**, i.e., "righting a wrong" or "making it right" and preventing it from recurring in the future. There are **no predefined consequences**, as these might vary significantly, based on the individual incident. For example, if a student has a temper tantrum, flips a desk in a classroom, and overturns a supply table, a community of adults and peers may determine that the student must clean the classroom during lunch for a week in addition to offering a public apology to the teacher and classmates.

CLASSROOM MANAGEMENT

Classroom management refers to the strategies that teachers use to maintain order in the classroom and establish an environment conducive to learning. Classroom management is effective in preventing and addressing **minor disciplinary problems**. A teacher who demonstrates effective classroom management considers student behavior and management in all aspects of the instructional process, including lesson planning, lesson delivery, room arrangement, procedures, and more. For example, a teacher may use **diverse instructional practices** to engage students and prevent disengagement or off-task behavior during a lesson. A teacher may also design a lesson so that students can get out of their seats and **move** to different areas of the classroom at various points. Classroom management also involves having clear **expectations** for student behavior, established **procedures** for all instructional activities, and strategies for effective **redirection** of students who misbehave. Teachers with effective classroom management also build **rapport** with students and utilize **parental communication** to preserve the learning environment.

DISCIPLINE APPROACHES

School discipline approaches range from lax to very stringent. A **lax approach** does not mean that school discipline does not exist; it means that discipline is often determined on an individual basis, reflective of the circumstances and individuals involved. This may include practices such as teen or peer courts and restorative justice models. Some discipline approaches combine **individualized disciplinary strategies** with **set disciplinary policies**. These approaches may offer flexibility in disciplinary options for relatively minor offenses and more defined options for more severe offenses. The most **stringent discipline approaches** have strict, pre-determined consequences for student misbehaviors. The most common example of this type of discipline approach is a zero-tolerance policy. In **zero-tolerance policies**, the consequences associated with particular behavioral infractions are administered without regard to the individual offender, context, or other variables within the situation. Many schools implement discipline approaches that fall within the midrange of this continuum, but a school leader should determine the best discipline approach for the campus based on student needs.

PARENTAL COMMUNICATION

Parental communication is an asset when addressing student discipline problems. It is important that parents are aware of their children's behavior while at school. This awareness, fostered through consistent and effective communication between the school and the parent, can help build a **positive relationship and rapport**. Additionally, the parent can support the school in disciplinary efforts and vice versa to establish **consistency** in behavioral expectations of the student. Finally, communication provides parents with the opportunity to **intervene** in a child's misbehavior before those behaviors escalate to more severe behaviors or have a negative impact on the student's academic progress. Failure to communicate with a parent regarding a child's behavior can cause **negative consequences** for the school, such as complaints about how the discipline was handled by school administration or contesting of assigned consequences. Parents or guardians should always be part of the disciplinary process.

SEVERE DISCIPLINARY PROBLEMS

ROLE OF SPECIAL EDUCATION STATUS IN ADDRESSING DISCIPLINARY PROBLEMS

When a student who is identified as receiving special education services displays behavioral issues, it is important to take certain steps to meet the child's needs. Some students with this identification already have **behavioral plans** in place. Teachers and school leaders must abide by these plans, which may include specific strategies for correcting a student's behavior or predetermined disciplinary consequences decided by the special education committee, which may or may not be aligned to the general student code of conduct. If a student who receives special education services commits a **severe disciplinary infraction** that could warrant consequences such as suspension or expulsion, a special meeting must be held by the special education committee to determine if the behavior was a manifestation of the student's identified disability. If it is concluded by the committee that the behavior is a manifestation of the student's identified disability, that student would likely not be subject to the traditional disciplinary consequences outlined by the student code of conduct. On the other hand, if the committee determines that the student's behavior is not associated with the disability, the student would likely be subject to the outlined disciplinary consequences.

ROLE OF DISCIPLINARY ALTERNATIVE EDUCATION PROGRAMS

Suspension and expulsion are consequences for severe student behavioral infractions. **Suspensions** typically last one to three days, but for some offenses, students are removed from the traditional education setting for longer periods of time. The public school system provides a means of education for all students, even those who have been removed from their traditional school due to extended suspension or expulsion. Students in these situations may receive their education through an **alternative education program**. In these programs, students may be assigned to attend the program for a certain number of days, usually for no longer than a school year. School districts may establish alternative education programs within the district or work with a program operating in that region. Additionally, students who commit crimes punishable by law may attend a school operated by the local **juvenile justice department**. Like other alternative education programs, the assigned duration that a student must attend varies based on the offense, as deemed by the courts.

ROLE OF LAW ENFORCEMENT IN SCHOOL DISCIPLINE

Some student behavioral infractions are not only violations of school codes of conduct, but also of the law. Consequently, **law enforcement** has the right and responsibility to administer **legal consequences** in addition to local disciplinary consequences. For example, if students engage in a physical altercation on campus, they are subject to local disciplinary consequences which may include suspension, but they are also subject to the law, which may warrant a citation. Many school districts and school leaders have opted to maintain a **police presence** on campus at all times. A school district may have its own police department dedicated to its schools. This police presence is established for the safety of everyone on campus, but if students break the law, the police exercise their authority by addressing the infraction. The involvement of law enforcement is discretionary, at times, depending on the offense. Law enforcement is not a replacement for school discipline, but a supplement.

Personal and Professional Ethics

INTEGRITY

Integrity refers to being honest and trustworthy and exhibiting moral principles. A person with integrity is generally of good character. A school leader can demonstrate **integrity** by behaving in a **trustworthy** manner with district personnel, staff, students, parents, and community stakeholders. The school leader should behave **ethically** in regard to all aspects of the position, including finance, personnel issues, and student matters. A school leader with integrity will hold him or herself and others **accountable** for ethical behavior, will recognize when ethics have been breached, and will take appropriate action in response. A school leader will also implement systems and procedures to ensure that the **rights and confidentiality** of students and staff are maintained at all times.

CONFLICT OF INTEREST

A conflict of interest is a situation in which the school leader can obtain personal gain or harm from a decision made as a leader. For example, a school leader may determine that the school gymnasium needs to be repainted. A family member of the leader owns a company that provides such a service and offers a bid. This would present a **conflict of interest** for the leader because he or she would potentially derive a benefit from hiring a family member's business to complete the job. Other situations that could present a conflict of interest may include hiring or terminating staff, awarding or disciplining a student who is a family member, or voting in an official capacity for colleagues or family members. A school leader should be aware of potential conflicts of interest and **alert superiors** should such a situation arise.

Protecting Privacy and Confidentiality of Information

Laws and regulations have been enacted to protect the privacy and confidentiality of students and staff in schools. Specifically, the **Family Educational Rights and Privacy Act (FERPA)** is a federal law that protects the privacy of **student education records**. Any school that receives funds from the United States Department of Education is subject to this law. It provides guidelines for who can access or view student records, who can alter student records, and what student information can be disseminated without student or parental consent. School leaders must abide by this law and implement policies and procedures on campus that ensure other school personnel also abide by this law. Additionally, schools have the obligation to **inform** parents and students aged 18 or older of their rights under FERPA.

Issues of Ethics and Integrity

A school leader will find that many of the situations they encounter involve **issues of ethics and integrity**. These situations may involve students, parents, personnel, and community members. Situations regarding **students** may involve grades, retention or promotion, assigning consequences in discipline matters, awards and recognition, and others. Situations involving **parents** may be student related or involve fundraising, elections to committees, or others. Situations regarding **personnel** may involve reprimands or other discipline, promotions, pay, and others. Additionally, situations involving **community members** may involve voting and elections, awarding contracts, exchanging services, and more. The leader must also use ethics and integrity in their own **decision-making processes** in regard to budgeting, school academic and extracurricular programming, and business and community partnerships.

Transparency in the Decision-Making Process

Some school decisions require input from stakeholders. In these decisions, it is important to have a **transparent decision-making process** so that all stakeholders can be assured that the decision is made ethically and with integrity. First, stakeholders must be **notified in advance** of the decision to be made. They should also have **access to relevant information** for making the decision, in accordance with any privacy or confidentiality regulations. They should be notified in advance of any **public meetings** related to the decision and documented meeting minutes should be made available. Any **voting** related to the decision should also be documented for transparency. Finally, when the school leader has made a decision, it should be **shared** with stakeholders along with the rationale for it, such as community input, votes, and other information.

Equitable Treatment of Students and Staff

The best way that the school leader can ensure equitable treatment of students and staff is to develop **policies and procedures** and adhere to them. When there are policies and procedures in place, the school leader can refer to these to determine the **best course of action** when dealing with students and staff. For example, if a student has excessive school absences, a school attendance policy should dictate when and how to address absenteeism. Similarly, if a staff member dresses unprofessionally for work, an employee handbook should outline how to address the staff member. In a situation with no guiding policy, the school leader should use **discretion** in handling the situation and subsequently develop a **guiding policy** for future incidents. This can be in the form of memorandums or addendums to existing student and staff handbooks. While there may be extenuating circumstances that require the school leader's discretion, policies and procedures ensure that all are treated equitably.

ETHICAL BEHAVIOR

A leader can ensure that others are acting ethically by **communicating expectations** regarding ethical behavior. The leader can provide staff with **documents and training** that explain these expectations. Employees should acknowledge receipt of such documentation by signing to confirm that they have received them as well as signing in at training sessions to confirm participation. The leader can also **monitor employee behavior**. This can be done in person by walking around and observing performance or remotely by instructing others on the leadership team to observe employee behavior or monitoring with security cameras. Security cameras are useful in areas that are most prone to unethical conduct, such as places where money is exchanged, entrances and exits, records storage, and areas on campus that are not frequently trafficked. Additionally, the leader can implement **consequences for unethical behavior** and address such behavior swiftly. Employees may be encouraged to behave ethically to avoid consequences for unethical behavior.

CONSEQUENCES OF UNETHICAL BEHAVIOR

Consequences for an employee's unethical behavior can vary, depending on the severity of the offense. For a minor offense, the employee may receive a **verbal or written reprimand** to be included in his or her personnel file. This type of situation may require a formal conference with the school leader or other school district staff. More severe offenses can result in **suspension**, **reassignment**, or **termination of employment**. For example, if an employee has behaved in an unethical manner involving exchange of money, he or she may be reassigned to a position that does not require interaction with money. Severe offenses can result in the suspension or revocation of state licensure. Ethical offenses that involve breaking the law can also result in **legal consequences** such as fines, probation, or even imprisonment as determined by city, state, and federal law.

ETHICAL VIOLATIONS

If a school leader has been made aware of an ethical violation, it is his or her responsibility to act immediately. In many cases, there are **procedures or guidelines** that a school leader should follow, as determined by the school district. These procedures may include notifying district personnel, initiating an investigation, conferencing with the offending employee, drafting a formal note of reprimand, and other actions. There should also be guidance from the school district on notifying **outside authorities or organizations**, such as law enforcement or Child Protective Services. In some instances, district personnel or an entity acting on their behalf handle the situation and the school leader takes on a role of **support and facilitation**. It is important for a school leader to take reports of unethical behavior seriously and act quickly and appropriately. Additionally, the school leader should maintain thorough **documentation** of the events and timelines for audit purposes.

SOCIAL JUSTICE

Social justice refers to the **fair and equitable treatment of all people**, regardless of their status in society. Factors such as socioeconomic status, race, ethnicity, place of residence, and others influence the **privileges** that certain people may have in society. These privileges, or lack thereof, can be reflected in the school system as well. The concept of social justice as it relates to education means that all students, regardless of their social status, socioeconomic status, race, ethnicity, religion, sexual orientation, or any other identifying factor, are entitled to an **equitable education** and access to **educational resources**. For example, it is considered a social injustice for children in poverty to have outdated textbooks and a lack of access to technology in schools. Social justice in education refers to advocating for children who are typically **marginalized and disenfranchised** so that they can receive the same educational opportunities as other children.

ADVOCATING FOR ALL CHILDREN

A school leader is in a unique position to be an **advocate for all children on campus**. First, the school leader needs to ensure that the **academic and extracurricular programming** is accessible to all children and reflective of the needs of all children on campus. Next, the school leader should ensure that all **special programming** is properly funded and implemented on campus. This can include programs such as Title I, special education, gifted and talented programs, English as a Second Language programs, career and technology programs, and many others. Finally, some inequities are the result of **governmental policy**, which affect the school. The school leader can use his or her voice and authority to influence policy and promote social justice in the school. Examples of these types of policy issues include school finance and funding, school zoning, school vouchers, and many others.

COMMUNICATING EXPECTATIONS

The school leader must communicate expectations to staff and students to increase the likelihood that staff and students will meet those expectations. It is difficult for staff and students to meet expectations if they are unaware of them. This can result in **unintentional disregard of expectations**. For example, teachers may decide to leave campus during an instructional planning period. If the teachers are unaware that the school leader expects them to remain on campus even when they do not have class, it will be difficult for the school leader to hold them accountable for that behavior. Likewise, the school leader should communicate **expectations of behavior** to students before a presumed offense is committed. A school leader must effectively communicate expectations so that students and staff will know what behavior to demonstrate and so the school leader can hold them accountable for those behaviors.

WAYS TO COMMUNICATE EXPECTATIONS

A school leader has many opportunities to communicate expectations to staff and students. These expectations can be written and shared in **employee and student handbooks** or **codes of conduct**. These documents can be printed as well as made available online. The school leader may require that staff and students provide a signature acknowledging receipt of such documents. Additionally, expectations for behavior can be communicated or reinforced during **announcements**, in **assemblies or meetings**, and in **individual conversations**. Many school leaders post expectations for behavior on posters in school hallways and classrooms. These often take the form of classroom rules for behavior, hallway expectations, cafeteria expectations, and so on. When correcting behavior that does not meet expectations, the school leader can reinforce expectations for the offender. For example, the school leader may verbalize to an employee that he or she is late to work and remind him or her of the expected arrival time.

Protecting and Advocating for Students

PROTECTING AND ADVOCATING FOR STUDENTS

A school leader should have systems in place for the protection and advocacy of students. These systems should be based on the needs of the student population and should be responsive to the changing needs and concerns of these students. A school leader will know if these systems are **appropriate and effective** in various ways. First, there should be a **student culture of safety** in school. This culture involves students feeling free to engage in the academic program, social activities, and extracurricular activities. Also, students should have an **adequate voice**. An appropriate and effective system for protection and advocacy will allow various avenues for students to contribute their ideas and voice their concerns. Additionally, there will be evidence that students are **supported** in times of need or crisis. This means that socio-emotional needs are identified and addressed quickly so that students can engage in the school program. These systems are effective and appropriate only if they benefit all students. If some groups of students are **marginalized or neglected** on campus, the school leader must revisit the appropriateness and efficacy of the school's systems.

> **Review Video: Crisis Management and Prevention**
> Visit mometrix.com/academy and enter code: 351872

OPPORTUNITIES TO SERVE AS AN ADVOCATE

Advocacy for students is necessary whenever any group of students is or has the potential to be **marginalized**. These groups are commonly students of low socioeconomic status, minority status, immigrant status, or a different sexual orientation. However, any student or group of students can need advocacy at any given time. There is an opportunity to advocate for these students when their **right to an equitable education in a safe environment** is threatened. For example, a school leader may observe that an academic program offered in the district consistently leaves out students who receive special education services. The school leader may advocate for that group of students by calling for a review of the application and acceptance criteria to drive change. Opportunities for student advocacy can occur on campus, within the school district, or within the local, state, and federal political arenas.

CONFIDENTIALITY

MAINTAINING STUDENT CONFIDENTIALITY

A school leader must maintain student confidentiality according to the Family Educational Rights and Privacy Act (FERPA). This involves keeping **student information and records** confidential. However, when advocating for students, the school leader may be informed of student information by other staff members, parents, or the students themselves that should also be kept confidential. Keeping the students' confidentiality means not sharing **private information** with outside parties unnecessarily. This fosters **trust** between the school leader and the student or other stakeholders. Establishing this trust helps to create a school culture in which students and their families are willing to share sensitive information with the school staff to help **advocate** for a student. For example, a parent may inform the school leader that the family has recently become homeless. Certain documents must be completed and certain staff need to be informed of this information to advocate for the homeless student, but the school leader must ensure that the sensitive information remains as private as possible. There are circumstances in which the student's confidentiality may need to be breached, but the school leader should make an effort to maintain that confidentiality.

SITUATIONS IN WHICH STUDENT CONFIDENTIALITY MUST BE BREACHED

A school leader and other school staff must do their best to maintain the confidence of students, but under some circumstances a student's confidentiality must be **breached**. If students confide in a staff member that they are being **harmed**, pose **harm to themselves**, or pose **harm to others**, school staff members have the responsibility to act on that information for the protection of those students or others. For example, a student may confide in a teacher that he or she is contemplating suicide. The teacher would then break the student's confidentiality and inform the school leader of the student's intentions. The teacher and the school leader would then contact the student's parents and the proper authorities to obtain immediate help for the student. Other examples that warrant a breach in student confidentiality include information related to **child abuse or neglect** or **threats of violence to others**.

Motivating Students

INTRINSIC MOTIVATION

Intrinsic motivation is motivation that comes from **within**. It is a person's own drive to succeed or to accomplish a goal. For students, this **intrinsic motivation** may be the result of education and career goals, family expectations, social influences, and more. Intrinsic motivation may drive students to meet or exceed academic performance expectations, participate in and excel in extracurricular activities, or choose certain education and career pathways. Intrinsic motivation is affected very little by **outside influences** because the drive comes from within. For example, a high school student may desire to become a writer and consequently excels in English Language Arts classes. This student may have an English Language Arts teacher that he or she does not get along with, but because the drive to become a writer is intrinsic, the student may still work hard and perform well in that class. Intrinsic motivation is considered more effective than extrinsic motivation. Students who excel in school, especially in the face of obstacles and challenges, are often intrinsically motivated.

EXTRINSIC MOTIVATION

Extrinsic motivation is motivation that comes from an **outside source**, such as another person, and is in the form of a reward. The reward can be **tangible**, such as money, prizes, or gifts, or it can be **intangible**, such as an experience, recognition, or approval. Teachers and other staff often use extrinsic motivation to encourage students to perform at a certain level or behave in a certain way. For example, a teacher may tell her third-grade class that all students who complete their homework will receive stickers. The students will be motivated to complete their homework and earn stickers. **Extrinsic motivation** can be effective with students, especially when they are lacking intrinsic motivation. However, extrinsic motivation is considered less effective than intrinsic motivation because in the absence of the reward, motivation significantly decreases. Additionally, if the reward loses its appeal, motivation will decrease. For example, if the third-grade teacher were to stop offering stickers for homework, the number of completed homework assignments might decline. Similarly, students may be less excited about receiving stickers for homework near the end of the school year, resulting in fewer completed homework assignments.

MOTIVATING STUDENTS

School staff can create **systems of rewards** to motivate students to engage in the academic program, perform at higher levels, and behave in an acceptable manner. Rewards can be given for individual and collective behaviors. Some schools have used **point systems** or **merit systems** to reward and motivate students. Students can redeem points for prizes, participation in field trips, or participation in other school activities. Some schools use stickers, tickets, or other means of reinforcing positive student behaviors, which can be redeemed as well. For example, a student may earn a ticket for participating in class discussion, which can be redeemed for a prize. This reward would encourage the student to increase participation in class discussion. Students may also be motivated by public recognition, such as receiving an award at an awards ceremony, being identified on the school website or a classroom bulletin board, or having their names announced during school announcements. Students are **motivated** when rewards systems are clear, fair, and consistent and when expectations are clearly outlined.

ASPECTS OF THE SCHOOL THAT CAN DEMOTIVATE STUDENTS

Perceived negative aspects of the school can decrease student motivation, causing them to disengage in the school program. If a student perceives school as **unsafe**, he or she may have poor school attendance or arrive late to school. If a student perceives the teacher to be **unfair or ineffective**, the student may not desire to perform well in that class, resulting in poor grades and possibly behavioral problems. When students perceive **school rules or policies** as unfair or inequitable, they may be discouraged from abiding by those policies or engaging in the programs that the policies or procedures apply to. For example, a student may desire to audition for a role in the school play. However, the student views the audition process as unfair and believes that certain students will be chosen for the roles regardless of who auditions. Consequently, that student will choose not to audition for the play or engage in the theater program. School leaders must identify aspects of the school and school program that may **demotivate** students and remedy these where possible.

Transparent Decision-Making

TRANSPARENT DECISION-MAKING

Transparent decision-making is the act of making sure that the process, logic, and rationale used to make a decision are **clear and open** to others. When decision-making is transparent, any **critical information** used to inform that decision is also readily available to others for review. This transparency allows others to understand **how the decision was made**. For example, if a school leader were to decide whether or not to eliminate the art program, a transparent decision-making process would allow stakeholders and team members to observe and understand how the school leader makes the decision. The process may start with publicly making known that the decision needed to be made. Then, data relating to the art program would be provided, including data related to any other programming that may be compared to the art program. Additional rationale could be documented, such as evaluating the position of the art program in relation to the school vision and goals. Based on this relevant information, observers of the decision-making process would be able to **understand** and even **predict** the decision that the leader would make.

DATA-SUPPORTED DECISIONS

Data is essential to offering transparency in decision-making. Data is **objective**, which makes it less refutable. Stakeholders may question or contest a school leader's decisions in some cases, but are less likely to question or contest the **data influencing those decisions**. Data that is shared may include financial data, student performance data, or data related to school demographics such as enrollment, attendance, or discipline. When data is shared with stakeholders, it is easier for them to understand the **basis and determining factors** for decisions. For example, if a school leader decides to eliminate a school program based on poor student participation, the school leader can be transparent and provide the attendance and participation data for that program to the stakeholders. As a result, the stakeholders will understand that the decision is based on objective data. Additionally, basing decisions on data will encourage the school leader to make sound decisions based on concrete data whenever possible because the school leader will be aware that the decision-making process will be observed by stakeholders.

SUPPORTING STAFF DECISIONS WITH DATA

Providing data is an essential component of transparency in decision-making. The school leader can share data such as **school performance data** and **individual student data** to demonstrate how a decision was made. Teachers and staff understand and are able to look at student data as employees working directly with students. This data can help them understand why decisions are made about certain curricular programs, school discipline procedures, and other aspects of the school program. Also, the school leader can use data to **support conversations with staff** regarding individual performance, which can lead to decision-making. For example, a school leader may determine that a third-grade reading teacher should be reassigned to a fourth-grade classroom. The leader can use student performance data and the teacher's performance evaluation data to explain the decision to the teacher. A school leader should always protect the **confidentiality** of students and personnel when applicable.

SUPPORTING COMMUNITY STAKEHOLDERS WITH DATA

Providing data is an essential component of transparency in decision-making. When being transparent with stakeholders, the school leader must be careful to protect the **confidentiality** of school, student, and personnel data. As a result, the school leader should be selective about the data that is shared with stakeholders and the manner in which it is shared. Data that is already public and is used to make a decision can be helpful when sharing data with stakeholders. The school leader should be prepared to **explain** the data, the measures used to obtain it, and its implications. Although the school leader cannot share individual student and staff data, the school leader can share **aggregates of the data**. For example, the school leader may provide data of third-grade student performance on a recent benchmark assessment. Data that is shared with stakeholders should be **clear, easy to understand, and purposeful** so that it adds to the transparency of the decision-making process.

Feedback and Reflection

IMPORTANCE OF FEEDBACK

Feedback is the process of gathering information from an outside source to **evaluate** or **correct** a particular course of action. A school leader should seek feedback to ensure that he or she is on the correct path when making decisions. Without feedback, a school leader may proceed with a course of action, only to realize later that it was a mistake. For example, a leader may decide to host parent meetings on Wednesday evenings. After hosting the first meeting with poor turnout, the leader may find that many families in the community attend church on Wednesday evenings. Had the leader gathered feedback, a different time might have been chosen. Gathering feedback can help the school leader make corrections or alter a course in a timely manner. Additionally, gathering feedback from stakeholders demonstrates that the school leader is **humble** and **receptive to feedback**. Perceived humility in the leader can help in team building and relationship building with the staff and the community. Gathering feedback also increases **buy-in** from those providing the feedback, such as members of the leadership team, key community members, or school district office personnel.

GATHERING FEEDBACK

A school leader can gather feedback from stakeholders in various ways to aid in their decision-making. A primary way of gathering feedback is presenting ideas and plans to the **campus leadership team**. The leadership team may include assistant principals, deans, or other leaders on campus. This team is effective in providing feedback because they know the campus, students, and community well and have demonstrated leadership skills and thinking. For example, the leadership team may provide feedback on a lunch schedule based on their experiences from lunch duty in the cafeteria. Also, **supervising district personnel** are often available to provide feedback to the school leader, especially in confidential matters. The school leader can also solicit feedback from **students, parents, and community members**. This type of feedback can help the school leader see situations and potential decisions from other perspectives. For example, a student may provide feedback that the proposed after school program does not interest the student body. Also, gathering and implementing feedback from **stakeholders** can increase stakeholder buy-in and support of the school's vision and goals.

RESPONDING TO NEGATIVE FEEDBACK

When a leader solicits feedback from students, staff, or stakeholders, it is possible that the feedback may be **negative**. The negative feedback may be in relation to aspects of the school program or in relation to the leader. When a leader receives feedback, he or she must avoid an immediate **emotional response** to the feedback. First the leader must determine whether the feedback has **validity**. People providing feedback can sometimes speak out of anger or frustration and deliver the feedback in a harsh way. However, delivery of the feedback does not necessarily determine whether the feedback is valid. Consequently, the leader must reflect upon his or her practice and identify whether the feedback identifies an area of improvement for the leader or the school program. If so, the leader must acknowledge this weak area and take steps to improve it. When improvements have been made, if possible, the leader should seek feedback once again to determine if the concerns of the stakeholders have been addressed.

RESPONDING TO POSITIVE FEEDBACK

Positive feedback from stakeholders can be encouraging for the school leader. Sometimes this feedback is solicited and other times it is volunteered. Positive feedback can be used for **reflection and improvement**. First, the leader needs to determine the **validity** of the feedback. Some people may feel the need to offer flattery or unsubstantiated positive feedback in an effort to favorably position themselves. Therefore, a leader must not assume that his or her performance or the school's performance is favorable because one or two people offered a compliment. Next, the leader must not become **overconfident** in the area that has received positive feedback. Instead, the feedback should encourage the leader to continue the actions that led to the favorable outcome to continue to achieve good results. Positive feedback can also be **shared** with other staff so they can be assured that they are performing well in the identified area.

HONEST SELF-REFLECTION

Honest self-reflection is a component of growth and efficacy as a school leader. A school leader should set aside time to reflect on **personal performance as a leader**, based on identified leadership **expectations and standards**. There are many models of leadership that the school leader can use for comparison, but most school districts select or develop a **tool for leadership evaluation**. These evaluation tools include the expectations for leadership skills, performance, and behaviors. School leaders can use the tools to identify their own strengths and weaknesses. Also, any time a leader is reading professional materials such as books or articles related to leadership, it is an opportunity to reflect on how he or she measures against the skills identified in the resource. Often, stakeholders such as parents or community members offer criticisms of the leader. The school leader should reflect upon the **validity of those criticisms** to determine areas for improvement. For example, during a parent conference, a parent may complain that the leader is a poor communicator. Even though the parent may have made the statement in a moment of frustration or anger, the school leader should take the opportunity to reflect upon his or her communication skills and how those skills were used in that situation.

Addressing Weaknesses

Once a leader has identified weaknesses through self-reflection, he or she can take several steps to **address** them. First, the school leader can read **books, articles, and other resources** related to the areas of weakness. For example, if the school leader has difficulty with time management, he or she can identify resources that can help to cultivate better time management skills. A leader can also participate in **training or professional development** related to the identified areas of weakness. A variety of professional organizations provide workshops and training related to various leadership competencies. The leader can also seek assistance from a **supervisor or other district staff person**. A supervisor can offer suggestions or guidance for improvement in a deficient area. Additionally, the school leader can obtain **mentors and coaches** outside of the school organization that can provide objective skill building in the school leader's deficit areas. Mentors may be retired principals or other types of leaders who are in the school leader's network and are willing to share their expertise. Mentors do not typically require payment. In contrast, coaches are often hired to help with targeted skill-building and professional growth.

Effect of Leader's Self-Reflection on the Leadership Team

A leader's self-reflection can affect the leadership team in a number of ways. First, it sets an example as a school leader that **self-reflection** should be a part of leadership practice. This also demonstrates to the leadership team that the leader is aware that he or she is not perfect and is making efforts to **address identified weaknesses**. The leadership team should be comprised of people who help to **compensate** for the leader's weaknesses. Therefore, when a leader identifies his or her weaknesses, this can lead to **adjustment** of the leadership team. For example, if the leader determines that his or her leadership in math and science is weak, the leader may identify a person who is strong in math and science to be a part of the leadership team. Additionally, a leader's self-reflection can lead to **shifting roles and responsibilities** on the leadership team and reflection about the strengths and weaknesses of the entire team.

Effect of Leader's Self-Reflection on Stakeholders

A leader's self-reflection can affect how he or she is **perceived** by stakeholders as well as the leader's **relationship** with stakeholders. When stakeholders observe the leader committing to self-improvement and making changes, they may conclude that the leader is humble and willing to improve the practice and the operation of the school. This can build hope and trust among stakeholders. For example, the leader may communicate to stakeholders that he or she is working on improving communication skills and is committed to doing a better job of returning phone calls and responding to emails. Similarly, engagement in self-reflection and self-improvement demonstrates that the leader is **responsive to feedback**. It is difficult to engage with a leader who believes that he or she knows everything, does not want feedback, and cannot receive criticism. In contrast, a leader who reflects and improves can encourage stakeholders to engage with the leader and the school, and relationships can be built between the leader and stakeholders.

Chapter Quiz

Ready to see how well you retained what you just read? Scan the QR code to go directly to the chapter quiz interface for this study guide. If you're using a computer, simply visit the bonus page at **mometrix.com/bonus948/nystcescbl109110** and click the Chapter Quizzes link.

NYSTCE Practice Test #1

Part 1

EXTENDED PERFORMANCE TASK
INSTRUCTIONAL LEADERSHIP FOR STUDENT SUCCESS

Use the information and documents below to answer the questions that follow them. You have 60 minutes to complete the assignment.

DESCRIPTION

You have just accepted the position of school principal at Ragsdale Middle School, a public school for grades 6-8, situated near a suburb that is fairly affluent socioeconomically. The school's enrollment has totaled about 800 students for the past several years, during which time the faculty has remained the same. Roughly one-quarter of the students receive free or price-reduced school meals.

Ragsdale Middle School is in a school district whose superintendent is new this year. In the past year, three local companies employing many residents have either closed or relocated, causing a mild to moderate decrease in the local economy. Local families and other community members strongly support the school. All school employees work hard to furnish students and their families with a positive environment that promotes learning and senses of welcome and community.

You have been instructed by the new superintendent to develop a plan for instructional change. Following reevaluation, Ragsdale Middle School has recently redesigned its curriculum in math to align with the Common Core Learning Standards (CCLS). This includes basing each grade's math content to reflect focus topics identified by the CCLS. Professional development at the school has recently devoted much time to monitoring student progress by examining formative assessment results, and to planning collaboratively to integrate more challenging math content across the curriculum. The redesigned curriculum has been receiving enthusiastic support from the teachers, who are also requesting professional development to support them in implementing it.

One quarter into the new school year, you have the first installment of data from teachers' classroom formative assessments.

Document 1

Ragsdale Middle School: Student Performance Indicators

State Standardized Assessment:

Two-Year Comparison – All Students

In this table are the percentages of all students who scored ≥ Level 3, "meets proficiency standard."

SUBJECT	SCHOOL – 2 Years Ago	SCHOOL – Last Year	DISTRICT – 2 years Ago	DISTRICT – Last Year	STATE – 2 Years Ago	STATE – Last Year
ELA	63%	68%	63%	60%	56%	57%
MATH	47%	48%	47%	49%	48%	50%

In this table are the percentages of students, disaggregated by grade and several demographic groups, who scored ≥ Level 3, "meets proficiency standard."

GROUP	% of Student Body	ELA – 2 Years Ago	MATH – 2 Years Ago	ELA – Last Year	MATH – Last Year
Female	48%	68%	43%	73%	43%
Male	52%	58%	51%	61%	53%
Grade 6	32%	63%	54%	71%	53%
Grade 7	35%	64%	51%	72%	52%
Grade 8	33%	60%	44%	63%	47%
Low-Income	25%	51%	40%	52%	43%
Limited English Proficiency	20%	41%	37%	37%	38%
Students with Disabilities	21%	42%	31%	45%	35%

Document 2

ELA and Math – Formative Assessment Results

ELA Formative Assessment Results for Grades 6 – 8
Percentage of students responding correctly to >65% of formative assessment items – End of First Quarter

	Grade 6	Grade 7	Grade 8
Close Reading and Writing to Learn	52%	51%	48%
Using Evidence	51%	50%	48%
Researching for Understanding	49%	54%	56%
Formulating Positions	46%	49%	46%

Math Formative Assessment Results for Grade 6
Percentage of students responding correctly to >65% of formative assessment items – End of First Quarter

Ratios and Proportional Relationships	62%
The Number System	50%
Equations and Expressions	43%

Math Formative Assessment Results for Grade 7
Percentage of students responding correctly to >65% of formative assessment items – End of First Quarter

Ratios and Proportional Relationships	54%
The Number System	35%
Equations and Expressions	33%

Math Formative Assessment Results for Grade 8
Percentage of students responding correctly to >65% of formative assessment items – End of First Quarter

Equations and Expressions	28%
Functions	36%
Geometry	39%

DOCUMENT 3

Ragsdale Middle School Student Survey: Last Year's Results

Grades 6-8 ELA and Math Classes

STUDENT SURVEY DATA: AVERAGE % AGREEING

ITEM STATEMENT	ELA Classes, Grade 6	ELA Classes, Grade 7	ELA Classes, Grade 8	Math Classes, Grade 6	Math Classes, Grade 7	Math Classes, Grade 8
This teacher cares about me as a person.	93%	87%	82%	73%	68%	56%
Students don't waste time and stay busy in this class.	85%	82%	89%	91%	87%	85%
This teacher clearly explains difficult things.	76%	74%	71%	46%	42%	37%
This teacher expects me to make clear what I think and why, and to explain my answers.	51%	40%	34%	33%	35%	29%
This teacher makes me enjoy learning.	75%	63%	54%	37%	31%	26%
This teacher creates interesting lessons.	83%	81%	77%	27%	34%	21%
This teacher makes the time to gives us a summary of every lesson and what we learned.	41%	45%	49%	64%	61%	50%

DOCUMENT 4

Last Year's Teacher Survey – Excerpted Responses

RAGSDALE MIDDLE SCHOOL
ANONYMOUS TEACHER OPINION SURVEY RESULTS

In your experience of Ragsdale Middle School for the last three years, how much do you agree with each statement?	ELA Teachers - % of "Strongly Agree" or "Agree" Responses	Math Teachers - % of "Strongly Agree" or "Agree" Responses
I enjoy working here.	82%	74%
I feel effective in my position.	80%	72%
All students receive instruction suited to their needs.	67%	52%
I want to develop my skills in achieving all student goals via professional development.	77%	85%
I have access to ideas, materials, and support for differentiating instruction by ability level effectively.	71%	50%
I have the knowledge and skills required to assist students from every family and socioeconomic background to make sufficient, timely academic progress.	63%	46%
I have the knowledge and skills to assist ELL students make sufficient, timely academic progress.	57%	45%
This school welcomes and appreciates diverse students.	88%	85%
ELL students receive effective instruction in general.	60%	51%
This school furnishes high-achieving students with suitable enrichment opportunities.	71%	77%

DOCUMENT 5

Data from Teacher Evaluations – All Teachers:

Last Year's Composited Evaluation Scores

(Using multiple measures, including local student achievement measures, other teacher effectiveness measures, state-supplied growth scores, etc.)

Grade(s) and Subject(s)	# of Teachers	Ineffective		Developing		Effective		Highly Effective	
ELA Grade 6	8	1	12.5%	1	12.5%	3	37.5%	1	12.5%
Math Grade 6	5	0	0.0%	0	0.0%	3	60%	2	40%
Special Education Grade 6	3	0	0.0%	1	33.3%	1	33.3%	1	33.3%
Gifted, Library Media, Health Grade 6	3	0	0.0%	1	33.3%	1	33.3%	1	33.3%
ELA Grade 7	5	0	0.0%	0	0.0%	3	60%	2	40%
Math Grade 7	5	0	0.0%	1	25%	2	40%	2	40%
Special Education Grade 7	4	1	25%	1	25%	1	25%	1	25%
Science, Social Studies, Foreign Language Grade 7	10	0	0.0%	2	20%	5	50%	3	30%
ELA Grade 8	5	0	0.0%	0	0.0%	3	60%	2	40%
Math Grade 8	5	0	0.0%	1	20%	3	60%	1	20%
Special Education Grade 8	3	0	0.0%	0	0.0%	2	66.7%	1	33.3%
Science, Social Studies, Foreign Language Grade 8	11	0	0.0%	0	0.0%	6	54.5%	5	45.4%
PE, Art, Music, Family and Consumer Science Grades 6-8	10	1	10%	2	20%	5	50%	2	20%

Document 6

Summary of Last Year's Teacher Observation Data

Number of teachers scoring on teacher practice rubric at each performance level

Key:

U	Unsatisfactory
B	Basic
P	Proficient
E	Exemplary

		# Unsatisfactory	# Basic	# Proficient	# Exemplary
Domain 1 – Planning and Preparation	ELA	U = 1	B = 2	P = 10	E = 5
	Math	U = 1	B = 4	P = 11	E = 2
Domain 2 – Classroom Environment	ELA	U = 2	B = 3	P = 9	E = 4
	Math	U = 4	B = 4	P = 8	E = 2
Domain 3 – Instruction	ELA	U = 1	B = 4	P = 10	E = 3
	Math	U = 2	B = 5	P = 9	E = 2
Domain 4 – Professional Responsibilities	ELA	U = 1	B = 3	P = 10	E = 4
	Math	U = 3	B = 5	P = 6	E = 4

SHORT ANSWER QUESTIONS

Using the information given above, write a response about 600-800 words long in a format you prefer (e.g., an outline, a list of bulleted items, prose paragraphs). In addressing the items below, give very specific details and cite evidence from the description and documents that support your answers.

1. Identify one of this school's particular strengths and three specific need areas in the school's instructional program. Cite evidence to support the strength and need areas you identify.

2. Identify which one of the three need areas you would give the first priority and explain why it should be addressed first. Also identify two major questions that you need to answer in addressing the need area you prioritized and explain the reason(s) answering each question is significant.

3. Describe individually how you will find answers to each of the two questions you identified in #2 above. Identify which actions you would take for addressing the need area you prioritized and explain why.

4. Explain how you could make use of the school strength you identified in #1 above for addressing the need area you prioritized in #2 above. In addition, identify some potential challenges that could arise as a result of the actions you take, and some things you could do to prevent, mitigate, or respond to those challenges.

SHORTER PERFORMANCE TASK 1
SCHOOL CULTURE AND LEARNING ENVIRONMENT TO PROMOTE EXCELLENCE, EQUITY, AND SOCIAL JUSTICE

Use the information from the scenario and documents below to complete the task following them. You have 30 minutes to complete the assignment.

DESCRIPTION

At a city middle school with 1,189 students in grades 6-8, you have just accepted the position of the next school building leader. This school's district includes several elementary schools with programs for the gifted and talented. Students from these programs now make up the majority of participants in the middle school's own gifted and talented educational program, which features weekly pull-out enrichment ELA and math classes.

At the end of summer before school starts, you receive a visit from a group of students' parents wanting to discuss the admission criteria for the middle school's gifted and talented program. You have previously met with school teams and faculty members in your building. Ms. H., the teacher specializing in gifted and talented students, was one of these faculty members. She informed you that she has been in charge of the school's gifted and talented program for six years; about 52 students were included when she started, and today there are about 126. Ms. H. also explained that a combination of diagnostic screening assessment scores and nominations by teachers forms the criteria for selecting students to participate.

As you conducted daily building walk-throughs and visited classrooms during the first several weeks of the school year, you became acquainted with the students, teachers, and other staff members. One observation you made was that the composition of students in the gifted and talented program does not reflect the considerable cultural, linguistic, and economic diversity of the overall student body. After reviewing data on current gifted and talented program participants, you constructed the table (Document, below) shown.

In visiting the general education classrooms, you observed several students whose verbal skills, content knowledge, and conceptual understanding seemed very advanced. They asked questions of their teachers and responded articulately to teacher prompts and questions in ways that demonstrated in-depth insight about the subjects of study. You find it obvious that more challenging instruction would benefit these students. When you met with Ms. H., she had told you that because their scores on the screening instruments used for identifying program eligibility were too low for program criteria, some of these advanced students are not eligible for the gifted and talented program.

Document

GIFTED AND TALENTED PROGRAM: STUDENTS PARTICIPATING THIS YEAR

Student Category	% of Student Population	% of Students in G&T Program
Limited English Proficiency	28%	5%
Economically Disadvantaged	53%	16%
Students with Disabilities	12%	2%

SHORT ANSWER QUESTIONS

Using the information given above, write a response about 300-400 words long, in a format you prefer (e.g., an outline, a list of bulleted items, prose paragraphs). In addressing the items below, give very specific details and cite evidence from the description and data that appropriately support your answers.

1. Identify the main issue in this situation and explain why. Identify two questions that are significant to answer for analyzing this issue, and explain the significance of each.

2. Explain how you will answer each of the two questions you identified above, including identifying some challenges you may encounter in answering them. Also identify one potential finding you may discover, and what possible action(s) are indicated by that finding.

Shorter Performance Task 2
School Culture and Learning Environment to Promote Excellence, Equity, and Social Justice

Use the information from the scenario and document below to complete the task following them. You have 30 minutes to complete the assignment.

Description

At a K-12 school with about 500 students in a rural district, you have just become the new school building leader. The teachers at this school have an average of 5-10 years of teaching experience, and staff turnover has been minimal for the last six years. When you reviewed teachers' formative assessments of student progress and state-level standardized assessments, you found that student performance levels in ELA and math have been the same for two years in a row.

You observe after a few months of school that students in third through fifth grades are being referred at a comparatively high rate for uncooperative behaviors, unacceptable language, talking too much in class, physical scuffles, and other minor disciplinary issues. The document below summarizes the data related to these referrals. Behavioral guidelines and consequences for unacceptable behaviors are defined in the school's code of conduct. Before your appointment as school building leader, teachers have developed their individual classroom expectations and rules based on this code of conduct.

You had requested your school leadership team members to plan a series of classroom management discussions for the next teachers' professional development day. These discussions were to refer to the school district-adopted teacher practice evaluation rubric. You then asked the teachers to reflect on these discussions and on their own classroom practices. Following these activities, you made short observational visits to each of the grade 3, 4, and 5 classrooms. While observing teacher approaches to optimizing classroom learning opportunities and student interaction and behavior, you noticed the majority of teachers appeared to care about and have genuine relationships with students, but also that some teacher-student interactions seemed nearly too informal to be appropriate.

You also observed some of the disciplinary issues while visiting classrooms. Some teachers interrupted their lessons to apply consequences immediately for each behavior, detracting significantly from instructional and learning time. Other teachers continued their instruction, ignoring misbehaviors. In two classes, many students were off-task, and equal numbers were too distracted by the off-task classmates to engage and participate well in learning activities. Across and within classes, the teachers generally displayed a variety of responses to disruptive behaviors.

Document

First and Second Quarters, This Year: Disciplinary Referrals in Grades 3-5 per Teacher

Behavior	Talking	Language	Uncooperative	Physical	Disrespectful	Disruptive	TOTAL
Grade 3 Teacher A	0	2	0	3	0	1	6
Grade 3 Teacher B	4	0	3	4	2	2	15
Grade 4 Teacher C	7	2	9	4	3	6	32
Grade 4 Teacher D	0	1	2	0	3	5	11
Grade 5 Teacher E	0	1	8	2	0	1	12
Grade 5 Teacher F	12	3	7	6	4	12	44
TOTAL	23	9	29	19	12	27	120

Short Answer Questions

Using the information given above, write a response about 300-400 words long, in a format you prefer (e.g., an outline, a list of bulleted items, prose paragraphs). In addressing the items below, give very specific details and cite evidence from the description and data that appropriately support your answers.

1. Identify a major issue relating to the learning environment and school culture that this situation reflects, and explain its significance. Identify two main questions you need to answer to examine this issue, and explain the importance of each question.

2. Describe how you will proceed to find answers to each of the questions you identified above. Identify some challenges you may encounter in seeking these answers. Also identify one potential finding you may discover, and its implications for possible action(s) to take.

MULTIPLE CHOICE QUESTIONS

Use the information from the scenario and documents below to answer the questions that follow them. You have two hours to complete these questions.

DESCRIPTION

In a school district located within a city, Mr. R. has been the school building leader of Main Street High, a public high school with roughly 1,900 students, for about five years. The faculty includes a majority of teachers who have taught there for at least 10 years or longer. Most of the teachers have regularly received "Effective" and "Highly Effective" ratings; however, 19 percent have received ratings of "Developing" or "Ineffective" at least once during Mr. R.'s tenure.

In general, Main Street High's students have performed below their district's and state's averages. Mr. R. spearheaded a school-wide initiative for implementing the district's Data-Driven Instruction and Inquiry (DDI) system with increasing student achievement as a goal about three years ago. This system included analyzing data at departmental meetings and conducting quarterly and inventory assessments adopted by the district. Student achievement on standardized tests overall has risen since, especially in math, which Mr. R. attributes largely to math teachers' consistent DDI application. However, students are still performing below average in English Language Arts (ELA).

Mr. R. starts a new school year making it a priority to improve ELA student achievement. To analyze instructional needs, he reviews data from teachers' formative assessments in both ELA and math, plus the students' state Regents exam scores for the past three years, and asks the assistant principal to collect and report information about faculty and staff DDI efforts.

DOCUMENT 1

Previous School Year: Formative Assessment Results

(Students correctly answering ≥65% of items)

	First Quarter	Second Quarter	Third Quarter	Fourth Quarter
ELA:				
Grade 9	79%	83%	80%	82%
Grade 10	78%	76%	77%	80%
Grade 11	81%	83%	82%	83%
Grade 12	83%	78%	81%	84%
MATH:				
Grade 9	69%	75%	78%	80%
Grade 10	60%	65%	70%	74%
Grade 11	65%	70%	72%	78%
Grade 12	67%	70%	75%	80%

DOCUMENT 2

State Regents Examinations: Scores over Past Three Years

(Entire Student Body)

TEST SUBJECT	3 YEARS AGO: Students scoring 65% - 84%	3 YEARS AGO: Students scoring ≥ 85%	2 YEARS AGO: Students scoring 65% - 84%	2 YEARS AGO: Students scoring ≥ 85%	LAST SPRING: Students scoring 65% - 84%	LAST SPRING: Students scoring ≥ 85%
English	56%	5%	59%	5%	57%	6%
Algebra	46%	1%	52%	6%	62%	10%
Geometry	40%	2%	47%	8%	55%	11%
Trigonometry	*	*	*	*	*	*
World History, Geography	50%	5%	50%	10%	53%	12%
American History, Government	65%	12%	68%	12%	69%	14%
Environmental Biology	54%	10%	54%	11%	59%	15%
Earth Sciences	39%	7%	45%	9%	49%	13%
Chemistry	35%	3%	39%	8%	45%	10%
Physics	*	*	*	*	*	*

KEY: * signifies data for <5 students are not disclosed here to protect individual student information confidentiality.

Document 3
Report from Assistant Principal on Last Year's ELA Department DDI Efforts

TO: Principal R.
FROM: Assistant Principal P.
RE: Report on ELA Department DDI Efforts – Update

Observational Notes on recent ELA Department Meeting:
The ELA Department held this meeting to review the results of formative assessments conducted during the first quarter in all grades. I observed a significant number of absentees, even though this meeting was called for all ELA faculty. Although those attending demonstrated the best intentions and serious commitment during their discussion, the meeting was inadequately focused, and their data analyses did not go into sufficient depth to provide insight into student performance. I noticed that the eleventh- and twelfth-grade teachers especially appeared to focus on the numbers of incorrect student responses at the expense of examining the content of those responses and the reasons for them. In closing the meeting, the department chairperson urged the teachers to find time for greater data exploration on their own.

Discussion with ELA Department Chairperson:
The chairperson and I conversed separately from the meeting described above. Although the chairperson seems committed to DDI, and the department's action plans we reviewed used the indicated district templates, I found the plans superficial in content. The department chair also did not appear to prioritize her role in assuring that teachers participate in DDI. She expressed her opinion that holding DDI meetings regularly was prohibited by teacher and student demands on her time combined with her administrative responsibilities.

Individual ELA Teacher Conversations:
In talking with teachers one on one, I learned that only three teachers regularly inform their lesson planning with DDI in their classrooms; these were the only ELA faculty with a thorough grasp of data's significance. The majority of ELA teachers, particularly those teaching juniors and seniors, plan and adjust their instruction based on their own intuition and experience, seldom examining or applying student data. Some teachers were concerned that if students already performed poorly on tests, making instruction more rigorous would discourage students and lower their achievement and interest even more. I look forward to your advice regarding these findings and will be glad to discuss them more with you as you see fit.

1. When Mr. R. compares the ELA formative assessment results and the state Regents Exam English scores, which of the following should be of most concern?

a. Formative assessment results are probably significantly less reliable than Regents Exam scores.
b. Formative assessment results distinguish grades and quarters, but the Regents Exam does not.
c. Formative assessment results are of less rigorous content than Regents Exam-tested standards.
d. Formative assessment results test school curriculum less comprehensively than do Regents Exams.

2. Which of the following strategies should Mr. R. assign ELA faculty to implement *first* for improving their school's student learning and achievement?
    a. Inform action plans by applying standardized test data to identify curriculum areas of greatest student need.
    b. Develop classroom assessments more closely reflecting Regents and district formative assessment contents.
    c. Evaluate classroom instruction alignment with curriculum standards by finding more sources of student data.
    d. Compare the school assessment data to those of similar high schools both within and outside of their district.

3. To develop a plan for improving student ELA achievement, the principal can obtain more data that will be most informative by doing which of these things?
    a. Review school ELA formative assessment results for the past three years at a minimum.
    b. Survey the ELA teachers to ascertain their DDI-related professional development needs.
    c. Assess how much time ELA teachers currently spend on DDI by conducting a time study.
    d. Identify the school's currently available professional ELA teaching and testing resources.

4. According to the information given, the principal will need to provide administrative support to the ELA department chairperson in which area for improving student achievement in ELA?
    a. Developing trust and collegial atmosphere in the department
    b. Identifying departmental impact on the school community
    c. Identifying and obtaining more resources for the department
    d. Prioritizing DDI implementation despite departmental duties

5. A main priority for Mr. R. is to further DDI implementation in his school. As its instructional leader, what other main priority should he pursue?
    a. To make sure that the instruction by the ELA teachers is suitably rigorous for every student
    b. To review ELA teachers' reports on students' classroom progress and achievement regularly
    c. To set up academic expectations for the students in accordance with their ELA performance
    d. To campaign for ELA teachers to buy into his plan designed for improving instruction overall

6. Based on the information provided, the principal should lead the ELA faculty to change their focus in analyzing student test data in which of the following ways?
    a. How many of the test items students get wrong
    b. How many items students have right, not wrong
    c. What kinds of test items the students get wrong
    d. Overall student understanding, not items wrong

7. According to the information given, which of the following characteristics of ELA department meetings to review student data actually existed, and most indicated deficits in faculty understanding of the importance of data to instruction?
    a. The teachers attending the meetings did not mean well.
    b. The teachers attending were not enough of the faculty.
    c. The teachers attending were not committed to DDI use.
    d. The teachers attending would rather analyze data alone.

8. Which of the following most accurately defines a key factor inhibiting the ELA department's implementation of DDI in the interest of improving student ELA achievement?
   a. The department chair lacked any real commitment to implementing DDI.
   b. The department action plans did not apply the correct district templates.
   c. The department chair made it a priority to get the teachers to apply DDI.
   d. The department action plans for using DDI did not go into enough depth.

9. Based on the information available, which choice best describes a perception that some of the ELA teachers experienced relative to using DDI to inform making their instruction more rigorous?
   a. That underachieving students would lose both engagement and achievement from greater rigor
   b. That underachieving students would perform better but be less engaged by increasing the rigor
   c. That underachieving students would be more engaged but perform worse through greater rigor
   d. That underachieving students would both be more engaged and perform better with more rigor

INSTRUCTIONAL LEADERSHIP FOR STUDENT SUCCESS
DESCRIPTION

As the principal of a middle school in a suburb of a medium-sized city, you and other building leaders have been apprised by your superintendent of significant demographic changes in your community and school district: a large influx of immigrants from other countries has recently occurred, and all of these arriving families with school-age children have enrolled them in local schools.

The superintendent wants all school administrators and faculty to prepare for the increased numbers of English language learner (ELL) students they will have in the coming school year. Previously your school had very few ELL students, and currently has only one teacher specializing in teaching them. The superintendent has charged school building leaders with the tasks of overseeing the administration of pre-assessments for incoming ELL students and resulting assessment data analysis, implementing professional development related to ELL instruction for faculty and staff, ensuring teachers know and apply instructional practices to promote success equally for ELL as well as other students, and leading progress-monitoring systems to ensure that instruction is effective for the new ELL students.

You review the preliminary data provided to you by the school district to learn more about ELL student distribution and characteristics. These include the results of preliminary assessments administered to incoming ELL students. You plan to meet with your faculty and staff before the school year begins to organize and coordinate school team and teacher efforts to meet new ELL students' educational needs while still maintaining their levels of meeting needs for all students.

DOCUMENT 1

Incoming Students: Demographics for Next School Year: Preliminary Report

	# of Students	% of All Students
New enrollments, all students	200	25%
New enrollments, ELL students	80	10%
ELL % of all new enrollments	-	45%
L1s of new ELL students:	# of Students	% of all ELL Students
Spanish	50	62.5%
Arabic	22	27.5%
Farsi	1	1.25%
Hindi	3	3.75%
Urdu	1	1.25%
Cantonese	2	2.5%
Mandarin	1	1.25%

DOCUMENT 2

Distribution of New ELL Students by Grade

GRADE	# ELL Students per Grade	# Classroom Subject Teachers per Grade	% of All ELL Students in Grade
6	24	2	30%
7	36	2	45%
8	20	2	25%

DOCUMENT 3

Pre-Assessment Results: Newly Enrolled ELL Students

Skills Areas Assessed	# ≤ 1 year below grade level	# ≥ 2 years below grade level
Basic Conversational English – Listening Comprehension	30	50
Basic Conversational English – Speaking Vocabulary and Fluency	20	60
Basic Conversational English – Reading Comprehension	18	62
Basic Conversational English – Writing Skills	13	67
Academic English – Listening Comprehension	8	72
Academic English – Speaking Vocabulary and Fluency	5	75
Academic English – Reading Comprehension	2	78
Academic English – Writing Skills	0	80

10. Extrapolating from the data shown above, how many total students attend this middle school?

   a. Around 800
   b. About 1,000
   c. Around 200
   d. About 2,000

11. Assuming equal class sizes across classrooms and grades, the classroom teachers in which grade will have the largest proportion of new ELL students?

  a. Sixth-grade teachers
  b. Eighth-grade teachers
  c. Seventh-grade teachers
  d. No difference in teachers

12. Based on the information given, which of the following should you do *first* to meet incoming ELL student instructional needs?

  a. Hire interpreters for each L1 spoken
  b. Identify all existing bilingual teachers
  c. Hire more teachers who are bilingual
  d. Identify volunteers who can interpret

13. How do preliminary assessment results conform to typical second-language acquisition patterns?

  a. ELLs acquire listening skills sooner for academic than for basic English.
  b. Listening and speaking develop sooner than reading and writing skills.
  c. A few ELL students always arrive with grade-level English literacy skills.
  d. Receptive language skills develop before expressive language skills do.

14. In implementing additional professional staff development to help teachers meet ELL and all student needs, which should you focus on primarily?

  a. Intensive crash courses for every new student L1
  b. Coordinating interpreting services with teaching
  c. How to differentiate instruction in the classroom
  d. Training a few teachers for classrooms of all ELLs

15. You have discovered several bilingual teachers already on your faculty. Which information would you need to help inform classroom placement potential for matching student L1s with teachers?

  a. Document 1 numbers disaggregated by grade
  b. A conflation of data from Documents 1 and 2
  c. The information in Document 2 provides that
  d. Which L1s the teachers in which grades speak

16. Which of the following can you NOT determine from the data provided above?

  a. How many ELLs will be in every grade
  b. How many ELLs will be in every class
  c. How many teachers in every grade
  d. How many grades will have ELLs

17. Which instructional format should you encourage your teachers to use to meet the needs of all students most efficiently and equitably?

  a. Whole-class instruction
  b. Separate classes for ELLs
  c. Small homogeneous groups
  d. Small heterogeneous groups

Use the information below to answer the questions that follow.

Description

You have just taken the job of school building leader at an elementary school with grades K-5 in a rural school district. The faculty, staff, and student population have been stable overall for a number of years. With strong community ties and support, the school is fortunate to have a dedicated group of volunteers, including members from community businesses and organizations (some of which have knowledge about, work with, or advocate for disabilities), as well as parents of students with disabilities.

Two new developments will affect the upcoming school year: some new students entering the school include several with disabilities, adding to the small number already attending, all of whom will be or are mainstreamed into regular education classrooms; and the school has received a federal government grant to fund the purchase of adaptive equipment and other resources for disabled students.

The funds are most needed and welcome, but they have their limits. As is the case in most public schools today, not all resources that would help existing and new students with disabilities can be afforded with the federal grant plus any other budget allocated for those purposes. You will need to make some decisions as to which resources take priority and which may be postponed, or which needs may be addressed using less expensive solutions.

To inform these decisions, you have met with classroom teachers and students' parents and have collected information about the needs of current and new students with disabilities, and which accommodations and modifications are required for them to access equal opportunities to learn as all other students. You have identified which disabilities these students have. At your request, your special education teacher and other specialists, who are few in number but excellent in quality, have provided you with lists of adaptive equipment, devices, and classroom accommodation and modification strategies pertaining to the disabilities of your current and incoming students. You also review the educational histories and records of the incoming students with disabilities, which your special educators and classroom teachers are also reviewing.

Document 1

Checklist of Disabilities Eligible under the IDEA

NOTE: Under IDEA regulations, for a student to satisfy the definition of a "child with a disability" and be eligible for special education and related services, the disability must adversely affect the student's educational performance.

IDEA DISABILITY CATEGORY	OUR STUDENTS	NUMBER OF STUDENTS
Autism Spectrum Disorder	✓	1
Deaf-Blindness		0
Deafness	✓	1
Developmental Delay		0
Emotional Disturbance		0
Hearing Impairment	✓	1
Intellectual Disability	✓✓	2
Multiple Disabilities		0
Orthopedic Impairment	✓✓	2
Other Health Impairment	✓	1
Specific Learning Disability	✓✓	2
Speech or Language Impairment	✓✓✓✓	4
Traumatic Brain Injury		0
Visual Impairment (including Blindness)	✓	1

Document 2

Excerpts from Special Educators' Lists:
Classroom Accommodations and Modifications

TYPE	EXAMPLES
Presentation accommodations	Audio recordings instead of reading
	Videos, movies, digital media instead of reading
	Large-print materials
	Fewer items per line or page
	Oral directions instead of written
	Designated readers
	Audio-record lessons instead of taking written notes
	Share classmate notes
	Provide lesson outlines
	Pictures, visual organizers, word webs instead of verbal material
	Written lists of directions
Response accommodations	Response in easiest form for the student (oral, written, etc.)
	Dictate responses to a scribe
	Dictate responses into an audio-recorder
	Use an electronic spell-checker or spelling dictionary
	Electronic word processors for responses or class notes
	Calculators or math facts tables
Setting accommodations	Alternative work/test settings (quiet rooms, fewer distractions)
	Preferential seating (e.g., near teacher or board)
	Special acoustics and lighting
	Small group settings for taking tests
	Sensory tools (e.g., exercise bands on chair legs for quiet kicking)
Timing accommodations	Allow more time to finish a test or assignment
	Allow more time for processing oral directions or information
	Allow frequent breaks (e.g., after each task completion)
Schedule accommodations	Allow more time to finish a project
	Take tests over several days or several timed sessions
	Take test sections in a different order
	Take tests at specified times of day
Organization accommodations	Aid time management using an alarm
	Highlight important parts of text
	Help student coordinate assignments in a planner or notebook
	Instruction in specific studying skills
Assignment modifications	Different or fewer homework items than classmates
	Write shorter papers or essays
	Different or fewer test questions
	Alternative assignments or projects
Curriculum modifications	Learn different material than classmates
	Different standards for assessment or grading than classmates
	Being excused from specific assignments or projects

DOCUMENT 3

Excerpts from Special Educators' Notes:

Student Needs

We still have wheelchair ramps previously installed in the building for a former student. However, our two new students with orthopedic impairments use wheelchairs that will not fit through some of our building's interior doorways.

Our new student with visual impairment is not totally blind but needs accommodations for low vision. As reflected in her educational records, this student has always performed at grade level in every subject area.

Of our new students with intellectual disabilities, one has always been placed at the same grade levels as other students his age; the other is starting kindergarten. Both will need curriculum modifications to perform successfully in grades for their chronological ages.

Of our new students with specific learning disabilities, one has a reading disability and one has a central auditory processing disorder.

Of our new students with speech or language impairment, two have delayed language development and two have mild articulation disorders. All have previously received and will continue receiving speech-language pathologist (SLP) services. All these students are in grades K-2.

Our new deaf student communicates using American Sign Language (ASL).

Our new students who are hard of hearing does not use ASL, but wears hearing aids and has advanced speechreading skills.

Our new student with autism spectrum disorder (ASD) has excellent skills in attentional task focus and sustained work time, but is easily agitated by bright lights, certain colors, loud noises, interruptions, and transitions.

Our new student in the Other Health Impairment category has Type 1 diabetes, requiring direct supervision during all exercise, as well as approved snacks and blood sugar checks, both regularly and at specified times during the school day.

18. In view of budgetary considerations, which of the following expenses should you give priority?

a. Widening doorways in the building
b. Hiring a full-time interpreter in ASL
c. Constructing ramps for the building
d. Designating alternate setting rooms

19. Which of the new students with disabilities is most likely to need the accommodation of an alternative setting for taking tests or completing assignments?

a. The deaf student
b. The ASD student
c. Visually impaired
d. Hearing impaired

20. The student described with hearing impairment is most likely to benefit from which of the following classroom accommodations?

a. An ASL interpreter
b. Specialized lighting
c. Time-of-day testing
d. Preferential seating

21. Based on the information given, what is the most likely need for the student with visual impairment?
   a. Braille copies of all textbooks to enable her to read material
   b. Curriculum modification to enable grade-level performance
   c. Magnifiers or large print to enable her to read material
   d. Receiving explicit instruction for development of study skills

22. Four new students will continue receiving the SLP services they need. For which of these students are those services *most* important at the present time?
   a. The students with delayed language development
   b. The students diagnosed with articulation disorder
   c. The students with both, but only kindergarteners
   d. The students with both, but only first- or second-graders

23. The special educators mentioned curriculum modifications for the students with intellectual disability. Which of the following is an example of these?
   a. Different kinds or fewer numbers of math homework problems
   b. Receiving explicit and direct instruction to develop skills in studying
   c. Continuing work on addition while others progress to multiplication
   d. Being allowed longer times for completing tests and assignments

24. Of the following categories represented, which student(s) is/are most likely to need someone—whether a school staff member or a volunteer who has been trained—to provide daily one-on-one assistance?
   a. Speech/Language Impairment
   b. Other Health Impairment
   c. Hearing Impairment
   d. Visual Impairment

25. The new student with a central auditory processing disorder will benefit most from which type of classroom accommodation?
   a. Presentation accommodation with a designated reader
   b. Presentation accommodation with audiobooks for text
   c. Timing accommodation for completing any written test
   d. Timing accommodation for a teacher's spoken directions

Use the information in the scenario and documents below to answer the questions that follow them.

DESCRIPTION

Perinton Middle School, with sixth through eighth grades, is situated in a suburb. Of about 600 students enrolled, around half are qualified for price-reduced or free school meals. The economy and demography of the school's surrounding community have not changed much in the past several years, and the school has retained the same staff for about five years. Ms. M. has just accepted the position of the new building leader for Perinton Middle School. Perinton is part of a school district that was recently assigned a new superintendent.

When the district first hired Ms. M., she met with the superintendent to obtain information about his goals for Perinton Middle School and about its background. The superintendent communicated that despite many students' demonstrating satisfactory academic achievement, there remained an achievement gap between them and the school's lower-income students, which the superintendent expected Ms. M. to eliminate or reduce.

In response to the superintendent's wishes, Ms. M. reviewed all student scores on the most recent state-level standardized assessment. In these data, she saw evidence of consistently lower academic performance by economically disadvantaged students than by the rest of the student body. She also reviewed student responses to an opinion survey that school counselors had given in classrooms last spring, and teacher responses to a survey they were given at the end of the last school year. Additionally, in reviewing data collected over the last few years, she observed that rates of school attendance by eighth-grade students from low-income families had regularly been lower than the rates of attendance by the overall student body.

DOCUMENT 1

Last Year's State Standardized Assessment:

Student Results, Aggregated and

Disaggregated by Two Categories

Percentages of all students, students with Limited English Proficiency (LEP), and Low-SES students who scored ≥ Level 3 = "Meets Proficiency Standards"

	ELA	Math	Science	Total # of Students Assessed
GRADE 6				
All Students	68%	67%	N/A	175
LEP Students	32%	49%	N/A	13
Low-SES Students	44%	47%	N/A	78
GRADE 7				
All Students	63%	69%	N/A	185
LEP Students	35%	49%	N/A	15
Low-SES Students	37%	44%	N/A	93
GRADE 8				
All Students	57%	59%	71%	202
LEP Students	30%	49%	43%	17
Low-SES Students	33%	41%	54%	96

Document 2

Student Opinion Survey – Last Year, Fourth Quarter: Excerpted Data from Aggregated Results

(c. 90% of Students Responding)

How much do you agree or disagree that the adults in our school:	% "Strongly Agree" or "Agree"
Respect and support the students?	54%
Care about all students a great deal?	57%
Listen to what each student has to say?	44%
Believe all students can succeed?	47%
Challenge you and all students to do your best?	32%
In your experience of school over this year, how much do you agree or disagree that:	
Your teachers have helped you to learn?	54%
You have liked school very much?	64%
You have made a real effort in school?	32%
It is important to you to get good grades?	44%
You are comfortable sharing your thoughts and ideas in classes?	54%
In this school, you have felt that people valued you?	48%
Your teachers have helped you academically when you needed it?	53%
Your expectations for yourself in school are high?	36%
Your teachers give equal opportunities to participate in classroom activities and discussions to all students?	55%

DOCUMENT 3

Anonymous Survey of all Teachers: Excerpted Data

Last Year, End of School Year

(c. 80% of teachers responding)

How much do you agree or disagree with each statement?	% "Strongly Agree" or "Agree"
All students can become motivated to learn.	41%
All students can be academically successful.	43%
Teachers can positively affect each student's learning.	51%
Teachers can ensure each student's active engagement in learning.	57%
Teachers play the main role in determining what their students can achieve.	37%
Teachers have significant ability to counter influences outside school that adversely affect student learning.	34%
Student attitudes about learning and school are influenced most by teachers.	29%

Survey's open-ended comments section: ≥ 5 teachers expressed the following opinions:
When students don't come to class, the teacher can't accomplish much.
Getting good grades, or school overall, seem unimportant to some student groups.
It would be hard for many students to catch up and get passing grades because they are already so far behind.
Some of my students have great attitudes toward school, and some show total apathy.
Although my doing what I am able seems to work for some student groups, what I do is never enough for other groups.

26. According to the information available here, on which of the following considerations should Ms. M. focus her analysis *first*?

    a. Whether any subject curriculum needs change to meet student needs and align with standards more
    b. How to make sure teachers use equitable instructional strategies that motivate all students to excel
    c. Why the students are performing better in some subjects like science than in ELA and mathematics
    d. Whether to establish school procedures for addressing attendance and other disciplinary problems

27. Ms. M. reviewed data from the state standardized assessment and the student survey. To obtain additional insight into the school's current issues, what else could she do regarding data analysis?

    a. Correlate state test data with report card grades and classroom results.
    b. Interview a random sample of the students surveyed in greater depth.
    c. Compare state test data with data of similar middle schools statewide.
    d. Disaggregate the student survey responses by categories of students.

28. Based on the responses of the teachers to the survey, following up on which of these characteristics in the faculty she will be leading should be of *most* concern to Ms. M.?
    a. Limitations in understanding the part that student motivation plays relative to student learning
    b. Habits of overly emphasizing student grades as ways of measuring how successful students are
    c. Lack of understanding of how the performance of students is affected by excellence in teaching
    d. Habits of overly focusing on differences among students versus commonalities among students

29. As part of her initiative to meet diverse student learning needs, Ms. M. decides to implement regular department and faculty meetings. Based on the information given, on which of the following should she focus these meetings to attain this goal?
    a. Instructional strategies they can develop and refine to enhance diverse groups' learning
    b. Instructional objectives they can develop and clarify to suit diverse student populations
    c. Instructional theories emerging that they can discuss about how diverse students learn
    d. Instructional assumptions they can examine about what helps or hurts diverse learning

30. In which academic subject did the same proportion of students with limited English proficiency meet the standard in all three middle school grades?
    a. English Language Arts
    b. Mathematics
    c. Science
    d. None

31. Which of the following statements is true about student performance, based on the data provided?
    a. More low-SES students than LEP students met the math standards in all the middle-school grades.
    b. Both low-SES and LEP students in grade 8 tested better in science than in math, and worst in ELA.
    c. The largest achievement gap between LEP students and all students in the seventh grade is in ELA.
    d. The same proportions of low-SES met ELA standards in Grade 6 as met math standards in Grade 7.

32. From the information given, which two factors appeared to have the strongest positive correlation?
    a. How much students expected of themselves and how much adults respected them
    b. How much teachers helped the students and how much effort students expended
    c. How much students felt challenged in school and how hard students tried in school
    d. How much teachers cared about students and how much students cared about grades

33. Across data sources, which two factors appeared to have the strongest inverse correlation?
   a. How much teachers cared about students and how much they felt they could engage them
   b. How much teachers could affect student attitudes and how much students enjoyed school
   c. How much teachers listened to students and how important grades were to their students
   d. How much teachers felt they could help all students learn and how much students felt teachers did it

Use the information below to answer the questions that follow it.

DESCRIPTION

Following the retirement of the previous long-time principal, you have taken over the position of building leader of a suburban high school. You learned in meeting with the superintendent of schools that the previous principal had initially emphasized inclusive education strongly and a welcoming and equitable school environment. Over the years, this environment, combined with social trends of increasing demographic diversity in the U.S., gradually led to a more diverse than average student population. This includes students of different races, ethnicities, cultures, SES, sexual and gender identification, and students with various disabilities, including emotional and behavioral disorders.

You also learned that currently, the school experiences regular problems with students bullying other students. This appears to have developed gradually along with the increasing diversity. Additionally, other student maladaptive behaviors have risen. Many of these are displayed by the larger proportion of students with emotional and behavioral disorders, and others by other students whose teachers are struggling with classroom management. The previous principal had adopted a zero tolerance policy against bullying in the school. However, this has backfired in a number of instances. Examples are given in a document below.

Having completed a professional development course in School-Wide Positive Behavioral Support systems (SWPBS, aka Positive Behavioral Interventions and Supports or PBIS) and consulted with a school psychologist, you want to implement this type of system in the school, as research has demonstrated it to be more effective than zero tolerance policies. The structure and content of a three-tiered SWPBS model are described in a document below.

Some students' parents are resistant to instituting this different approach as they fear it will be "not strict enough"; they prefer maintaining the zero tolerance policy because they think it projects a more definitive attitude against bullying. Since these parents are unaware of research findings or of actual results of this policy in their school, you plan to present some of these school incidents at your first parent meeting. You additionally plan to have a school psychologist present a summary of the American Psychological Association (APA) Task Force on Zero Tolerance Report illustrating its limitations and also a summary of research findings about the effectiveness of SWPBS.

You are planning professional development for all school faculty and staff members to train them in classroom behavior management, and in the organization and implementation of the three-tiered SWPBS system. Based on APA recommendations, you have issued a brief list of new general guidelines for all teachers already. They are to start following these immediately, and will receive additional instruction and reinforcement for these during and after training.

DOCUMENT 1

Notes for Parent Meeting:

Examples Against Zero Tolerance Policy

Incidents in Our School and District

When long-term verbal and emotional abuse of a student finally escalated to physical violence and the victim fought back in self-defense, the principal was forced to suspend or expel all students involved, *including the victim*, because the policy prohibited physical violence regardless.

Instead of being able to resolve minor classroom incidents, use them as teachable moments, and prevent bullying, teachers have been required to report them to administrators, who then addressed them as major incidents.

A student from a neglectful and abusive home who was diagnosed with a behavioral disorder was suspended for threatening a teacher, but managed to sneak back in the same day because he found the school a safer environment than his home.

A freshman, whose mother had packed a knife in her lunch for cutting an apple, turned in the knife to a teacher knowing it was against school rules; the teacher praised her action, but the student was then expelled for having a weapon in school.

Colleagues at other schools in our district report students have received identical treatment regardless of age, even though student intentions and behaviors differed. For example, a middle school student who threatened to shoot the principal and a kindergarten student who brought a toy gun to school in his backpack were both expelled.

These are just a few examples of numerous incidents wherein the existing policy has backfired. While zero tolerance was initially a law to expel students bringing guns to school, it has since spread to many other behaviors in our school. Its imposition of harsh consequences often hurts more than helps, as illustrated by these examples.

Document 2

School-Wide Positive Behavioral Support System:
3-Tiered Model

School building leaders, administrators, faculty, and staff define positive expectations and teach these to all adults and students, which researchers find develops a positive school culture.

TIER 1	
% of Students	Approximately 80-85%
Summary	Universal screening, instruction, and intervention School sets positive behavioral expectations. Operationalize positive behaviors; instruct students in them. Ensure staff and families understand expectations as well as students. Teachers model expected behaviors. Teachers interact with students pro-socially. Give faculty formal behavior management training. Form school leadership team to support SWPBS. Implement a student behavior data-collection system to inform interventional and other decisions.
Procedures	Teach positive expectations at the beginning of the school year. Post goals in classrooms; familiarize students; re-teach goals all year. Make goals understandable and measurable; give students examples. Keep expectations five or fewer at a time; students will forget more. Adjust behavioral expectations for setting, group size, other contexts. <u>Positive Reinforcement:</u> Specifically praising good behaviors will increase them. Determine which rewards are reinforcing for which students. <u>Student Engagement:</u> Prevent off-task behavior with instructional materials at appropriate difficulty levels for students (neither too easy nor too hard). Increase student ownership of learning experience by giving students choice in study materials. Increase student engagement in learning material by incorporating student interests into the curriculum.
TIER 2	
% of Students	Approximately 10-15%
Summary	Students not responding to Tier 1 receive secondary-level interventions like social skills instruction in small-group format. First Steps to Success (Walker et al., 1997) and other research- and evidence-based programs recommended.

Procedures	Instruction in small groups for classroom behavior management and improvement
Small-group socioemotional skills training – Examples:
Self-management training
Anger management training
Conflict resolution training
Specialized social skills training
Mentoring programs
Establish daily check-in and check-out procedures to monitor student behavior and give feedback. Base monitoring criteria on school behavior expectations.
Consult with school psychologist for data collection and functional behavior analysis. Determining behavior functions identifies student needs to inform effective and appropriate interventions.
Engage families: Communicate consistently and inform of school problem-solving plans to recruit family support of group interventions.
TIER 3	
% of Students	Approximately 5-7%
Summary	Students not responding to Tier 2 interventions receive tertiary-level, individualized, evidence-based programs based on behavior data and functional behavior analysis (FBA). Consultation with school psychologists, special education teachers, and others with FBA expertise is important, as most classroom teachers are not trained in FBA or functional assessment.
Procedures	Each student receives intensive, individualized interventions.
Principals, school psychologists, teachers, and special educators form problem-solving teams that regularly meet, collaboratively determining suitable interventions for students needing more support.
To design applicable, function-based interventions, first determine purposes of student behaviors by conducting functional behavior assessments.

Document 3

New General Guidelines for Our Teachers

(Adapted from APA Recommendations)

Set rules that are clear and specific, not vague or generalized. For example, define "respectful" behavior by giving students examples of specific behaviors.
Only set rules that you are actually willing to enforce.
Do not let student behaviors breaking classroom or school rules continue by ignoring them.
Treat unacceptable behaviors consistently and clearly, not irregularly or ambiguously.
Only deliver punishments accompanied by support. Do not give humiliating or overly harsh punishments.
Do NOT subject students to any corporal (physical) punishment.
Whenever possible, do not suspend students. (Refer to APA Task Force on Zero Tolerance Report.)
For serious student behavior problems, do not attempt to solve these alone; refer students to school psychologists or special education professionals.

34. In addition to the supports and interventions described, what else should you as the new school building leader *most* do to improve the school environment and student behavior?

a. Model respectful behavior for faculty who will then naturally model that for students.
b. Inform faculty of your expectations that they model respectful behaviors for students.
c. Model respectful behavior and state your expectations of it from faculty and students.
d. Inform faculty of your expectations for respectful behavior—from them and students.

35. When implementing a SWPBS system, why it is important to collect student behavior data?

a. To ensure school accountability
b. To ensure objective reporting
c. To ensure staff participation
d. To ensure student conduct

36. According to the information provided, how can schools best establish a positive school culture?

a. By defining the consequences for misbehaviors
b. By defining behaviors that will not be tolerated
c. By defining the functions for student behaviors
d. By defining and teaching positive expectations

37. Based on the information given, why is it important to conduct Functional Behavior Analysis (FBA) for upper tiers of SWBPS, as well as for behavior management in general?

a. To determine more adaptive ways for students to achieve functions
b. To determine the impacts of behaviors on school-wide functionality
c. To determine how functional each of the student's behaviors can be
d. To determine whether a student's behavior has any functions or not

38. If a teacher encounters a major, serious student behavior problem, what is recommended according to the information given?
   a. Refer to nobody else; it is a primary responsibility of the teacher to solve these problems.
   b. Refer to another professional only as a last resort, after trying to solve the problem alone.
   c. Refer to the school psychologist only, whether they are special education students or not.
   d. Refer to the school psychologist or special educators with special education students.

39. The student described in item #3 of Document 1 would most likely benefit from which of these in the SWPBS program outlined?
   a. The intervention described as Tier 1 would be most effective.
   b. The intervention described as Tier 2 would be most effective.
   c. The intervention described as Tier 3 would be most effective.
   d. The intervention described as suspension was most effective.

40. Teachers at this school have been struggling with classroom behavior management. The more interested students are in their learning, the fewer behavior problems they tend to exhibit. Among aspects of learning materials, students' lack of ownership of their learning is most attributable to which of these?
   a. Teachers are offering students excessively easy materials.
   b. Teachers were offering students overly difficult materials.
   c. Teachers are not offering students choices as to materials.
   d. Teachers were not including student interests in materials.

41. Which of the following most accurately reflects estimates of student distribution among SWPBS tiers, based on the information provided?
   a. About twice as many students need Tier 2 supports as those needing Tier 3 supports.
   b. About half as many students need Tier 2 supports as those who succeed with Tier 1.
   c. About equal proportions of students, if not responding to Tier 1, need Tiers 2 and 3.
   d. About twice as many students need Tier 3 supports as those needing Tier 2 supports.

Part 2

Note: Part 2 of the NYSTCE School Building Leader exam includes an extended performance task requiring the test taker to evaluate a 15-minute video recording of a teacher's classroom instruction. After watching the video, the test taker is asked to score the teacher based on a provided rubric and note evidence from the recording to support the feedback. Because we are unable to provide a reasonable simulation of this exercise in our text study guide format, we recommend visiting the NYSTCE website and familiarizing yourself with the observation rubric on which you will be evaluating the recorded instructional session.

(http://www.nystce.nesinc.com/Content/STUDYGUIDE/NY_SG_Vid_107_subtest2.htm)

EXTENDED PERFORMANCE TASKS
DEVELOPING HUMAN CAPITAL TO IMPROVE FACULTY AND STAFF EFFECTIVENESS AND STUDENT ACHIEVEMENT

Use the information and documents below to complete the task that follows. You have 70 minutes to complete this assignment.

DESCRIPTION

You have just become the new school principal of Henrietta Elementary, a K-5 school with an enrollment of about 275 students. For more than 10 years, enrollment at this school has been relatively stable.

High student achievement characterizes Henrietta Elementary School's history. Four years ago, the state education department introduced more rigorous educational standards. Since then, the students in most grades and classes have demonstrated continuing performance improvements on formative and standardized state assessments. After being hired, you had met with the superintendent of schools, who expressed great pride in the school's student and staff accomplishments and her expectations for you to build on that successful status.

Of Henrietta Elementary School's 13 classroom teachers, most have taught there for 10 years or longer. In the past six years, one teacher relocated out of the district and one retired, and two new teachers were hired to replace them. Otherwise, the school has minimal staff turnover. From talking with your teachers before the school year began, your impressions included that teachers were highly committed to providing each student with excellent, effective learning experiences, and that teacher morale was also high.

You recently reviewed the available school building data on student assessments, teacher evaluations, and teacher responses to a survey taken the previous school year. These are summarized in the documents below.

Document 1

Henrietta Elementary School:
Student Performance Indicators
Two-Year Comparison: All Students, Grades 3-5
State Standardized Assessment Results

Percentages of all students who scored ≥ Level 3, "Meets Proficiency Standard," on state assessment:

Subject	School Building Level		School District Level		State Level	
	2 Years Ago	Last Year	2 Years Ago	Last Year	2 Years Ago	Last Year
ELA	74%	77%	70%	72%	55%	57%
Math	81%	83%	78%	79%	63%	65%

Two-Year Comparison: All Students, Grades 3-5, By Grade
State Standardized Assessment Results

Percentages in each grade and three-grade totals of all students who scored ≥ Level 3, "Meets Proficiency Standard," on state assessment:

	2 Years Ago		Last Year	
	ELA	Math	ELA	Math
Grade 3	81%	88%	84%	90%
Grade 4	70%	77%	73%	78%
Grade 5	77%	85%	80%	88%
Total Grades 3-5	76%	83%	79%	85%

DOCUMENT 2

Last Year's Teacher Evaluation Data:

All Classroom Teachers – Composited Scores

(Assessed using state-issued growth scores, local student achievement measures, and other teacher effectiveness indicators among multiple instruments)

* Teachers specializing in Art, Music, Physical Education, Gifted and Talented, and Non-English Languages are not included in these data. *

Teacher Ratings		Ineffective		Developing		Effective		Highly Effective	
Grade	Total # Teachers	#	%	#	%	#	%	#	%
K	3	0	0%	0	0%	2	66.7%	1	33.3%
1	2	0	0%	0	0%	2	100%	0	0%
2	2	0	0%	1	50%	1	50%	0	0%
3	2	0	0%	0	0%	1	50%	1	50%
4	2	0	0%	1	50%	1	50%	0	0%
5	2	0	0%	0	0%	2	100%	0	0%
TOTAL	13	0	0%	2	15.4%	9	69.2%	2	15.4%

Teachers – Grades 4 and 5: Adjusted Mean Growth Percentiles (MGP)

Teacher	Grade	Adjusted MGP	Range of Confidence Intervals – Adjusted MGP		Teacher Growth Rating
			Lower Limit	Upper Limit	
Teacher J	4	60	56	64	Effective
Teacher K	4	42	39	46	Developing
Teacher L	5	50	44	46	Effective
Teacher M	5	64	60	68	Effective

Document 3

Grades K-2 Teachers: Excerpted Summary Data from Observations Using Teacher Practice Assessment Rubric

Domains, Selected Components	Teacher A (K)	Teacher B (K)	Teacher C (K)	Teacher D (1)	Teacher E (1)	Teacher F (2)	Teacher G (2)
Observational Ratings Overall	3	4	3	3	3	2	3
Planning and Preparation	3	4	4	3	2	2	3
Demonstrating content knowledge	3	4	4	3	3	2	3
Demonstrating pedagogical knowledge	3	4	3	3	3	2	3
Defining instructional outcomes	3	3	4	3	2	3	3
Coherent instructional design	3	4	4	3	2	2	3
Student assessment design	2	3	3	2	2	1	2
Classroom Environment	3	4	3	3	2	2	2
Establishing a learning culture	3	4	4	3	1	2	2
Classroom procedure management	3	4	3	2	3	2	3
Student behavior management	2	4	3	3	3	3	2
Instruction	3	4	3	3	3	2	3
Communication with students	3	4	3	3	3	2	2
Using discussion and questions	3	4	3	3	2	3	3
Engaging students in learning	3	4	3	3	3	2	3
Using assessment in teaching	2	3	3	2	3	1	2
Showing responsivity and flexibility	2	4	3	2	2	2	3
Professional Responsibilities	2	3	3	3	4	3	3
Reflection on teaching	2	3	3	3	4	3	3
Professional community participation	2	3	2	3	3	2	2

Key: 1 = Unsatisfactory   2 = Basic   3 = Proficient   4 = Exemplary

Document 4

Grades 3-5 Teachers:
Excerpted Summary Data from Observations
Using Teacher Practice Assessment Rubric

Domains, Selected Components	Teacher H (3)	Teacher I (3)	Teacher J (4)	Teacher K (4)	Teacher L (5)	Teacher M (5)
Observational Ratings Overall	3	4	3	2	3	3
Planning and Preparation	3	4	2	2	3	3
Demonstrating content knowledge	4	4	3	3	3	3
Demonstrating pedagogical knowledge	3	4	3	2	3	3
Defining instructional outcomes	3	4	2	1	3	2
Coherent instructional design	3	4	2	2	3	3
Student assessment design	3	4	2	2	3	2
Classroom Environment	2	4	3	2	2	4
Establishing a learning culture	2	4	3	2	3	4
Classroom procedure management	2	4	2	2	3	4
Student behavior management	3	4	3	2	2	4
Instruction	3	4	3	2	3	3
Communication with students	3	3	3	3	3	4
Using discussion and questions	3	4	3	2	3	3
Engaging students in learning	2	3	3	2	3	3
Using assessment in teaching	3	4	2	1	2	3
Showing responsivity and flexibility	2	4	2	1	2	3
Professional Responsibilities	3	4	3	2	3	3
Reflection on teaching	2	4	3	2	3	3
Professional community participation	3	3	2	2	2	2

Key: 1 = Unsatisfactory   2 = Basic   3 = Proficient   4 = Exemplary

DOCUMENT 5

Last Year's Teacher Survey:

Excerpted Results

(100% of Teachers Responding)

Survey Statement	% "Strongly Agree" or "Agree"
I enjoy teaching at this school.	93%
School leaders are responsive to my work needs.	78%
Clear performance expectations are defined for teachers.	86%
School leaders support and encourage me and my efforts.	86%
School leaders acknowledge my work and contributions.	86%
I have the support and resources to give my students a very effective learning environment.	73%
Reasonable planning time is afforded by my work schedule.	68%
I have sufficient professional development opportunities.	78%
I have the knowledge and skills to inform my teaching decisions by analyzing data on my students' performance.	62%
I have the knowledge and skills to attain all of my students' instructional goals.	70%
I meet diverse student needs by regularly differentiating instruction.	55%
I collaborate actively with other teachers of the same grade.	49%
I collaborate actively with other teachers of other grades.	42%
I analyze data from my formative assessments routinely.	57%
I analyze data from formative assessments with other teachers routinely to inform my instructional design and choices.	49%

Short Answer Questions

From your school building leadership understanding and the information supplied, address the following tasks:

1. Write a response about 100-200 words long, in a format you prefer (e.g., an outline, a list of bulleted items, prose paragraphs, etc.), addressing this question and these prompts:

In which area is additional human capital development the most imminent need at Henrietta Elementary School? Explain what you would do to develop this area and why you think this would work. In identifying the need area and how you would address it, give clear definitions and specific details. Cite evidence in support of your answers.

2. Write a response around 100-200 words in length, in a format you prefer (e.g., an outline, a list of bulleted items, prose paragraphs, etc.) to the following:

To improve human capital at Henrietta Elementary School, which two actions you could take are the most important? Explain why these would benefit the school in the long term. Describe your proposed actions clearly and specifically. Cite pertinent evidence to support your answers.

3. Write an answer about 100-200 words long, in a format you choose (e.g., a list of bulleted items, an outline, prose paragraphs, etc.) responding to the following:

Describe clearly and specifically what you would do to help Teacher K to develop more effectiveness as a teacher, and explain why you would do those things. Support your answers by citing pertinent evidence.

4. Write a response about 100-200 words in length, in a format of your choice (e.g., prose paragraphs, an outline, a list of bulleted items, etc.) to the following:

Which professional development opportunities would you recommend for Teacher H, and why? Describe these opportunities clearly and specifically, and support your answers by presenting pertinent evidence.

SHORTER PERFORMANCE TASK
FAMILY AND COMMUNITY ENGAGEMENT

Use the information and documents below to complete the task that follows. You have 40 minutes to complete this assignment.

DESCRIPTION

Last spring you accepted the position of school principal in anticipation of the coming school year at X High School, with grades 9-12. This school's large district, located in the suburbs, responded to falling high school enrollments and government budget cuts at the end of the last school year by closing its other secondary school, Y High School, and incorporating its student population in that of X High School. Consolidating the two schools into one means that this fall, your school will have a 4,000-student enrollment, having added 1,000 more students from the former Y High School, as well as three assistant principals, 30 teachers, several school counselors, and additional staff members.

Before the new school year started, you and the superintendent of schools met to talk about the school consolidation and pinpoint which issues you will most need to confront as the new principal. The superintendent informed you that before consolidation, X and Y high schools had been major sports opponents, and that the two schools have had significantly different demographic characteristics. The former Y High School was less successful academically, with fewer AP classes, fewer graduates, fewer of those graduates attaining State Regents Diplomas with Advanced Designation, and fewer attending college. Members of the surrounding community also have always perceived X High School as superior.

You reviewed both high schools' survey data during the summer to gain more insight into local family perceptions of them. One thing you observed immediately was that 60 percent of X High School's families responded to the survey, whereas 35 percent of Y High School's families did.

Also during the summer, families and other community members from both high schools contacted or visited you to discuss their concerns related to the consolidation. These concerns included that class sizes could become excessive; students could be crowded in the single building space; some transferring students would have to commute miles farther and up to half an hour longer; how consolidation would affect the school's athletic program; and, for parents from X High School, the possibility that teachers would need to slow their instructional pace to accommodate lower-achieving students or confront behavioral problems due to transfers from Y High School.

The input and feedback you have received during the summer have illustrated for you the tenuous position of the newly consolidated high school. You have thus committed to discovering means for unifying the blended school student body, faculty, and staff; fostering new school community partnerships; and furthering learning at your school.

DOCUMENT 1

Comparison of Two High Schools (Pre-Consolidation)

Indicators	X High School	Y High School
# of Advanced Placement classes	14	3
% of students graduating	95%	75%
% of graduates earning State Regents Diploma with Advanced Designation	60%	20%
% of graduates attending college	90%	48%

DOCUMENT 2

Last Year's (Pre-Consolidation) Data from Family Perception Survey by School

Survey Questions	X High School - % "A great deal" or "A good deal" responses	Y High School - % "A great deal" or "A good deal" responses
1. How much do students feel a sense of belonging at school?	84%	75%
2. How much does your school offer activities meeting your student's interests?	79%	63%
3. How well are your student's learning style(s) matched by teachers' instructional methods?	77%	52%
4. How well do you think your school is preparing your student for the next school year?	85%	65%
5. How frequently do you meet with your student's teachers?	53%	30%
6. How much do you believe teachers can motivate your student to do his/her best in school?	67%	25%
7. How comfortable are you with communication and involvement with the school?	75%	47%
8. How welcome as a parent does the school make you feel?	63%	45%

SHORT ANSWER QUESTIONS

Using the information given above, write a response about 400-500 words long, in a format you prefer (e.g., an outline, a list of bulleted items, prose paragraphs). In addressing the items below, give very specific details and cite evidence from the description and data that appropriately support your answers.

1. Identify two significant issues you can expect in the new school year with the consolidated school. Describe some reasons and ways that engaging families in addressing these issues would have benefits.

2. Identify which actions you would take to involve families in each of the two issues you identified above, and explain why these would work. Identify some new challenges that could result from your actions, and how you would manage them.

Multiple Choice Questions

Use the information and documents below to complete the task that follows. You have 60 minutes to complete these questions.

Family and Community Engagement

Description Ms. C. has just become the new principal of Seneca Elementary, a K-5 school in the suburbs with about 500 students enrolled. Seneca Elementary has a reputation for strongly emphasizing instruction in foundational skills, and for high rates of involvement by many students' families. In general, its students achieve higher than or equal to the averages for their school district and state. Last year, the school implemented a new curriculum, aligned with the New York State Common Core Learning Standards (NYSCCLS), which its district had adopted. Students maintained their high achievement rates during curricular changes that year.

Seneca Elementary has been collaborating with a local college for the past several years on a tutoring program, Reading for All. The college's undergraduate teacher preparation program partners with the elementary school, assigning students from its advanced course in reading instruction to tutor Seneca Elementary students who struggle with reading. Requirements for course completion include tutoring for four hours weekly at the elementary school. The course is taught by several members of the college faculty, who take turns with teaching rotations. College faculty teaching the advanced reading instruction course typically do not have formal meetings with Seneca Elementary personnel; instead, at the beginning of every school year, a college faculty coordinator meets with Seneca's administrators and ELA coordinator, and they meet again during the year as needed.

Seneca Elementary staff and school community were enthusiastic about implementing the tutoring program initially, and students participating in tutoring sessions have demonstrated improved reading performance by all assessment measures over the last four years. Currently the program involves about 80 students receiving tutoring from the college students. When Ms. C. started leading Seneca Elementary, she met with 25 participating students' parents, who attributed their children's increased confidence in their own reading skills, improved attitudes about reading, and third- through fifth-graders' increases of two to three hours weekly in voluntary home reading time to the tutoring, and unanimously expressed their support of the program.

Despite these salutary results, in her first meetings with her staff Ms. C. discovered teachers had become somewhat less supportive of the tutoring program than initially. Concerns expressed by individual teachers included that college faculty members appeared to have lost some of their original engagement, and that the program was "losing steam." Ms. C. wants to revitalize school staff's support for the Reading for All program, and to reinforce the school-college partnership. To inform pursuit of these goals, she reviews data from a yearly school survey of teachers about the tutoring program, and data from teachers' formative assessments of student literacy skills and progress. She also reads a letter written by her predecessor to the college's faculty coordinator after the program had been operating for one year.

DOCUMENT 1

Seneca Elementary School

Grades 1-5 Literacy Skills Formative Assessment Data:

Fourth Quarter

Percentage of students correctly responding >65% of formative assessment items

Skills Areas by Grade	5 Years Ago	3 Years Ago	Last Year
GRADE 1			
Print Concepts	78%	85%	86%
Phonological Awareness	73%	79%	81%
Phonics, Word Recognition	71%	77%	76%
Reading Fluency	67%	72%	72%
Identifying Main Ideas, Supporting Details	63%	69%	70%
Structure and Craft	58%	65%	64%
Integrating Ideas and Knowledge	62%	67%	68%
GRADE 2			
Phonics, Word Recognition	77%	81%	81%
Reading Fluency	71%	75%	74%
Identifying Main Ideas, Supporting Details	66%	71%	71%
Structure and Craft	62%	68%	67%
Integrating Ideas and Knowledge	65%	70%	69%
GRADE 3			
Phonics, Word Recognition	82%	85%	86%
Reading Fluency	76%	80%	80%
Identifying Main Ideas, Supporting Details	69%	73%	72%
Structure and Craft	64%	69%	69%
Integrating Ideas and Knowledge	67%	72%	71%
GRADE 4			
Phonics, Word Recognition	86%	88%	87%
Reading Fluency	81%	84%	84%
Identifying Main Ideas, Supporting Details	70%	75%	75%
Structure and Craft	68%	73%	71%
Integrating Ideas and Knowledge	71%	75%	74%
GRADE 5			
Phonics, Word Recognition	87%	91%	91%
Reading Fluency	85%	88%	87%
Identifying Main Ideas, Supporting Details	72%	77%	76%
Structure and Craft	67%	73%	73%
Integrating Ideas and Knowledge	71%	76%	77%

Document 2

Seneca Elementary School

Teacher Survey Data Comparison:

Teachers with Students Participating in

Reading for All Tutoring Program

Survey Item Statement	% of Teachers Responding "Strongly Agree" or "Agree"	
	3 Years Ago*	Last Year**
The Reading for All program benefits the struggling readers in my class.	91%	81%
The tutors assigned to my class know how to instruct struggling readers effectively.	75%	64%
The tutors assigned to my class demonstrate effective responses to the varying learning needs of my students.	80%	69%
The tutors assigned to my class demonstrate familiarity with the ELA curriculum at Seneca Elementary School.	70%	44%
My students who struggle with reading look forward to their tutoring sessions.	85%	78%
Working with the tutors assigned to my class is easy for me.	75%	59%
The tutors assigned to my class are available for consultation about my students' reading and their tutoring activities.	75%	64%
To instruct my students effectively, the tutors assigned to my class need more training.	20%	46%
The Reading for All program's college coordinator is available as needed for communicating with me.	56%	44%
The Reading for All program's college coordinator responds to my concerns and comments.	66%	49%
Teachers at Seneca would benefit from the following:		
Opportunities for collaborating with college partners on planning and designing instruction for reading	51%	59%
Having college faculty in the Reading for All program lead professional development activities at our school	61%	66%

Key

* = 89% of teachers with students in the tutoring program responded.

** = 95% of teachers with students in the tutoring program responded.

DOCUMENT 3

Letter from preceding Seneca Elementary School principal to college Faculty Coordinator

Dear Dr. L.:

I am pleased to see the success of our partnership in the Reading for All tutoring program during its first year. Your college's contributions to our school community have brought great benefits to the students of Seneca Elementary School.

Throughout the school year we had 75 students in several grades receiving one-on-one tutoring from your tutors, 24 of whom visited our school regularly. Their efforts have had excellent results. All participating students have demonstrated improvement in reading skills. They have also been excited to work with your tutors and have genuinely enjoyed their sessions. Our school staff gave a good reception to our collaborative partnership and the effort contributed by your faculty and students. Our students' parents, and indeed the whole school community, have supported the tutoring program enthusiastically. We can all feel proud of our considerable accomplishments in this program.

My staff and I find some of your and other faculty's suggestions for expanding the program very exciting and look forward to exploring them in the coming school year. Having some of your faculty in the tutoring program also lead professional development activities at Seneca is an idea my teachers find especially appealing. I believe this would greatly enhance teachers' exposure to current best practices and research findings in reading instruction. Another of your ideas we want to pursue is giving our teachers more opportunities for consulting with your college faculty on effective, appropriate reading instruction for all our students. Such consultation would not only reinforce the strong partnership we have developed this year; it would also give our school staff an excellent source of support.

We very much appreciate all of the commitment, time, and energy that you, your faculty, and your students have devoted to our tutoring program. Please accept my thanks and congratulations, and share them with your colleagues.

Sincerely,
Mr. J., Principal
Seneca Elementary School

Use the information and documents below to complete the task that follows.

1. Ms. C. plans a first meeting with the college's current faculty coordinator for the tutoring program. According to the information given, which issue should she focus on during this meeting first and most?

    a. Working on identifying more instructional strategies for Seneca teachers
    b. Working on improving the responsivity of college faculty to Seneca staff
    c. Working on improving the knowledge of tutors about Seneca curriculum
    d. Working on examining formative assessment data from Seneca students

2. To increase college faculty engagement in continued planning of the tutoring program, Ms. C. intends to share Seneca school data with them. To attain this goal, which should she do with these data?

    a. Offer formative assessment data for every school year since program inception.
    b. Disaggregate formative assessment data for students in vs. not in the program.
    c. Identify individual tutors in every classroom along with the teacher survey data.
    d. Reorganize the teacher survey data to clarify areas of teachers' major concerns.

3. To revitalize Seneca teacher support for the reading tutoring program, which school strength area can Ms. C. leverage most, according to the information given?
   a. Parental reports of their children's improved reading times and attitudes
   b. Student increases in literacy skills performance since program inception
   c. College faculty's interest in leading professional development activities
   d. Percentage of teachers reporting good classroom experiences with tutors

4. To promote the vitality and efficacy of the Reading for All tutoring program as it continues, which of these actions that Ms. C. could take is likely to be the most useful?
   a. Ensure teacher contact to college faculty about tutoring issues by setting up procedures.
   b. Ensure information by offering available state and formative reading assessment results.
   c. Ensure collaboration by inviting periodic college faculty, tutor, and teacher conferencing.
   d. Ensure continuing, regular school-college faculty communications by setting up a system.

5. Which of the following should Ms. C.'s first priority be to reinforce the school-college partnership in the next several years?
   a. Evaluating the partnership's ongoing support of the school goal of enhancing student achievement
   b. Increasing opportunities for direct school staff collaboration with college teacher education faculty
   c. Ensuring that teacher education college undergraduates have sufficient preparation for being tutors
   d. Inviting Seneca teachers to attend the college to obtain professional development for reading

6. Which of the following best characterizes the relationship of teacher support for the program with student results from program participation?
   a. Student results and teacher support appear to show a positive correlation.
   b. Student results and teacher support appear to show no visible correlation.
   c. Student results and teacher support appear to show an inverse correlation.
   d. Student results and teacher support appear to show a variable correlation.

7. In terms of the teachers' perceptions, which of these has *decreased* over the past two years?
   a. Teacher perceptions that the tutors assigned require additional training to aid their students
   b. Teacher perceptions that professional development from college faculty will benefit teachers
   c. Teacher perceptions that consulting with college faculty will aid designing reading instruction
   d. Teacher perceptions that their feedback and concerns get good college coordinator response

8. Where in the information presented can you identify that teachers have lost faith in tutors' skills for differentiated instruction?
   a. In the Description only, not any actual school data
   b. In the students' decreased enjoyment for tutoring
   c. In less perceived efficacy for varied learning needs
   d. In lower perceived college coordinator availability

9. Over a period of two years, teacher attitudes regarding the tutoring program have changed the MOST about which factors?
   a. Tutor preparation status and tutor knowledge of school curriculum
   b. Tutor availability for consultations and cooperation from the tutors
   c. Tutor instructional knowledge and student anticipation for tutoring
   d. Tutor efficacy and college faculty help in professional development

10. Based on the available information, the predominant patterns of change in student literacy skills were _____ from five years ago to three years ago and _____ from three years ago to one year ago. Which choice correctly completes this statement?
   a. Falling 1-2 points; rising 2 points, flat, or falling 1 point
   b. Rising >1 point; rising 1 point, flat, or falling 1-2 points
   c. Rising <2 points or flat; rising by 1 point or staying flat
   d. Falling or rising 1 point; staying flat or rising by 1 point

11. To manage the school organization using information and communication technology (ICT), which of these do principals LEAST need to have today?
   a. An understanding of available technologies
   b. An understanding of applying ICT in schools
   c. An understanding of every aspect or all aspects of ICT
   d. An understanding of specific advice sources

12. Among ways that information and communication technology (ICT) has changed school leaders' work, which of the following is the most transformative?
   a. Developing budgets by using spreadsheets
   b. Communicating with others utilizing email
   c. Writing by using word processing software
   d. School planning by using MIS as core tools

13. Some advantages of standardizing technology in a school include saving money and increasing discounts on bulk purchases. It can also *increase* which of these?
   a. Parts and supply inventory
   b. Systems compatibility
   c. Time spent in training
   d. Need for tech support

14. Technology not only facilitates school principals' duties like preparing budgets; technology advances can also save schools money on technology itself. For example, some leaders realize significant savings by using Google Apps for Education and similar web-based programs. In which area(s) would such applications save schools and districts money?
   a. In software but not in hardware
   b. In storage but not in printing
   c. In storage and printing only
   d. In support and the others

15. Among sources of funding, which supplies the *most* for K-12 public schools in the United States?
   a. State governments
   b. Local governments
   c. Federal government
   d. Private fund sources

16. Regarding what federal education programs require of state education departments, which of these is true?
   a. Some federal education requirements are unfunded.
   b. States must accept federal education program funds.
   c. The laws only apply if states voluntarily accept funds.
   d. Federal funds have been declined by many U.S. states.

17. An essential part of school organizational management is the principal's use of effective internal controls, including procedures to ensure (reasonably) the school's attaining its objectives in several areas. Of these, the area of reliability in program reporting is reflected by which of the following?
   a. Meeting financial goals
   b. Preparing audits for ED
   c. The performance goals
   d. Protection of resources

18. The U.S. Department of Education (ED) supports school use of electronic data processing (EDP), and of "reasonable safeguards" against fraud and other abuse of student information systems as internal controls that school leaders must apply. Which choice accurately reflects one of these safeguards?
   a. Limiting staff access to necessary functions for assigned duties
   b. Assigning staff to unique IDs and passwords that never change
   c. Informing staff of use guidelines without their signing anything
   d. Issuing school-wide, not individual, use policies and procedures

19. In a school principal's effective time management, which of these is most related to prioritization?
   a. Scheduling to-do lists by their importance
   b. Scheduling duties to the appropriate staff
   c. Scheduling their own "closed door" times
   d. Scheduling to accommodate each request

20. Researchers have found which of these about how much of their time school principals typically use for various instructional activities?
   a. Formal teacher evaluations use principals' time more than informal classroom walk-throughs.
   b. Principals of lower-achieving and low-income schools use less time for instructional activities.
   c. High school principals use more time for instructional activities than elementary principals do.
   d. Elementary principals use more time for professional development than secondary principals.

21. When developing school Emergency Management Plans (EMPs), school principals should plan for their schools to be prepared for all types of hazards. For example, a custodian routinely mops floors in high-traffic areas between periods in a high school. This is an example of which type of hazard?
    a. Natural
    b. Biological
    c. Community
    d. Environmental

22. Which of the following is true about the National Incident Management System (NIMS)?
    a. All schools are required by federal law to adopt the NIMS.
    b. The NIMS enables better coordination by standardization.
    c. No schools are required under any law to adopt the NIMS.
    d. The NIMS is for military use and not to be used in schools.

23. According to research findings, how does maintaining safe, efficient, effective school physical plant facilities relate to student achievement?
    a. It can influence student achievement more than family background and behavior in combination.
    b. It can influence student achievement more than either socioeconomic status or attendance does.
    c. It can influence student achievement more than family, behavior, SES, and attendance combined.
    d. It can influence student achievement more than any single one of these factors does individually.

24. In defining effective school facilities maintenance plans, the U.S. Department of Education includes which of the following understandings by school administrators about these plans?
    a. That they require school-wide coordination more than collaboration of stakeholders
    b. That they affect building appearance and operations more than health and learning
    c. That they help school physical and financial well-being but also require funding
    d. That they have proper staff implementation and evaluation without demanding this

25. The principal of a middle school must decide whether or not conducting a search of a student's backpack for a potential illegal substance is justified. Which choice identifies the minimum legal requirement for doing this?
    a. Observation of an unlawful activity by the student
    b. Verbal consent from the student to make a search
    c. Parent consent to and presence during the search
    d. Reasonable suspicion that the student has a substance

26. Which legislation *most* protects the rights of students who have disabilities?
    a. IDEA
    b. NCLB
    c. WEEA
    d. Title VI

Answer Key and Explanations for Test #1

Part 1

EXTENDED PERFORMANCE TASK
INSTRUCTIONAL LEADERSHIP FOR STUDENT SUCCESS

Sample Response:

Because there is no single best way to respond to the extended performance items, the best way for us to help you to determine how well you did with your response is to direct you to NYSTCE's scoring rubrics for the extended response questions.

http://www.nystce.nesinc.com/Content/STUDYGUIDE/PDFs/SBL_Rubric1_Part1_Assignment1.pdf

http://www.nystce.nesinc.com/Content/STUDYGUIDE/PDFs/SBL_Rubric2_Part1_Assignment2.pdf

http://www.nystce.nesinc.com/Content/STUDYGUIDE/PDFs/SBL_Rubric3_Part1_Assignment3.pdf

http://www.nystce.nesinc.com/Content/STUDYGUIDE/PDFs/SBL_Rubric5_Part2_Assignment2.pdf

http://www.nystce.nesinc.com/Content/STUDYGUIDE/PDFs/SBL_Rubric6_Part2_Assignment3.pdf

MULTIPLE CHOICE QUESTIONS

1. C: Examinees must apply knowledge about monitoring student progress by using assessment data for this question. Although about 78.5 percent (averaged) of students responded correctly to >65 percent of ELA formative assessment items last spring, during the same period only 63 percent (added) of students responded correctly to ≥65 percent of English items on the Regents Exam. This difference implies that the formative assessment content was less rigorous than the standards tested by the Regents Exam. This should concern Mr. R. because to analyze and improve instruction and learning, the school must align its formative assessments with state standards.

2. A: This question tests examinee application of skills and strategies in leading collaborative educator work in developing plans to enhance student learning using assessment data. The teachers must first find ELA curriculum areas where students need the most help in order to determine how to change curriculum and instruction accordingly. Since their formative assessments are not currently aligned with state standards tested in the Regents Exam, analyzing standardized assessment data is the most useful strategy for informing action plans.

3. B: This question tests examinee knowledge of data collection and analysis strategies to use for developing action plans toward school goal attainment. Since DDI is proven to increase student achievement, ELA teachers must start using it more. The assistant principal's report reveals most of them currently make little or no use of DDI. The principal can remediate this by providing them professional development (PD) in DDI. Surveying ELA faculty will yield data informing their PD needs.

4. D: Examinees must apply knowledge of strategies for supporting and supervising research- and evidence-based rigorous best instructional practices to answer this question. The assistant principal's report identifies the department chair's opinion that teacher and student demands plus administrative responsibilities prohibit holding DDI meetings regularly. However, DDI is a school building and district priority, so the principal needs to support the chairperson in finding ways to address departmental duties that still allow her time to lead her department in implementing regular DDI. This support can also develop the department chair's teacher-leader skills.

5. A: This question tests examinee ability to apply knowledge of strategies to ensure that teachers' instructional practices further every student's academic success. From Documents 1 and 2, school formative assessments in ELA appear less rigorous than the state Regents Exam; from Document 3, some ELA faculty are concerned that more rigorous instruction will affect some students adversely. Together, these imply low ELA teacher expectations for some students. Since research finds lower teacher expectations can correlate with lower student performance, Mr. R. should prioritize suitable instructional rigor for every student, enabling all students' higher academic achievement.

6. C: The assistant principal reports observing that ELA teachers, especially in upper grades, focus on students' incorrect test responses instead of what content they are mistaken about and why. If the principal leads the ELA teachers to focus more on which test items and what types and categories of test questions the students are answering incorrectly, this will give them information about specific areas or elements of ELA wherein students have the greatest learning deficits and instructional needs, enabling the teachers to change their instruction to address these.

7. B: The lack of full attendance at a meeting for all department faculty most indicates lack of understanding of the importance of data to instruction. The assistant principal reported that those attending demonstrated the best intentions (a) and serious commitment (c). This document also reports that from conversations with individual teachers, most did not use data; and from observing the meeting, the department chair urged teachers to explore data on their own more. Since most had not been doing this, one can infer they would rather not analyze data alone (d) than together.

8. D: The assistant principal reports in Document 3 that the ELA department chair seemed committed to DDI (a), and the department's action plans used the correct templates (b). He also reports that the department chair did not appear to prioritize getting her teachers to participate in applying DDI (c). The only correct choice identifies the assistant principal's impression that the content of the department's action plans was superficial (d).

9. A: According to the assistant principal's report, some of the ELA teachers had the perception that making their instruction more rigorous would decrease both engagement and achievement for already underachieving students. This perception, among other factors, detracted from their basing instruction on data analysis. Their concerns were not that doing so would improve those students' performance at the expense of their interest (b), or vice versa (c). If they believed that increased instructional rigor would improve both (d), they would not be concerned.

10. A: Since all newly enrolled students = 200, which = 25 percent of all students and all newly enrolled ELL students = 80, which = 10 percent of all students, the total student population must be around 800 students. If it were (b), then total new enrollments would be 20 percent. (c) is the total of new enrollments, not the total of all students. (d) is double the correct number.

11. C: Document 2 indicates the largest number and proportion of new ELL students are in seventh grade, but each grade has the same number of teachers; therefore, the seventh-grade teachers will have more new ELL students in their classes than the sixth-grade teachers (a), who will have the second largest number; and eighth-grade teachers (b) will have the lowest number, so (d) is incorrect.

12. B: Identifying existing bilingual faculty requires no new hiring or expenditures, and you may be able to place some new ELL students with teachers speaking their L1s. If the budget allows, hiring more bilingual teachers (c) might be a second step. Hiring interpreters for every L1 (a) could be impracticable, in terms of both funding and availability, considering some of the L1s identified. However, finding volunteers to interpret (d) as a later step would cost nothing, and could include some new ELLs' family as well as other community members.

13. D: In second-language acquisition as in first-language acquisition, receptive language skills (listening and reading) typically develop before expressive language skills (speaking and writing). Hence (b) is incorrect. ELLs typically acquire all skills for basic conversational English far sooner than for academic English, not vice versa (a). According to the data provided, (c) cannot be "always" true, as none of the ELL students represented arrived with grade-level English literacy skills.

14. C: Professional development should focus on differentiating instruction so teachers can most effectively meet all student needs within their classrooms in the time allowed. While it can make ELLs feel welcomed and included if every teacher learns a few words of their L1s, the point is to help them learn English language and academic content in English, not for teachers to learn every student L1 intensively (a). Adjusting instruction for each student's needs supersedes interpreting (c), and segregating ELLs (d) is not inclusive education.

15. A: Document 1 gives numbers of ELL students speaking each language, but not in each grade, which is the information you would need. Document 2 gives numbers of all ELL students per grade, but not which L1s they speak (c), so conflating Documents 1 and 2 (b) would not yield this information. Knowing which L1s the teachers speak in each grade (d) would be insufficient without also knowing which L1s the students speak in each grade.

16. B: Document 2 identifies how many ELLs will be in each grade (a), how many teachers each grade has (c), and the fact that all three grades will have ELL students (d). However, you can NOT determine how many ELL students will be in each class (b) because the numbers of ELL students in each grade may be distributed unevenly among classes (and teachers).

17. D: Because of the increased diversity recently introduced to your school, whole-class instruction (a) is unlikely to meet all students' educational needs efficiently or equitably. Segregating ELLs (b) is not equitable. When ELL and native English-speaking students interact, both benefit: ELLs have role models for using English; native English-speaking students gain exposure to new linguistic and cultural information and perspectives; and both increase their social skills repertoires and develop greater tolerance. Thus heterogeneous groups (d) are better than homogeneous (c), and small groups enable differentiated instruction and cooperative learning.

18. A: While this may be among the most expensive changes, widening doorways takes priority to enable new students in wheelchairs to access the same rooms and spaces as others. Only one deaf student communicates using ASL, and the school has a very strong group of volunteers, including those with knowledge of disabilities, so seeking volunteer interpreters could come before hiring a paid one (b). According to the special educators' notes, the building already has wheelchair ramps (c). Designating rooms as alternative settings (d), assuming available space, should cost little or nothing.

19. B: The special educators' notes state that the student with ASD is easily agitated by a variety of sensory stimuli, to which this student is hypersensitive. Hence this student is most likely to need a quieter room, where bright lights and colors have been removed or modified and interruptions are less likely, for taking tests or completing assignments.

20. D: The student with hearing impairment is described as having excellent speechreading skills and wearing hearing aids. Therefore, being seated close to the teacher or board is most likely to benefit this student. The student does NOT use ASL as the deaf student does, so (a) does not apply. Specialized lighting (b) is more applicable to students with visual impairment or ASD. Testing at certain times of day (c) applies more to students taking medication, having hyperactivity or attention deficit disorders, ASDs, intellectual disability, etc., than hearing impairment.

21. C: The information given includes identifying this student as not totally blind, and there is no indication that she can read Braille, so (a) is inappropriate. The special educators describe her as needing accommodations for low vision. Magnifiers and large print are included in the list of such classroom accommodations. The special educator notes also state that this student has always performed at grade level, so (b) and (d) do not apply.

22. A: Delayed language development has a significant impact on all school learning and achievement; the earlier the intervention, the more effective it is. The articulation disorders (b) are identified as mild; also, age norms for correctly producing a number of speech sounds are higher than Grade 2 (e.g., age 8-9), so some articulation disorders spontaneously resolve with maturation, and others resolve sooner with therapy than they otherwise would. Since either or both may apply to these students, (c) and (d) are incorrect.

23. C: Different types or fewer numbers of math homework problems (a) is an *assignment* modification, i.e., a change in what the teacher expects from or teaches to students. An accommodation is a change in format, modality, etc., enabling students to circumvent or overcome disabilities without changing teacher expectations or curriculum content. Explicit, direct instruction to develop studying skills (b) is an organizational skills accommodation. Learning different material (c) is a curriculum modification. Allowing longer times to complete work (d) is a scheduling accommodation.

24. B: The student in the Other Health Impairment category has Type 1 diabetes, requiring blood sugar monitoring and permitted snacks regularly at specified times of the day, as well as supervision during all exercise. Especially in elementary school, this requires someone to provide daily one-to-one assistance. The categories and descriptions of students in the other choices are less likely to require regular one-to-one attention.

25. D: Students with central auditory processing disorder have difficulty understanding the spoken language they hear. This can also affect their reading, because decoding written words has an auditory basis. A designated reader (a) could help the student with the reading disability, but not this student. Audiobooks for text (b) would give this student more difficulty, not less. The student does not necessarily need extra time for written tests (c) as much as extra time for processing directions spoken aloud by the teacher (d). Adding printed or visual directions to spoken can help further.

26. B: Significant achievement gaps exist among three student groups (Document 1). Significant percentages of students do not feel the school motivates, supports, or cares about them (Document 2). Many teachers lack belief in all students' potential and in their own ability to help all students (Document 3). These imply inadequate teacher expectations or insufficient instructional design for all students' needs and success. Thus Ms. M. should first focus on teachers' using equitable instructional strategies to motivate all students to do their best.

27. D: There is a substantial achievement gap among low-SES students, LEP students, and the rest of the students at Perinton Middle School. To inform herself about the sources and characteristics of this gap, Ms. M. could explore similarities and differences in perceptions about school among these student categories. However, Document 2 only gives responses from all students, precluding analysis by categories. If these data were disaggregated by category, she could learn more about the achievement gap, lower attendance in low-SES eighth-graders, and possibly whether and how these relate.

28. C: From Document 3, many Perinton Middle School teachers do not believe that they can overcome outside influences on student academic difficulties, that all students have the ability and motivation to learn, or that teachers can play central parts in student engagement and achievement. Therefore, Ms. M. should be most concerned on following up with her teachers who do not understand the effects of excellent teaching on student performance.

29. A: To create a learning environment that meets all student needs and supports all students' best achievement, educators must know and use a wide variety of instructional strategies. From the documents, many teachers do not, since significant achievement gaps among student categories show their instruction is not meeting some groups' needs. Ms. M. can make the department and faculty meetings she plans most effective to attain that goal by focusing them on developing and refining instructional strategies that further learning for diverse students.

30. B: According to Document 1, of the students with LEP who took the state standardized assessment last year, 49 percent scored above or at the level required to meet the proficiency standard in math in grades 6, 7, and 8. The percentages of LEP students meeting the standard in ELA (a) were 32 percent in grade 6, 35 percent in grade 7, and 30 percent in grade 8. Students in grades 6 and 7 were not tested in science (c). Therefore, (d) is incorrect.

31. D: On the state assessment, 44 percent of low-SES sixth-graders met ELA standards; 44 percent of low-SES seventh-graders met math standards. More LEP than low-SES students met math standards in all three grades, not vice versa (a). Although both low-SES and LEP eighth-graders tested worst in ELA, LEP students tested better in math than science, while low-SES students tested better in science than math (b). The largest achievement gap is between LEP students and all students in ELA in the *sixth* grade, not the seventh (c).

32. C: Positive correlation means that two variables occur in the same or similar amounts in the same situation. Document 2 shows 33 percent of the students responding felt challenged to do their best, and 33 percent felt they tried hard. This is a perfect positive correlation. Thirty-seven percent of students felt they had high expectations of themselves; 55 percent felt adults in school respected them (a). Fifty-four percent perceived teachers helped them academically when needed; 33 percent of students perceived trying hard (b). Fifty-eight percent felt teachers cared about students; 45 percent of students cared about high grades (d).

33. B: Of teachers surveyed (Document 3), 30 percent felt teachers most influenced student attitudes; of students surveyed (Document 2), 65 percent liked school a lot—respectively the lowest and highest values in each document. Inverse correlation means two variables occurring together are opposite, i.e., as one rises, the other falls. These two factors have the strongest *inverse* correlation. The values in (a) were 58 percent for both, 45 percent for both in (c)—both perfect *positive* correlations. In (d), they were 52 percent (item 3) and 55 percent—not equal, but still strongly *positively* correlated.

34. C: School building leaders must expect AND model respectful behavior for faculty AND students. They cannot assume modeling this for faculty will cause teachers to model it automatically for students (a). Leaders cannot get teachers to be models for their students unless the leaders are models for their teachers (b). They cannot get teachers or students to "do as I say, not as I do," i.e., to engage regularly in behaviors that leaders say they expect yet do not actually demonstrate themselves (d).

35. B: In addition to determining student behavior functions for identifying suitable interventions, schools must collect behavior data for SWPBS systems to ensure that behaviors are reported objectively (e.g., frequency, intensity, duration, times, places, settings, situations, antecedents, consequences, etc.) rather than receive unverifiable staff complaints that vary individually in frequency, consistency, accuracy, etc. This data collection is not to satisfy government mandates (a), procure staff buy-in (c), or threaten students to keep them in line (d).

36. D: As stated at the beginning of Document 2 and shown throughout its procedures, schools can best establish a positive school culture by defining and teaching positive expectations to all adults and students in the school. (a) is important for clarifying classroom and school rules. (b) is an example of the previous policy, which has been ineffective. (c) is important for identifying suitable interventions.

37. A: All behavior has a function; thus (d) is incorrect. Some psychologists succinctly summarize the function of all behaviors as to get something or get away from something. For example, a student being ignored acts out and is scolded. Although scolding seems like punishment, the student wants attention so much that he or she prefers aversive attention to none. FBA does not determine how behaviors affect school operations (b) or whether specific student behaviors are "functional" in terms of being adaptive (c); maladaptive behaviors are functional in terms of accomplishing some purpose.

38. D: As stated, the new general guidelines for teachers in Document 3, which reflect APA recommendations related to positive behavior support and classroom behavior management, include warning teachers NOT to attempt to solve serious student behavior problems themselves (a), not even initially (b), but rather to refer them to the school psychologist or special education professionals (d) if they are special education students. Hence (c) is also incorrect.

39. B: The referenced description states this student threatened a teacher. This suggests difficulties with self-management, anger management, conflict management, and social skills. Tier 2 intervention includes training in all these. Since the student also has an unsafe, neglectful, abusive home, the mentoring programs included in Tier 2 would benefit him. Tier 2's recommended daily check-in and check-out procedures would also provide monitoring, considering that this student sneaked back into school right after being suspended—although that should not be punished, as his finding the school safer is beneficial when unsafe at home.

40. C: In Document 2 under Tier 1 procedures, recommendations for student engagement in learning include offering materials at appropriate difficulty levels for students, i.e., neither too easy (a) nor too hard (b), to prevent off-task behavior; including student interests in curriculum, to augment student engagement with learning materials (d); and offering students choices among materials, to increase their taking ownership of their learning (c).

41. A: Document 2 identifies c. 80-85 percent of students as able to meet classroom behavioral expectations through receiving Tier 1 supports; c. 10-15 percent of students as needing Tier 2 supports to achieve this success; and the remaining c. 5-7% of students as requiring Tier 3 supports to succeed. Hence between one-sixth and one-sixteenth of students need Tier 2 supports as those who succeed in Tier 1, not half (b). Students needing Tier 3 are about half of those needing Tier 2, not equal proportions (c). The correct answer is reversed by (d).

Part 2

MULTIPLE CHOICE QUESTIONS

1. C: This item tests applying knowledge of skills and strategies to meet school needs through developing productive partnerships with higher education institutions. The Description reports Seneca Elementary implemented a new curriculum aligned with NYSCCLS last year. Document 2 shows only 44 percent of surveyed teachers agreed tutors were familiar with the curriculum last year (vs. 70 percent three years ago). Hence Ms. C.'s priority at the first meeting with the program's college faculty coordinator should be improving tutor knowledge of current Seneca curriculum.

2. B: Examinees must apply knowledge of community engagement strategies for supporting planning and implementing changes to answer this question. Offering data showing the tutoring program's specific strengths and weaknesses can help Ms. C. increase college faculty engagement in continuing program planning. Document 1 shows formative assessment data for all students, not students in the program. Disaggregating data enables both focusing on program participant students' performance, and comparing this to non-participating students' performance, helping college faculty identify program strengths and weaknesses and improve the program accordingly.

3. A: To support implementing school change, principals need to apply strategies for family engagement. According to the Description, teachers have lost some support for the tutoring program. According to the formative assessment data, student performance improvement appears to have leveled off in the past two years. In contrast, all parents of students in the program strongly support it, so Ms. C. can most leverage this to revitalize teacher program support by informing teachers of parental reports about improved student attitudes to reading, and moreover, increased student time reading voluntarily at home.

4. D: Principals must apply knowledge about effective school-community communication systems to address any issues timely and acceptably to both, and meet both partners' expectations and needs. As the Description identifies, school staff do not meet with college faculty; only school administrators and the ELA coordinator meet with a single college coordinator, and only infrequently. Since teacher concerns are increasing and support for the program decreasing, creating a system for continuing, regular school-college faculty communications (e.g., monthly meetings, weekly conference calls, etc.) would promote continuing program vitality and efficacy.

5. B: According to the preceding principal's letter to the program's college faculty coordinator, they had discussed increasing opportunities for teachers to consult and collaborate with college faculty. According to the teacher survey data, many teachers with students in the tutoring program feel this would benefit them; many want greater college responsivity and communication; and many could address program issues they encounter better by interacting with college partners more. Greater opportunities for direct interaction can fulfill all these needs, reinforcing the partnership.

6. A: Positive correlation means the two factors change in concert; i.e., if one increases, the other does too, or if one decreases, so does the other, and often in comparable amounts or degrees (the more similar, the stronger the positive correlation). Hence the two are not unrelated (b). Inverse correlation means if one factor increases, the other decreases and vice versa, so (c) is false. The correlation is more consistent than inconsistent (d), with decreases over time in both student results (Document 1) and teacher support (Document 2).

7. D: This answer can be found in Document 2's teacher survey data comparison. In the past two years, teacher perceptions have *increased* that assigned tutors need more training (a); that professional development from college faculty will benefit them (b); and that it will help them design reading instruction to consult with college faculty (c). In contrast, over the same time period, teacher perceptions have *decreased* that the tutoring program's college coordinator is responsive to their feedback and concerns (d).

8. C: In Document 2, the third survey item is "The tutors assigned to my class demonstrate effective responses to the varying learning needs of my students." Differentiated instruction enables educators to respond effectively to learning needs that vary across students. Teacher perceptions of this have declined 11 percent in two years. This specific information is NOT in the Description (a). Teachers feel student enjoyment of tutoring has decreased (b), but cannot be attributed to lack of differentiated instruction from available information—or to lower perceived college coordinator availability (d).

9. A: The teacher survey shows that in two years, opinions that tutors needed more training rose by 26 percentage points; opinions of tutors' school curriculum knowledge fell by 26 percentage points. Opinions of tutor consultation availability fell by 11 percentage points and of tutor cooperation, i.e., ease working with tutors, by 16 percentage points (b). Opinions of tutor instructional knowledge for effectively teaching struggling readers fell by 11 percentage points and of students' tutoring anticipation, by 7 percentage points (c). Opinions of tutor effectiveness with varied student learning needs fell by 11 percentage points; opinions that college faculty would help professional development rose 5 percentage points (d).

10. B: According to Document 1, from five years ago to three years ago, the percentages of students achieving >65 percent on formative assessments in every grade and skill area all rose more than 1 point; from three years ago to one year ago, all percentages either went up 2 points, stayed the same (flat), or fell by 1 or 2 points. More specifically, from three years ago to one year ago, a total of four percentages rose 1 point; a total of 12 percentages stayed the same; a total of 10 percentages fell 1 point; and one percentage fell 2 points.

11. C: Today's school principals must understand which technologies are available to their schools (a), how to apply ICT in school settings (b), and where to obtain expert advice about specifics (d) like providing classroom Internet access, developing internal school networks, etc. However, while they must have technological expertise, principals need NOT know everything about all aspects of ICT (c) to apply it for effective organizational management.

12. D: School planning using management information systems (MIS), which are far more sophisticated than any methods of school planning without technology, as core tools is the most transformative change in school leaders' work. Using spreadsheets for budgets (a), email for communication (b), and word processing software for writing (c) are all more simply improvements upon traditional practices.

13. B: By standardizing a school's technology services, equipment, and services, the school leader can *decrease* school inventory of parts and supplies (a), time spent training staff to use varied products (c), and need for technical support (d). However, technology standardization (e.g., via single-point purchases) can *increase* compatibility, e.g., among new and existing or legacy systems (b), also saving money.

14. D: Using web-based applications can save schools money in software AND hardware (a) AND in storage AND printing (b), not only in the latter two (c), by using Internet clouds instead of computer hard drives, which also saves on support costs (d) by reducing maintenance needs. For example, one school leader (Johnson, 2011/2012) estimated that his district, with 3,000 computers and 7,300 students, saved roughly $2,000 annually in these four expense areas by using Google Apps for Education.

15. A: Consistent with U.S. historical emphasis on local control of schools, the most funding for K-12 public schools is supplied by each state's government. The second largest source is school districts' local governments (b). The third largest source is the federal government (c). The remaining funds from private sources (d) are mainly for private, not public, schools.

16. C: According to the U.S. Department of Education (ED), there are no unfunded federal education program mandates or requirements (a), because U.S. states and other grant recipients are not required to accept federal program funds (b). States must only adhere to federal program requirements if they voluntarily accept that program's funds (c). If they do not want to meet the requirements, they can decline the funding. The majority of states use federal funds; only a few have ever declined them (d).

17. B: Preparing audits, financial statements, other fiscal reports, and operational reports that schools are required to submit to the U.S. Department of Education (ED) reflect school objectives in the area of reliability in program reporting, which good internal controls promote. Effective internal controls also promote meeting school financial goals (a), performance goals (c), and resource protection (d), which are all school administrative objectives in the area of operational efficiency and effectiveness.

18. A: ED recommends internal controls as "reasonable safeguards" against potential fraud or other abuse of electronic student information systems, including limiting staff access to functions needed to complete their assigned duties; assigning unique IDs and passwords to staff members AND frequently changing passwords (b); informing authorized user staff of system use guidelines AND having them sign statements acknowledging their responsibilities (c); and issuing policies and procedures for correct system use and security not only on a school-wide level, but also extending to the level of each individual user (d).

19. A: Doing things in order from most to least important is a time-management strategy related to prioritizing tasks. Scheduling duties to the most appropriate staff members to handle (b) is a time-management strategy related to delegating responsibilities. Scheduling "closed door" times for themselves (c) is a time-management strategy related to minimizing interruptions. Trying to accommodate every request they receive (d) is impossible, not a time-management strategy, and to be avoided; principals must be able to say "no" sometimes (or delegate) to manage time efficiently.

20. D: Researchers (Grissom & Loeb, 2013) have found that principals they studied spent more than *twice* as much time on informal classroom walk-throughs as on formal teacher evaluations, not less (a); principals of lower-achieving schools and schools with more low-income students spend *more* time on instructional activities, not less (b); elementary school principals spend more time on instructional activities than high school principals do, not vice versa (c); and elementary school principals spend *more* time on professional development (d).

21. D: Natural (a) hazards include major storms, heat waves, droughts, earthquakes, etc. Biological (b) hazards include infectious diseases, food contamination, spilled bodily fluids, student or staff medical conditions, etc. Community (c) hazards include nearby storage facilities for hazardous materials, prisons, military installations, railroads, dams, airports, etc. Environmental (d) hazards include unsafe practices, like the example described; incorrect building maintenance and poor building design; and environmental features like loose light fixtures, bookshelves, room dividers, trophy cases, unreinforced masonry, etc.

22. B: The NIMS is mandated by a Homeland Security Presidential Directive (HSPD-5) for managing domestic incidents; however, not all schools are required by federal law to adopt it (a): only districts or schools receiving federal grants for emergency preparedness are. Thus (c) is false. However, because the NIMS standardizes emergency response principles and terminology, it enables schools and community responders to coordinate emergency management better (b), so school safety experts recommend all schools adopt it. Hence (d) is false.

23. C: According to the U.S. Department of Education (ED), research findings indicate that physical school conditions can influence student achievement more than family background, socioeconomic status, student behavior, and school attendance combined—not just more than two of these combined (a), or more than one of two of these individually (b), or more than any one of them individually (d). These findings illustrate the importance to student performance of maintaining optimal physical conditions in schools.

24. C: ED identifies effective school facilities maintenance plans as including administrators who understand and do the following: coordinating maintenance activities school-wide while understanding that these plans also require expertise and input from a wide variety of stakeholders (a); maintaining school facilities affects building appearance, operations, AND student and staff health and student learning (b); maintaining school facilities contributes to school physical and financial well-being, and also requires funding (c); and demanding that staff properly implement and evaluate these plans, not simply assume they do (d).

25. D: The United States Constitution's Fourth Amendment guarantees the right of US citizens to freedom from unreasonable search and seizure of property without probable cause. But regarding students specifically, the U.S. Supreme Court ruled in the 1985 case of *New Jersey v. T.L.O.* that unlike probable cause, reasonable suspicion is enough for school officials to search student property. Hence a reasonable suspicion that a student has an illegal substance is the minimum legal requirement to justify searching the student's backpack.

26. A: The Individuals with Disabilities Education Act (IDEA) guarantees students with disabilities a free, appropriate public education in the least restrictive environment possible. The No Child Left Behind (NCLB) Act (b) holds schools accountable for student achievement and provides grants funding various school needs. The Women's Educational Equity Act (WEEA) prohibits gender discrimination in elementary and secondary schools (c). Title VI of the Civil Rights Act (d) prohibits discrimination, including based on national origin, protecting the rights of ELL students.

NYSTCE Practice Test #2

Part 1

EXTENDED PERFORMANCE TASK
INSTRUCTIONAL LEADERSHIP FOR STUDENT SUCCESS

Use the information and documents below to answer the questions that follow them. You have 60 minutes to complete the assignment.

DESCRIPTION

You were just hired to serve as the principal for Western High School, a public high school in a midsize suburban school district. Western High School is the only high school in the district and serves families from a variety of socioeconomic backgrounds. Approximately 7% of students qualify for free and reduced lunch, while many others come from middle-class or affluent backgrounds. There are currently 1,210 students enrolled in the school, and it serves children in grades 9-12. In general, the school performs well academically, and the graduation rate of 97.2% is above the state average of 86.4%. Approximately 46% of students enrolled in the school come from backgrounds that are categorized as historically underperforming: English language learners (ELLs), special education students, or economically disadvantaged students.

Following your hiring, you are invited to meet with the district superintendent. Although the school's overall scores on Advanced Placement (AP) exams are generally above the state and national average, the superintendent is concerned that students from historically underperforming groups have been unable to find success on AP exams in general. Furthermore, very few students from these groups enroll in AP courses. The superintendent indicates that your predecessor was not concerned with such students demonstrating proficiency on the exam (earning a score of 3 or better) and instead focused his attention on higher-performing students.

The superintendent encourages you to develop a plan in which a greater number of historically underperforming students not only enroll in AP courses but also successfully do well on the exams. He expects you to report your findings back within the next month. To guide the development of such a plan, you analyze student performance data, classroom teaching strategies, and available courses from the last school year. Furthermore, you choose to send out surveys to students and staff to further inform the planning process.

DOCUMENT 1

Percent of Students Demonstrating Proficiency on the AP Exams (Last Year)

Subject	Western High School	State
AP English Language and Composition	78%	59%
AP Statistics	78%	64%
AP Biology	82%	68%
AP German Language and Culture	83%	82%
AP World History	73%	49%

Percent of Students Enrolled in Each AP Course who are from Historically Underperforming Groups (Last Year)

Subject	Total Number of Students Enrolled	Economically Disadvantaged	English Language Learners	Special Education
AP English Language and Composition	60	1.7%	0%	3.3%
AP Statistics	18	0	0	11.1%
AP Biology	11	0	9.1%	0
AP German Language and Culture	6	0	0	0
AP World History	40	5%	0	20%

Number of Historically Underperforming Students Demonstrating Proficiency on the AP Exams (Last Year)

Subject	Number of Historically Underperforming Students Demonstrating Proficiency	Total Number of Historically Underperforming Students Enrolled in AP Courses
AP English Language and Composition	0	3
AP Statistics	0	2
AP Biology	1	1
AP German Language and Culture	0	0
AP World History	1	8

DOCUMENT 2

ELA Formative Assessment Results for All Students: Grades 10-12

(Percent of Students Demonstrating Proficiency, 4th Quarter of Last Year)

	Grade 10	Grade 11	Grade 12
Use of Evidence	64%	66%	70%
Development of a Position	60%	57%	65%
Close Reading	68%	69%	71%
Analysis of Evidence	59%	63%	76%

ELA Formative Assessment Results for Historically Underperforming Students: Grades 10-12

(Percent of Students Demonstrating Proficiency, 4th Quarter of Last Year)

	Grade 10	Grade 11	Grade 12
Use of Evidence	29%	27%	39%
Development of a Position	31%	20%	38%
Close Reading	35%	30%	41%
Analysis of Evidence	19%	13%	28%

DOCUMENT 3

Results of Anonymous Survey Sent Out to all Teachers

Based on your teaching experiences over the last two school years, to what extent do you agree with the following statements?	All Teachers (Percent Who Agree)	Teachers with Five or Fewer Years of Teaching Experience (Percent Who Agree)	Teachers with Six or More Years of Teaching Experience (Percent Who Agree)
You use a variety of instructional materials.	89%	92%	86%
You differentiate effectively to meet the needs of students in your classes.	91%	94%	88%
You have measures in place that allow historically underperforming student groups to succeed.	70%	68%	72%
You have the resources necessary to best meet the needs of all students.	49%	55%	43%
You have received the training necessary to meet the needs of all students.	36%	40%	32%

Based on your teaching experiences over the last two school years, to what extent do you agree with the following statements?	All Teachers (Percent Who Agree)	Teachers with Five or Fewer Years of Teaching Experience (Percent Who Agree)	Teachers with Six or More Years of Teaching Experience (Percent Who Agree)
You are well versed at adapting and modifying instructional materials for students with diverse learning needs.	47%	49%	45%
You feel effective in your role as an educator.	89%	97%	81%

Document 4

Results of Anonymous Survey of Students Enrolled in AP Courses

Based on your experiences this year, to what extent do you agree with the following statements?	Students Enrolled in AP Courses (Percent Who Agree, Rounded)	Historically Underperforming Students Enrolled in AP Courses (Percent Who Agree, Rounded)	Students Enrolled in AP Courses Who Are Not from a Historically Underperforming Group (Percent Who Agree, Rounded)
My coursework is appropriately challenging.	89%	95%	88%
My teacher employs strategies that are engaging and help me to learn.	89%	76%	90%
The class is designed in a way that meets my needs and is at my academic level.	85%	64%	87%
I am confident in my ability to succeed in this course.	75%	48%	77%
The course material is overwhelming or too challenging.	28%	81%	23%

Based on your experiences this year, to what extent do you agree with the following statements?	Students Enrolled in AP Courses (Percent Who Agree, Rounded)	Historically Underperforming Students Enrolled in AP Courses (Percent Who Agree, Rounded)	Students Enrolled in AP Courses Who Are Not from a Historically Underperforming Group (Percent Who Agree, Rounded)
I feel confident that I am equipped to pass the AP exam at the end of the year.	59%	38%	61%
If applicable, I plan to take future AP courses next year.	91%	60%	94%

DOCUMENT 5

Composite Teacher Evaluation Data of Teachers in Subject Areas that have AP Courses (Last Year)

AP Subject Area	Total Number of Teachers	Ineffective (Number of Teachers)	Developing (Number of Teachers)	Effective (Number of Teachers)	Highly Effective (Number of Teachers)
ELA	7	0	2	3	2
Math	8	1	1	5	1
Science	6	0	1	4	1
World Language	4	0	0	3	1
History	6	0	0	4	2

DOCUMENT 6

Number of Teachers in Subject Areas that have AP Courses Scoring at Each Performance Level (Last Year)

	AP Subject Area	Unsatisfactory (Number of Teachers)	Basic (Number of Teachers)	Proficient (Number of Teachers)	Distinguished (Number of Teachers)
Domain 1: Planning and Preparation	ELA	0	2	3	2
	Math	0	2	6	0
	Science	0	1	1	4
	World Language	0	1	1	2
	History	0	1	3	2
Domain 2: The Classroom Environment	ELA	1	1	4	1
	Math	1	2	5	0
	Science	0	1	4	1
	World Language	0	0	3	1

	AP Subject Area	Unsatisfactory (Number of Teachers)	Basic (Number of Teachers)	Proficient (Number of Teachers)	Distinguished (Number of Teachers)
Domain 3: Instruction	History	0	0	4	2
	ELA	1	1	5	0
	Math	1	3	4	0
	Science	0	0	5	1
	World Language	0	0	2	2
Domain 4: Professional Responsibilities	History	0	0	3	3
	ELA	0	0	6	1
	Math	0	0	6	2
	Science	0	0	4	2
	World Language	0	0	1	3
	History	0	0	4	2

SHORT ANSWER QUESTIONS

Using the information given above, write a response about 600-800 words long in a format you prefer (e.g., an outline, a list of bulleted items, prose paragraphs). In addressing the items below, give very specific details and cite evidence from the description and documents that support your answers.

1. Identify one strength of this school, citing evidence to support your response.

2. Identify three areas of need in the instructional program, citing evidence to support each need.

3. Which area of need would be your highest priority? Explain why.

4. What are two important questions you must answer to address your highest priority area of need? Explain why each question is important to address.

5. How will you go about getting answers to each question?

6. What actions would you take to address the school's priority need? Explain why.

7. How would you leverage the identified strength of the school to address the priority need?

8. What possible challenges might your actions create, and what are some ways that you could manage these challenges?

SHORTER PERFORMANCE TASK 1
SCHOOL CULTURE AND LEARNING ENVIRONMENT TO PROMOTE EXCELLENCE, EQUITY, AND SOCIAL JUSTICE

Use the information from the scenario and documents below to complete the task following them. You have 30 minutes to complete the assignment.

DESCRIPTION

You are the building leader at a suburban middle school on the fringe of a major US city. The school has a current enrollment of 1,270 students. Although this is your third year at the school as a building leader, you previously taught seventh-grade science in the same building for a total of 10 years. Throughout your tenure you have observed marked demographic changes take place within the school. When you started teaching 13 years ago, 92% of students were white, 2% were Asian or Pacific Islander, 4% were black or African American, and 2% were multiracial. This school year 53% of students are white, 8% are Asian or Pacific Islander, 22% are black or African American, 11% are Hispanic or Latino, and 6% are multiracial.

The majority (94%) of 53 teachers and staff who work in the school are white, with only 4% classified as black or African American and 2% as Asian or Pacific Islander. Although there is a lack of diversity among the teachers and staff, most report that they are able to effectively meet the needs of all of their students and can relate to them on an academic and personal level. Teachers and staff state that the school is welcoming and accepting of all students and that differences are celebrated among students.

However, students and their families report multiple instances of discrimination and racism to you, with many of those instances occurring toward those who are from what are typically seen as minority groups. Students indicate that instances of racial intimidation, the use of derogatory terms, microaggressions, and passive exclusions are commonplace in the hallways and classrooms. Furthermore, families allege that most teachers and staff make little attempt to rectify such situations when instances of racial discrimination are brought to their attention.

You are concerned about the climate of the school and hope to develop a plan to promote acceptance and inclusion. In an attempt to inform the development of your plan, you survey both families and teachers, and those results are included below.

Document

School Inclusivity Survey: Teacher and Staff Results

	Agree	Disagree	Unsure
The school is an accepting environment where all students are made to feel welcome.	91%	4%	5%
I would step in immediately if I heard a student making disparaging remarks to another.	98%	0%	2%
I am cognizant of my own biases when planning and delivering instruction.	77%	2%	21%
I feel confident connecting to students of cultures and backgrounds different from my own.	77%	8%	15%
I effectively maintain an environment of acceptance and inclusion in my classroom.	85%	0%	15%
The minority students in our school are treated with dignity and respect.	81%	6%	13%

School Inclusivity Survey: Family Results

	Agree	Disagree	Unsure
The school is an accepting environment where all students are made to feel welcome.	38%	40%	22%
Teachers and administrators ensure that students engage with one another in a dignified and respectful manner.	26%	33%	41%
The school ensures that students are punished equitably, administering the same punishment for the same offense.	18%	12%	70%
Teachers and staff make an effort to learn about the cultural backgrounds of all students.	46%	51%	3%
The curriculum includes diverse authors and topics that draw connections to the uniqueness of the student body.	38%	8%	54%
Teachers and staff treat all students equitably.	32%	53%	15%

Short Answer Questions

Using the information given above, write a response about 300-400 words long, in a format you prefer (e.g., an outline, a list of bulleted items, prose paragraphs). In addressing the items below, give very specific details and cite evidence from the description and data that appropriately support your answers.

1. What is the primary issue presented in this scenario, and why do you believe this to be so?

2. What are two important questions you must address in order to explore this issue? Explain why each is important to address.

3. How will you go about getting answers to each question? What challenges might you face in getting answers to your questions?

4. Describe one possible finding of your inquiry process and the potential action that finding would imply.

SHORTER PERFORMANCE TASK 2

SCHOOL CULTURE AND LEARNING ENVIRONMENT TO PROMOTE EXCELLENCE, EQUITY, AND SOCIAL JUSTICE

Use the information from the scenario and document below to complete the task following them. You have 30 minutes to complete the assignment.

DESCRIPTION

You are the building leader at an urban elementary school that serves students in grades K-5. Currently, 560 students attend the school. The student body is diverse, with students coming from a variety of socioeconomic backgrounds. Approximately 46% of students are economically disadvantaged and 18% are English language learners (ELLs).

Over the last school year, bullying has become a major concern in the school. You have fielded multiple emails and phone calls from parents and guardians on the topic, and disciplinary referrals from teachers have increased by 62% in the past two years. Although the issue primarily seems to impact students in the upper grades, students in grades K-2 have also reported an increased rate of bullying behavior. A number of the reported cases occur with students who utilize district-provided transportation. Although only 18% of students rely on district transportation to travel to and from school, 28% of reported instances of bullying occur while students are riding buses. The remaining reports stem from bullying that has occurred in a variety of settings including lunch/recess (26%), classrooms (23%), bathrooms (12%), hallways (9%), and social media (2%). You are concerned that the school culture and the overall learning environment are becoming increasingly negative and harmful to students.

You spend the next several weeks maintaining an active presence outside the building before and after the school day, in the cafeteria during lunch periods, and in the halls when students are transitioning to different locations and classes. Additionally, you perform formal observations and informal walk-throughs to gain a better understanding of what is happening regarding student behavior.

You call upon your teacher leadership team in an attempt to develop a solution and discuss the possibility of implementing a positive behavioral interventions and supports (PBIS) program. The leadership team expresses concerns about the additional time required to implement the program, as well as the overall effectiveness of such a program in improving student behavior. To determine the overall perceptions of such a program and bullying in general, you decide to survey the staff. An excerpt of the survey results is listed below.

DOCUMENT

Teacher Survey Results on Occurrence of School-Wide Bullying and Implementation of PBIS

	Percent of Teachers Who Disagree	Percent of Teachers Who Are Neutral or Unsure	Percent of Teachers Who Agree
Bullying presents a significant behavioral concern within our school.	10%	32%	58%
Bullying occurs in my classroom.	70%	20%	10%
I handle instances of bullying immediately and follow all required anti-bullying protocols.	0%	4%	96%
I am willing to implement new strategies to reduce the amount of bullying experienced by students.	3%	41%	56%
I have heard about positive behavioral interventions and supports and am familiar with its benefits.	26%	35%	39%
Positive reinforcement for students who are following the student handbook is an effective way to improve behavior school-wise.	18%	51%	31%

SHORT ANSWER QUESTIONS

Using the information given above, write a response about 300-400 words long, in a format you prefer (e.g., an outline, a list of bulleted items, prose paragraphs). In addressing the items below, give very specific details and cite evidence from the description and data that appropriately support your answers.

1. What is an important school culture and learning environment issue presented in this scenario? Explain why the issue you chose is important.
2. What are two important questions you must address in order to explore this issue? Explain why each is important to address.

3. How will you go about getting answers to each question? What challenges might you face in getting answers to your questions?
4. Describe one possible finding of your inquiry process and the potential action that finding would imply.

MULTIPLE CHOICE QUESTIONS

Use the information from the scenario and documents below to answer the questions that follow them. You have two hours to complete these questions.

INSTRUCTIONAL LEADERSHIP FOR STUDENT SUCCESS

DESCRIPTION

Mr. J is the long-standing principal at a large, rural elementary school, Valley Elementary, that serves 1,250 students in grades K-6. The majority of students in the school are economically disadvantaged, with over 92% qualifying for free and reduced lunch. Additionally, 56% of students receive special education services, and 83% are reading below grade level. Attendance rates have declined over the last three years and are also below the state average. For example, in the last school year, 57.28% of students missed 10 or more days of school by the end of the fourth quarter. Furthermore, students generally perform below the state average on the Regents exams.

The staff at the school is dedicated to encouraging the academic success of their students. However, given the significant rates of poverty experienced by families in the district, teachers must often first focus on meeting the basic needs of their students that are overlooked or unable to be met at home. For example, many teachers provide snacks and hygiene products to students in their classes.

The superintendent meets with Mr. J and explains that he would like to see a marked improvement of test scores across the school. Although the superintendent is aware of the impact of poverty on students in the school, his primary concern is ensuring that test scores increase over the next three years and that student attendance rates increase. He suggests that Mr. J develop a plan that will ensure that this goal becomes a reality. Mr. J is worried that any potential solutions will ultimately fail as many students do not have access to basic necessities. He feels strongly that students' basic needs must first be met before academic growth can be promoted.

Mr. J calls together his leadership team to develop a plan of action that will ensure students' needs are met as well as promote overall academic performance.

DOCUMENT 1

Valley Elementary Attendance Data for the Last School Year

Grade	Percent of Students Missing 10 or More Days of School in the First Quarter	Percent of Students Missing 10 or More Days of School in the Fourth Quarter Alone	Total Number of Students per Grade
Kindergarten	23%	61%	180
1st	26%	50%	168
2nd	18%	31%	155
3rd	22%	45%	178
4th	30%	46%	192

Grade	Percent of Students Missing 10 or More Days of School in the First Quarter	Percent of Students Missing 10 or More Days of School in the Fourth Quarter Alone	Total Number of Students per Grade
5th	36%	51%	196
6th	45%	59%	181

Document 2

State Assessment Results by Grade: ELA (Last Year)

Grade	Percent of Students Testing Proficient on the ELA Assessment at Valley Elementary	Percent of Students Testing Proficient on the ELA Assessment in New York State
3rd	16%	45%
4th	31%	50.5%
5th	24%	46.9%
6th	9%	44.8%

State Assessment Results by Grade: Mathematics (Last Year)

Grade	Percent of Students Testing Proficient on the Mathematics Assessment at Valley Elementary	Percent of Students Testing Proficient on the Mathematics Assessment in New York State
3rd	12%	55%
4th	32%	52.3%
5th	26%	50.5%
6th	7%	45.5%

Document 3

Students Passing ELA in Grades 2-6 (Last Year)

(Traditional Grades Are Not Awarded to Students in K-1)

Grade	Percent Passing in Quarter 1	Percent Passing in Quarter 4	Total Number of Students
2nd	67%	38%	155
3rd	81%	49%	178
4th	90%	72%	192
5th	73%	44%	196
6th	78%	40%	181

Students Passing Math in Grades 2-6 (Last Year)

(Traditional Grades Are Not Awarded to Students in K-1)

Grade	Percent Passing in Quarter 1	Percent Passing in Quarter 4	Total Number of Students
2nd	70%	42%	155
3rd	83%	51%	178
4th	90%	74%	192
5th	76%	49%	196
6th	80%	30%	181

1. In reviewing assessment data, Mr. J should come to which of the following conclusions regarding student data at Valley Elementary?
    a. Third-grade students performed better on the ELA assessment, while sixth-grade students performed better on the mathematics assessment.
    b. Fourth-grade students performed the best overall on both the ELA and mathematics assessments.
    c. Overall, students attained higher rates of proficiency on the ELA assessment in comparison to the mathematics assessment.
    d. Students' overall proficiency increased as they progressed through the grades.

2. Which of the following should be the highest priority for Mr. J and the leadership team?
    a. Continuing to address the basic needs of students to provide the best opportunity for academic success
    b. Identifying and implementing more rigorous ELA and mathematics curriculum to improve performance on assessments
    c. Addressing the poor attendance rates of students in all grades
    d. Introducing an intervention period designed to focus on the test-taking skills necessary to achieve success on state assessments

3. Mr. J and his leadership team are working to develop a program that incentivizes good attendance, with students offered small prizes and rewards based on individual and group attendance goals. Which of the following practices should be implemented to offer the best chance for overall success of the program?
    a. Providing students with the opportunity to select their prizes and rewards
    b. In addition to rewards, connecting attendance to student grades so that families understand the importance of consistent attendance
    c. Making contact with businesses and organizations in the community that may be able to provide donations that can be used as program incentives
    d. Requesting parental input and discussing familial attendance barriers that can be eliminated

4. Mr. J and his team determine that new mathematics and ELA curriculum may lead to improved student academic performance. Which of the following steps would allow for a curriculum to be selected and implemented most effectively?

a. Selecting a curriculum that is research-backed and has brought about the greatest academic gains at schools where it has already been introduced
b. Allowing district-level administrators to select a curriculum based on the needs of the school as well as any financial stipulations
c. Presenting curriculum options to grade-level leaders so that teacher feedback can be incorporated during the selection process
d. Providing the teaching staff with the ability to research, recommend, and ultimately vote on a curriculum that best fits their needs

5. After reviewing the assessment data, Mr. J and his team should be most concerned about which of the following trends?

a. The low rate of proficiency on both the ELA and mathematics assessments for sixth-grade students
b. The decline in performance between fourth- and fifth-grade students
c. The overall low passage rates on both ELA and mathematics assessments
d. The inability of students at Valley Elementary to demonstrate proficiency at the same average rate as students across the New York State

6. When Mr. J is considering student grades in mathematics and ELA, which of the following questions is most important for him to address?

a. How can student grades in ELA and mathematics be improved?
b. Is another factor besides attendance leading to poor academic performance?
c. What other areas are students struggling in academically, and how might this connect to mathematics and ELA?
d. How can the curriculum be differentiated so that mathematics and ELA are more engaging and attainable for students?

7. What additional data would be most helpful for Mr. J to better understand academic performance and student growth at Valley Elementary School?

a. Assessment scores and academic records from the previous five school years
b. Information detailing the number of excused versus unexcused absences
c. Teacher evaluation records from the previous five school years
d. Teacher attendance records from the past school year

8. Following his review of attendance data and student grades, Mr. J should reach which of the following conclusions?

a. Poor attendance negatively impacts students' mathematics grades but not their ELA grades.
b. Poor attendance negatively impacts students' ELA grades but not their mathematics grades.
c. The number of days absent directly correlates to student pass rates in both mathematics and ELA across grade levels.
d. Although poor attendance appears to impact many students negatively and results in failing grades, the impact on fourth-grade students was not as significant as the other grade levels.

9. **Based on his review of student assessments, grades, and attendance data, Mr. J acknowledges that a structured five-year plan must be implemented to guide overall student improvement. Which of the following steps should Mr. J take first?**
   a. Develop a tiered system of attendance support in which students receive different levels of guidance based on their average number of days absent.
   b. Send a survey to families designed to determine the needs of students related to consistent attendance.
   c. Further analyze attendance data to identify which students are chronically absent so that specially designed support can be provided that meets their needs.
   d. Introduce a new curriculum that is more aligned with state assessments to help bring students to grade-level proficiency.

INSTRUCTIONAL LEADERSHIP FOR STUDENT SUCCESS
DESCRIPTION

Ms. B is in her fifth year as the principal at Thompson Middle School, a suburban school that serves students in grades 6-8. Approximately 780 students attend school at Thompson. Most of the school's teachers have been teaching for over 10 years, with the majority of staff having spent their entire careers at the school.

Through the course of Ms. B's time at Thompson Middle, students have typically scored over the state average on state assessments and demonstrated proficiency in both math and ELA. However, Ms. B and the district superintendent would like to see a greater percentage of students score in the Level 4: Exceeds Proficiency category. Last school year, 63.7% of students across grades 6-8 scored within the Level 3: Proficient category on the ELA state assessment, while 18.5% scored within the Level 4: Exceeds Proficiency category. Ms. B is concerned that the building scores are stagnating and that her students are not demonstrating adequate growth.

During the last school year, Ms. B completed walk-throughs as well as formal observations on all of her teachers. She observed that many teachers utilize traditional instructional methods such as teacher-delivered lectures. She saw only limited examples of engaging, student-centered learning. She is concerned that these traditional teaching methods are ineffective and wants to see the incorporation of student-centered learning activities across the board. Furthermore, Ms. B is concerned that the curriculum in many content areas is outdated and ineffective. For example, one teacher was using a US history book that had been published in 2005. In response, Ms. B scheduled department meetings with her staff. She discovered that many teachers were willing to explore new curriculum and teaching methods but were unsure where to begin.

Over the summer, Ms. B then held a few meetings with department heads to review new textbook options and professional development opportunities. She also decided to send out a survey to the staff as a whole to gain additional feedback as the building embarks on identifying and implementing new textbooks and curriculum. Ms. B will need to take a measured response and plans to focus on several content areas per school year, with the goal of new curriculum across the board within three school years. Consequently, she must determine how to prioritize which departments implement new curriculum first.

Document 1

2023/2024 School Year State Assessment Data: ELA

Grade	Percent of Students Scoring Within the Level 3: Proficient Category	Percent of Students Scoring Within the Level 4: Exceeds Proficiency Category	Total Students Attaining Proficiency on the State Assessment
6th	57%	16%	73%
7th	66%	20%	86%
8th	68%	19.5%	87.5%

2022/2023 School Year State Assessment Data: ELA

Grade	Percent of Students Scoring Within the Level 3: Proficient Category	Percent of Students Scoring Within the Level 4: Exceeds Proficiency Category	Total Students Attaining Proficiency on the State Assessment
6th	58%	14%	72%
7th	64%	21%	85%
8th	70%	18%	88%

2021/2022 School Year State Assessment Data: ELA

Grade	Percent of Students Scoring Within the Level 3: Proficient Category	Percent of Students Scoring Within the Level 4: Exceeds Proficiency Category	Total Students Attaining Proficiency on the State Assessment
6th	53%	18%	71%
7th	69%	16%	85%
8th	46%	13%	59%

Document 2

Teacher Survey Results on New Curriculum/New Teaching Strategies

Question	Percent of Teachers Who Agree	Percent of Teachers Who Are Neutral/Unsure	Percent of Teachers Who Disagree
I feel confident in incorporating student-centered approaches to learning.	15%	23%	62%
I understand the benefit of reducing teacher-centered teaching methods.	32%	49%	19%
I am willing to learn and apply new teaching approaches in my classroom.	87%	12%	1%

Question	Percent of Teachers Who Agree	Percent of Teachers Who Are Neutral/Unsure	Percent of Teachers Who Disagree
I have the skills needed to utilize new teaching approaches.	6%	53%	41%
I feel that my curriculum and/or textbook is adequate in meeting the needs of my students.	6%	2%	92%
I would like to explore new textbooks/classroom materials.	93%	1%	6%
I would like to be considered for the team who will decide on new curricular alternatives.	38%	18%	44%

Document 3

Summary of Walk-Through Data Last School Year: 2023/2024

	6th-Grade ELA	7th-Grade ELA	8th-Grade ELA	6th-Grade Math	7th-Grade Math	8th-Grade Math
Number of Classes Observed	7	5	5	7	7	6
Lecture/Direct Teacher-Led Instruction	5	3	3	5	3	5
Student-Centered Activities	0	1	1	0	0	1
Students Engaged in Independent Work	1	0	1	1	2	0
Students Engaged in Academic Discourse	0	1	1	0	0	1
Appropriate and Rigorous Learning Materials	2	0	1	3	2	3

10. Ms. B establishes a leadership team to focus on the issues she found in her reviews of curriculum, teaching, practices, and assessment data. Which of the following must be the highest priority for Ms. B and her team?
   a. Implementing new assessment tools designed to measure student growth and mastery
   b. Working with department leaders to identify and implement new curriculum
   c. Promoting a higher degree of collaboration among community members, staff, and families to ensure students' needs are adequately met
   d. Focusing on encouraging high levels of academic performance across grade levels

11. Which of the following pieces of information would be most helpful as Ms. B and her team attempt to better understand the assessment data?
   a. Student attendance data including the average number of days missed per quarter
   b. Access to teacher lesson plans to evaluate the presence of learning objectives that align to state standards
   c. The performance data for middle schools that are of a similar size and socioeconomic ranking as Thompson Middle School
   d. Student demographic data including economic and disability status

12. Based on the data above and her overall goals, Ms. B, in future post-observation conferences, should encourage teachers to adopt which of the following strategies?
   a. Continue to utilize teacher-centered strategies in classes such as math and history but encourage student-centered approaches in ELA and science.
   b. Utilize district-issued student laptops at a higher rate for classroom instruction.
   c. Differentiate based on the needs of students to ensure that both lower-level and higher-performing students are adequately challenged.
   d. Maximize the use of student-centered learning strategies in all classrooms.

13. How can Ms. B best encourage her staff to serve on the curriculum development team?
   a. Provide incentives that will promote greater teacher buy-in and lead to a higher rate of participation on the curriculum development team.
   b. Require that all staff must participate on the curriculum development team in some capacity.
   c. Provide staff with the time during the school day or provide professional development time to research and explore initiatives that best meet their needs.
   d. Offer workshops during the summertime when teachers have more time and availability to commit to curriculum development.

14. After Ms. B reviews the walk-through data, which of the following conclusions can she most reasonably reach?
   a. Teachers allow students to engage in off-task behavior during instructional time.
   b. Students are more likely to engage in academic discourse and student-centered learning activities in ELA courses than in math courses.
   c. Teachers are more likely to engage students in student-centered learning activities than independent tasks.
   d. Students instructed in a teacher-centered learning environment are more likely to engage in academic discourse.

15. Ms. B plans to complete an annual evaluation to determine if the team's curricular modifications are improving the academic performance of students. Which of the following would be most helpful in determining the overall effect of the changes?
   a. Anecdotal survey results from teachers and students
   b. The quarterly grades of students, as well as results of their final cumulative exams
   c. Walk-through data detailing the presence or absence of student-centered approaches
   d. Assessment data in the areas of ELA and mathematics

16. Ms. B is working to analyze the data from last year's walk-throughs. Based on the data, which strategy will most improve instructional strategies?
   a. Incorporating professional development that focuses on the use of student-centered learning activities
   b. Changing the evaluation structure so that all teachers receive more frequent observations throughout the school year
   c. Identifying teachers who could be content-level instructional coaches to provide feedback on teaching practices of their peers
   d. Informing staff that teacher-centered instructional practices are no longer acceptable in the classroom and must be replaced with student-centered practices

17. How can Ms. B best motivate any staff members that are hesitant to make instructional changes?
   a. Provide incentives to staff who incorporate student-centered learning strategies into their classrooms.
   b. Allow hesitant teachers to make changes at their own pace so that they can more easily transition to the new teaching style.
   c. Create a presentation that highlights the academic gains experienced by students in classrooms where student-centered approaches are prioritized.
   d. Require hesitant teachers to observe other teachers in the building who utilize student-centered approaches.

INSTRUCTIONAL LEADERSHIP FOR STUDENT SUCCESS
DESCRIPTION

Mr. S is the principal at Woodsen High School in a small rural school district. He has been working at the school, which serves approximately 520 students, for the past five years. Many of the students' parents work at the local mill; however, a large number of migrant families have recently moved into the district to work in the growing agricultural sector. Most teachers at the school are young and relatively inexperienced, with less than five years of work experience. Many teachers begin their careers at Woodsen and then move on to positions at higher-performing districts in larger metropolitan areas. In general, the school performs below the state average on state assessments. Furthermore, over the last two school years, the students at this school have performed significantly worse than other students on the ELA Regents Examination. While 81% of students statewide attained proficiency, only 20.17% of students at Woodsen attained proficiency.

Mr. S and his staff are presented with a number of challenges. As a result of the increasing number of immigrant families in the community, the rate of English language learners (ELLs) in the school has drastically increased. When Mr. S began working at Woodsen, ELLs were less than 1% of the school population. During the last school year, ELLs were 18% of the school population. Woodsen High School has struggled to attract and maintain an appropriate number of English as a second language (ESL) teachers to meet this growth.

Additionally, Mr. S has observed the number of students diagnosed with disabilities grow. The number of students with Individualized Education Programs (IEPs) has increased from 52 to 134 in the past five years despite a relatively stable total number of students. These students generally perform poorly on state assessments. Mr. S is also concerned that many ELLs are being incorrectly determined to be in need of an IEP. He is worried that students are not provided with adequate support to learn English and are being mistakenly identified as having disabilities.

Mr. S has two primary goals for the upcoming school year: to improve assessment scores for all students at Woodsen High School and to ensure that the school staff is appropriately differentiating instruction to meet the needs of all students. Although most teachers are willing to ensure that students' needs are met, Ms. S. worries that they are not fully prepared to make these changes in their classrooms. He decides to implement a leadership team that will work to develop a plan that is effective at providing individualized instruction to students based on their abilities. When the team meets, they review various data including assessment data, IEP qualification data, and teacher survey results. Mr. S hopes that he and the team can establish a differentiation plan that can be put into place by the start of the second semester of the new school year.

DOCUMENT 1

Individualized Education Programs by Disability Category

Disability Category	Five Years Ago		Three Years Ago		One Year Ago	
	ELLs	All Students with IEPs	ELLs	All Students with IEPs	ELLs	All Students with IEPs
Autism	0	5	1	6	3	11
Deafness or Blindness	0	0	0	0	0	0
Developmental Delay	0	0	0	0	2	5
Emotional Disturbance	0	4	0	0	0	0
Hearing Impairment	0	0	0	0	0	0
Intellectual Disability	0	2	0	3	1	1
Multiple Disabilities	0	0	0	0	0	0
Orthopedic Impairment	0	1	0	0	0	0
Other Health Impairment	0	8	0	16	5	18
Specific Learning Disability	1	21	10	32	40	78
Speech and Language Impairment	0	9	0	18	0	21
Traumatic Brain Injury	0	0	0	0	0	0

Disability Category	Five Years Ago		Three Years Ago		One Year Ago	
Visual Impairment	0	2	0	1	0	0
Total IEPs	1	52	11	76	51	134

Document 2

ELA Regents Exam Results (Administered to Students in 11th Grade)

	Percent of 11th-Grade Class Five Years Ago	Proficiency Rate Five Years Ago	Percent of 11th-Grade Class Three Years Ago	Proficiency Rate Three Years Ago	Percent of 11th-Grade Class One Year Ago	Proficiency Rate One Year Ago
Black or African American	6%	31%	12%	33%	11%	30%
White	92%	54%	78%	48%	69%	46%
Hispanic or Latino	2%	28%	10%	23%	20%	27%
Students Diagnosed with Disabilities	8%	15%	14%	12%	26%	12%
English Language Learners	0%	N/A	9%	10%	20%	6%

Document 3

Excerpt from Anonymous Teacher Survey on Differentiation Techniques

	Percent of Teachers Who Agree	Percent of Teachers Who Are Neutral/Unsure	Percent of Teachers Who Disagree
I am aware of differentiation strategies that will meet the needs of my students.	32%	22%	46%
I am confident in my ability to differentiate for different levels of learners including ELLs, students with disabilities, and gifted students.	28%	15%	57%
I utilize differentiation strategies on a daily basis.	30%	10%	60%

	Percent of Teachers Who Agree	Percent of Teachers Who Are Neutral/Unsure	Percent of Teachers Who Disagree
I can improve upon my ability to effectively differentiate for my students.	88%	10%	2%
I am willing to apply new strategies in my classroom to ensure the needs of my students are met.	66%	8%	26%
I feel that I have adequate training in the area of differentiation.	24%	17%	59%

18. Which of the following trends from the 11th-grade student assessment data should be most concerning to Mr. S?

    a. The decline in proficiency rates among black or African American students from three years ago to one year ago

    b. The stagnation of proficiency rates among students diagnosed with disabilities over the past three years

    c. The increasing rate of ELLs coupled with their declining proficiency rates over the past five years

    d. The overall decline in proficiency rates among students at Woodsen High School

19. Based on the results of the teacher survey, Mr. S should focus on which of the following areas when developing a plan designed to promote differentiation strategies across the building?

    a. Incentivizing teachers so that they are encouraged to try new differentiation strategies within their classrooms

    b. Highlighting the lack of differentiation across the building and the resulting negative impacts on students

    c. Increasing teacher understanding of differentiation strategies in hopes of promoting greater confidence and usage overall

    d. Helping staff to understand the necessity of improving and providing differentiation to students of all levels

20. Over the past five years, Woodsen High School has experienced a significant increase in its special education population. What should Mr. S's primary focus be in addressing this issue?

    a. Assessing staff on their ability to accurately identify the presence of a disability

    b. Focusing professional development on effective differentiation techniques to use in the classroom

    c. Providing professional development opportunities that focus on the proper identification of students with disabilities that are also ELLs

    d. Ensuring that each classroom has access to rigorous and effective curricular materials

21. Mr. S plans to review survey data with all school staff at the next faculty meeting. Which of the following is the best way for Mr. S to promote classroom improvements among the staff following the review sessions?
    a. Request that each teacher share his or her responses from the survey within a small group.
    b. Provide teachers with the opportunity to reflect on the survey responses and identify their highest priority to focus on.
    c. Lead a role-playing activity in which teachers take turns modeling various scenarios that call upon differentiation techniques.
    d. Call out specific teachers who differentiate appropriately and request that they share advice with their peers.

22. After reviewing the data above, which of the following conclusions should Mr. S reach about ELL students at Woodsen High School?
    a. Although ELLs serve as a minority group within the total student population, they are disproportionately represented among students with IEPs.
    b. ELLS are less likely to be diagnosed with a disability than any other demographic group at Woodsen High School.
    c. ELLs performed better overall on state assessments than those students diagnosed with disabilities.
    d. ELLs are not receiving instruction that has been appropriately differentiated.

23. As Mr. S and his team strive to improve assessment performance, finding answers to which of the following questions is most important?
    a. What, if any, relationship exists between socioeconomic status and assessment performance?
    b. How does a student's disability status impact his or her ability to demonstrate proficiency on state exams?
    c. How can barriers preventing assessment success be eliminated or reduced for ELLs?
    d. Will improved differentiation alone result in increased assessment scores, or do other changes need to be made?

24. At the culmination of the school year, Mr. S and his team plan to review the effectiveness of the differentiation program. What would be most helpful in determining the overall effect of the program?
    a. An overview of students' IEP goals and progress monitoring data
    b. Walk-through data detailing teacher use of differentiation strategies
    c. Curriculum-based assessment results for students from throughout the school year
    d. The English proficiency levels of ELLs who take the state assessment at the end of the school year

25. All of the following are steps Mr. S should take to ensure that ELLs are proportionately represented in the special education program EXCEPT:

a. Develop a robust ESL program that is effective in determining student needs and promoting English proficiency.
b. Adequately train staff on special education referral and evaluation protocols for all students, especially ELLs.
c. Promote the belief among staff members that it is better to under identify than overidentify ELLs with disabilities.
d. Ensure that classroom instruction is designed to meet the needs of all students regardless of disability status or English language proficiency.

SCHOOL CULTURE AND LEARNING ENVIRONMENT TO PROMOTE EXCELLENCE, EQUITY, AND SOCIAL JUSTICE

DESCRIPTION

Ms. L has just completed her fourth year as principal at McDonald Elementary, one of five elementary schools in a large suburban school district. In the school year that just finished, there were 820 students in grades K-5. The school is ethnically diverse and includes students from a variety of linguistic and cultural backgrounds. In this last school year, approximately 39% of the student body was Hispanic or Latino, 27% was black or African American, 18% was Asian or Pacific Islander, and 16% was white. Additionally, approximately 54% of students were considered economically disadvantaged, 31% were students who had been diagnosed with disabilities, and 41% were English language learners. On state assessments, students at the school have historically performed at, or slightly below, the state average.

The general demographics of McDonald Elementary have remained relatively consistent over the last several years. However, Ms. L and the district leadership team have noticed an increase in disciplinary infractions over the past two school years. The total number of disciplinary infractions and suspensions overall exceeds not only the state average but the rates of other schools in the district. It seems that Hispanic or Latino students disproportionately experience disciplinary consequences compared to other ethnic groups. Ms. L and the team are concerned that both the school's overall positive culture and learning environment are declining.

For the upcoming school year, Ms. L and the team decide that they will implement a positive behavior support program aligned with a positive behavioral interventions and supports (PBIS) framework. Additionally, Ms. L hopes to determine the reasoning behind the disproportionate percentage of Hispanic or Latino students facing disciplinary consequences.

Over the summer, Ms. L then reaches out to staff who may be interested in becoming members of the core PBIS team. She hopes to facilitate several training and planning sessions before the start of the school year so that the new program can be put into place by the start of the spring semester.

Document 1

Preliminary PBIS Plan for McDonald Elementary

School Name: McDonald Elementary

1. Behavior Expectations

Core Values of Program:

- Respect
- Kindness
- Safety
- Responsibility

Behavior Matrix:

Setting	Respect	Kindness	Safety	Responsibility
Classroom	Raise hand before speaking	Provide help to friends and teachers	Follow all rules	Complete classwork
Hallways	Speak quietly	Wave hello to those you know	Walk in the halls	Place personal items in lockers
Recess	Be respectful of equipment	Invite new friends to play	Follow game directions	Put away all items used at the end of recess
Lunchroom	Use inside voices	Make room for others	Don't share food or snacks	Take trash to the garbage cans

2. Collection/Review of Data

- Track all disciplinary referrals using a school-wide tracking system.
- Meet biweekly to review disciplinary referrals and other related data.

3. Professional Development

- Provide training for staff at the start of the school year as well as workshops throughout the year to discuss new strategies and identify areas of improvement.

4. Involvement of Families/Community Members

- Send out monthly newsletters outlining strategies families can reinforce or discuss at home.
- Work with local businesses to collect donations to use as incentives.

5. Recognition/Reward System for Students

- Students earn "Tiger" tickets for good behavior/display of core values. These can be turned in for a chance to win small rewards.
- Recognize all students each quarter who demonstrate positive behavior with larger rewards such as a movie day or outdoor activity.

6. Review/Adjust

- Survey staff, students, and families to determine effectiveness of program.
- Use data from disciplinary referrals to identify areas of need/adjustment.

DOCUMENT 2

Excerpt of Results from the Family Survey on School Culture

	Agree	Neutral/Unsure	Disagree
My child has been punished unnecessarily.	42%	20%	38%
The school punishes and rewards all children equitably.	17%	43%	40%
My child's teachers reach out with positive communication.	8%	16%	76%
My child enjoys going to school.	41%	15%	44%
The culture at McDonald Elementary is positive and welcoming.	22%	8%	70%
My child is rewarded for positive behavior.	16%	57%	27%

DOCUMENT 3

Disciplinary Referral Data for the Previous School Year

	Approximate Percent of Student Population	Total Number of Disciplinary Referrals	Percent of Referrals Resulting in Detention/Suspension
All Students		2,482	86%
Male	48%	1.264	90%
Female	52%	1.218	82%
Hispanic or Latino	39%	1,737	90%
Black or African American	27%	447	76%
Asian or Pacific Islander	18%	124	77%
White	16%	174	78%

26. When Ms. L and her team assess the PBIS program at the end of the school year, identifying the answer to which of the following questions should be the most important?

   a. Are families aware and supportive of the implications of the PBIS program?
   b. How can staff members be more effectively trained in PBIS initiatives?
   c. Has the program reduced the disproportionate number of disciplinary actions against Hispanic or Latino students?
   d. Are class and building-wide rewards adequate in encouraging student buy-in and participation?

27. The PBIS program included above is missing which of the following components that will help to ensure its successful implementation as a whole?

   a. Restorative justice practices
   b. Research-backed consequences
   c. Differentiated application of behavioral analysis
   d. Multitiered system of behavioral supports

28. Upon comparing the disciplinary data and parent survey results, Ms. L should reach which of the following conclusions?

   a. The handling of disciplinary issues at McDonald Elementary has led to a lack of confidence among families regarding the school's ability to promote a positive culture.
   b. McDonald Elementary families feel as if their children are treated fairly and equitably when it comes to disciplinary referrals.
   c. Families at McDonald Elementary feel that the school culture is welcoming despite the belief that certain students may be unfairly disciplined.
   d. All families feel that McDonald Elementary both refers and disciplines children of certain genders and ethnic backgrounds at a higher rate than students of other demographic backgrounds.

29. Although Ms. L believes that PBIS training will help to reduce disciplinary infractions and improve the school environment, the implementation of which of the following strategies would improve the chances of the team achieving their ultimate goal?

   a. Updating the student handbook so that it minimizes consequences for certain student behaviors
   b. Ensuring that students' basic needs are met through the incorporation of a free breakfast program
   c. Implementing professional development opportunities that train staff on culturally responsive practices
   d. Involving parents in disciplinary meetings so they can better understand the process by which students are disciplined

30. Which of the following should be the biggest concern for Ms. L and her team?

   a. Parental concerns regarding unequal treatment of students
   b. Increasing rates of disciplinary referrals among all demographic groups at McDonald Elementary
   c. The belief that the culture and learning environment at McDonald Elementary are negative and viewed as unwelcoming to many students
   d. Disproportionate disciplinary referrals for Hispanic or Latino students

31. Based on the results of the parent survey, families overall have a negative perception of the school culture at McDonald Elementary. Which of the following is the best action that Ms. L can take to improve this perception?
   a. Require that teachers offer additional conferences in the evening hours throughout the school year to provide greater opportunity for parental input and feedback.
   b. Provide additional volunteer opportunities for families to participate in general school activities as well as individual classroom tasks.
   c. Hold monthly school culture meetings where families are invited to attend informal online sessions where they can voice concerns and provide feedback on school culture initiatives.
   d. Develop a new survey that allows parents the opportunity to provide feedback and suggest strategies that will improve the school culture.

32. Ms. L will hold a staff meeting at the beginning of the school year to review concerns with school-wide disciplinary referrals. The meeting will most likely result in positive change if she takes which of the following approaches?
   a. Request that teachers stop writing disciplinary referrals for Hispanic or Latino students to reduce any disproportions.
   b. Detail how the data indicates discriminatory practices on the part of the teachers and school administrators in general.
   c. Present the data objectively and discuss potential reasons for the increase in referrals as well as the disproportionate focus on Hispanic or Latino students.
   d. Invite parents to the meeting to share their feelings on the topic as well as to discuss the implications of the practice on their children.

33. What additional information will most help Ms. L and her team in determining the effectiveness of the PBIS program at the end of the school year?
   a. The results of a parent survey sent to families after the PBIS program has been implemented
   b. Disciplinary referral data for the current school year
   c. Data that details which specific teachers are issuing student disciplinary referrals
   d. Student Individualized Education Program data broken down by demographic group

SCHOOL CULTURE AND LEARNING ENVIRONMENT TO PROMOTE EXCELLENCE, EQUITY, AND SOCIAL JUSTICE

DESCRIPTION

Mr. V has just begun his first year as principal at Britton High School. Britton is one of five high schools in a large urban school district. Britton serves approximately 1,876 students, many of whom come from diverse backgrounds. Approximately 47% of the school population is black or African American, 28% is Hispanic or Latino, 19% is white, and 6% is Asian or Pacific Islander. Students at Britton typically perform below the state average on state assessments.

Mr. V has worked at several other schools within the district. He most recently worked as principal at one of the magnet high schools, where students who are interested in the performing arts must apply to attend. The superintendent asked Mr. V to transfer to Britton to help improve student test scores as well as the overall culture and environment. The relationship between teachers and administrators at Britton is wrought with distrust and contention. Teachers at the school feel that the previous principal was not supportive and did not advocate for their needs as a building. They also feel that the superintendent unfairly targets their building as a result of poor test scores, which they feel they cannot change or improve as a result of poor attendance and an overall lack of parental support. Furthermore, relations between the teaching staff have often been poor and divisive.

When it comes to building relationships with families, the teachers have appeared to give up. Many families fail to respond to teacher emails and phone calls. Even fewer families attend events such as parent-teacher conferences, the school open house, or curriculum night. The teaching staff has grown accustomed to a lack of involvement from student families and often fails to maintain adequate communication avenues with the families that are engaged in their child's academic career.

At the request of the superintendent, Mr. V has implemented a number of initiatives to improve both communication and the professional community as a whole. On a weekly basis, Mr. V sends out a staff communication email that details upcoming events and includes an anonymous suggestion box. He also has already held a mandatory training on appropriate conflict resolution. Additionally, he has developed a school leadership team (SLT) that meets on a biweekly basis to discuss staff concerns as well as any new initiatives or ideas aimed at improving the school as a whole. Furthermore, Mr. V is planning to incorporate team-building activities into an upcoming professional development day. Although the staff was welcoming of Mr. V and hopeful that his initiatives would improve the school climate, the overall reception has been mixed. Many of the issues that existed over the last few years continue to persist as the staff has failed to buy in completely to the new strategies proposed by Mr. V.

DOCUMENT 1

Excerpt from Teacher Survey: June of the Previous School Year

	Percent of Staff Who Agree	Percent of Staff Who Are Neutral or Unsure	Percent of Staff Who Disagree
Certain teachers are treated preferentially and are provided with opportunities that others are not.	76%	8%	16%
I feel that I am respected by my coworkers and building administration.	8%	23%	69%
I am open to incorporating new practices into my professional practice that will improve the climate at Britton.	88%	6%	6%
The administrative team communicates effectively with members of the staff.	4%	7%	89%

	Percent of Staff Who Agree	Percent of Staff Who Are Neutral or Unsure	Percent of Staff Who Disagree
I feel that my opinions are heard and valued.	16%	12%	72%
I communicate frequently and effectively with families.	48%	26%	26%
My work environment is hospitable and welcoming.	12%	31%	57%
The administration values me as an employee and encourages input.	13%	7%	80%
I engage with my coworkers in an effective and respectful manner.	56%	22%	22%

Document 2

Beginning of the School Year Email Communication to Staff

Hello Everyone,

I have reviewed the results of the staff survey sent out in June and have developed a plan to address some of the concerns brought to my attention. I hope that this school year we are able to grow and develop as a building and improve our school culture as a whole. Please understand that this school year will be an adjustment, and we will all need to commit to making positive changes for both ourselves and our students. Take a moment to review the list of initiatives below that I plan to implement throughout the school year.

Open Door Policy

- Please stop in to see me with any concerns throughout the school year. My door is always open, and I am happy to discuss anything that will help improve our school community!

School Leadership Team (SLT)

- Principal-selected staff members will have the ability to participate in biweekly meetings aimed at discussing any concerns and upcoming initiatives.
- Members of the SLT will provide the administrative team with valuable information that will be considered in decision-making moving forward.

Community Leadership Team (CLT)

- Principal-selected staff members will discuss familial concerns and strategies to promote community engagement.
- Meetings will take place once per month.

Weekly Newsletter

- Review of important school-wide happenings and upcoming events
- Suggestion box for anonymous feedback, suggestions, or queries

Professional Development Opportunities

- Conflict resolution strategies
- Building positive relationships with families
- Team building
- Professional communication strategies
- Meeting the needs of diverse students and their families

DOCUMENT 3

Excerpt from Teacher Survey: End of Quarter 1

	Percent of Staff Who Agree	Percent of Staff Who Are Neutral or Unsure	Percent of Staff Who Disagree
The initiatives proposed by the administration are helping to improve the climate of Britton.	24%	8%	68%
I am utilizing the strategies proposed in my professional practice.	18%	20%	62%
I have adequate time to communicate with families as well as members of my school-based team.	3%	12%	85%
The administration values me as an employee and encourages input.	16%	10%	74%
The administrative team communicates effectively with members of the staff.	8%	8%	84%

	Percent of Staff Who Agree	Percent of Staff Who Are Neutral or Unsure	Percent of Staff Who Disagree
I am open to incorporating new practices into my professional practice that will improve the climate at Britton.	78%	10%	12%
My work environment is hospitable and welcoming.	10%	28%	62%
Certain teachers are treated preferentially and are provided with opportunities that others are not.	81%	12%	7%
I engage with my coworkers in an effective and respectful manner.	60%	24%	16%

34. As Mr. V assesses the overall effectiveness of the initiatives he introduced to improve the school climate, it is most important that he asks himself which of the following questions?

   a. Will parental involvement actually bring about a change in student engagement that can lead to an improved school climate?
   b. What other initiatives can be introduced to further improve the school climate?
   c. Which teachers appear to be the most discontented regarding both professional and familial relationships?
   d. Have the initiatives positively changed the building staff's perception of building leadership and the school environment?

35. At a monthly staff meeting, Mr. V discusses the importance of positive relationships between a student's home and school and begins by reviewing a list of specific parental complaints that have been submitted to the administration. Collectively, the staff becomes upset and disengaged. How could Mr. V have introduced the topic of positive relationships between home and school in a way that may have resulted in a more positive reception?

   a. By reiterating district-wide expectations for familial contact and relationship building
   b. By discussing the ultimate goal of meeting the needs of students and their families and promoting academic growth
   c. By reviewing the new policy that staff will be required to stay after school on conference days in the hope of promoting a greater rate of family attendance
   d. By providing evidence detailing the lack of family contact at Britton and the implication on student performance

36. Which of the following decisions by Mr. V will most likely result in increased discontent among staff members?

   a. The selection of staff members to participate in both the SLT and CLT
   b. The open-door policy to encourage communication between the administration and staff
   c. The introduction of team-building activities that will promote relationship building
   d. The acknowledgement by Mr. V that all staff members must demonstrate commitment to the new policies

37. Which of the following concerns should be the highest priority for Mr. V?

   a. General feelings of discontent about the workplace by staff members
   b. The lack of teacher utilization and ultimate buy-in of the new initiatives
   c. Poor relationships among teachers as well as their apparent inability to mediate disputes
   d. The sentiment among staff members that members of the administrative team fail to effectively communicate

38. Mr. V completes a comprehensive overview of the programs implemented throughout the school year. Which of the following pieces of information would be most helpful in gauging the ultimate improvement of the school environment?

   a. The data from quarterly family surveys on the topic
   b. Formal and informal observation data of staff members
   c. An anonymous and voluntary staff survey following the end of the school year
   d. Disciplinary records of students throughout the school year organized by teacher

39. Mr. V brings a team-building specialist to conduct the first professional development session of the year. The specialist leads staff members through a variety of fun and engaging activities designed to promote a more positive culture within the school. One staff member, Mr. K, complains loudly throughout the day and encourages negativity among his peers. How should Mr. V address the situation?

   a. Send out a general email communication that evening reiterating the importance of professionalism during in-service days.
   b. Immediately address the behavior in front of the group and discuss the justifications for incorporating team-building activities.
   c. Schedule a meeting with Mr. K during his preparation period to discuss the behavior as well as professional expectations.
   d. Speak privately with Mr. K during a break in activity and provide an opportunity for him to discuss his concerns on an individual basis.

40. Mr. V reflects on the progress of his initiatives at the end of the school year. Although the school climate as it pertains to the perceptions and actions of staff members has improved throughout the course of the year, Mr. V feels that more can be done. Which of the following strategies should Mr. V implement for the next school year to promote further growth in this area?

a. Develop a mentorship program where students can build improved relationships with staff members they may traditionally have little contact with.
b. Introduce department-level planning periods in which members of the same department can meet to develop strategies to improve their practice and communicate with families.
c. Encourage staff members to participate in school-wide community service programs such as collections for the local food pantry.
d. Provide opportunities for students and their families to participate in the decision-making process for different school-based programs.

41. Based on the results of the two staff surveys, Mr. V should reach which of the following conclusions?

a. The staff is unwilling to adopt the new initiatives that have been proposed at the school to improve the school climate.
b. The initiatives have proven to be ineffective in bringing about a change in mindset among staff at the school.
c. No positive effects have come about as a result of the initiatives introduced during the current school year.
d. Perceptions among school staff regarding issues that impact the school climate have not changed significantly over the course of the first quarter.

Part 2

Note: Part 2 of the NYSTCE School Building Leader exam includes an extended performance task requiring the test-taker to evaluate a 15-minute video recording of a teacher's classroom instruction. After watching the video, the test taker is asked to score the teacher based on a provided rubric and note evidence from the recording to support the feedback. Because we are unable to provide a reasonable simulation of this exercise in our text study guide format, we recommend visiting the NYSTCE website and familiarizing yourself with the observation rubric on which you will be evaluating the recorded instructional session.

(https://www.nystce.nesinc.com/Content/STUDYGUIDE/NY_SG_Vid_110.htm)

EXTENDED PERFORMANCE TASK
DEVELOPING HUMAN CAPITAL TO IMPROVE FACULTY AND STAFF EFFECTIVENESS AND STUDENT ACHIEVEMENT

Use the information and documents below to complete the task that follows. You have 70 minutes to complete this assignment.

DESCRIPTION

You are the newly hired principal at Crestview High School, a suburban school that serves approximately 540 students in grades 9-12. The suburban community in which it is located demonstrates a strong commitment to education and diversity. Overall, families in the community are supportive of their children's education and engage in a positive manner with staff at Crestview. The school has traditionally performed above the state averages on state assessments. Most teachers at the school have been employed at the district for over 10 years and are comfortable in their positions. That being said, Crestview is struggling with retaining new teachers. Approximately 86% of newly hired teachers move on to other districts within three years of being hired.

Five years ago, the former principal, Mr. S, launched an intensive school improvement agenda centered on increasing student engagement and improving student academic outcomes. Through Mr. S, teachers, support staff, and parents collaborated to create a shared vision of an inclusive school with high academic expectations. During the initial two years of the initiative, there were significant boosts in student achievement in the areas of advanced placement coursework, and there was an increased graduation rate. Many teachers and students welcomed the change, but others felt that they were being pushed too hard by the speed of implementation and that follow-up support was limited.

In the third year, the momentum began to dissipate, and achievement levels somewhat stabilized. By the fourth year of the program, it became apparent that levels of student performance were stagnating and did not demonstrate significant growth or decline. When you took over halfway through the fifth year of the program, following the resignation of Mr. S, it was obvious that changes needed to be made to promote continued academic growth. At the urging of the superintendent, you begin the process of implementing changes to the program. To guide these changes, you begin by reviewing student grades, school-wide assessment data, student attendance data, teacher observation results, and feedback from recent teacher and student surveys.

DOCUMENT 1

Overall Evaluation Scores from Previous School Year

Subject Area	Total Teachers	Ineffective	Developing	Effective	Highly Effective
English Language Arts	12	1 (8.3%)	3 (25.0%)	6 (50.0%)	2 (16.7%)
Mathematics	10	0 (0.0%)	2 (20.0%)	5 (50.0%)	3 (30.0%)
Science	6	0 (0.0%)	1 (16.7%)	4 (66.7%)	1 (16.7%)
Social Studies/History	7	1 (14.3%)	1 (14.3%)	4 (57.1%)	1 (14.3%)
Special Education	4	0 (0.0%)	2 (50.0%)	2 (50.0%)	0 (0.0%)
Specialty/Noncore Subjects	8	2 (25.0%)	1 (12.5%)	4 (50.0%)	1 (12.5%)
Total	47	4 (8.5%)	10 (21.3%)	25 (53.2%)	8 (17.0%)

DOCUMENT 2

Attendance Data from Previous School Year

Grade	Total Students	Attendance Rate (%)	Number of Students with 10 or More Absences	Number of Students with 20 or More Absences
9th	150	92.5%	15	5
10th	140	85.0%	25	12
11th	130	94.0%	10	2
12th	120	71.0%	15	8
Total	540	86.1%	65	27

Attendance Data from Three Years Ago

Grade	Total Students	Attendance Rate (%)	Number of Students with 10 or More Absences	Number of Students with 20 or More Absences
9th	145	95.0%	10	3
10th	135	90.0%	15	5
11th	128	96.0%	8	1
12th	115	80.0%	10	4

Grade	Total Students	Attendance Rate (%)	Number of Students with 10 or More Absences	Number of Students with 20 or More Absences
Total	523	90.7%	43	13

Document 3

Excerpt of State Assessment Results (11th Grade)

Subject	School Assessment Results (% of Students Passing)			State Assessment Results (% of Students Passing)		
	Five Years Ago	Three Years Ago	Last Year	Five Years Ago	Three Years Ago	Last Year
ELA	86%	89%	89%	83%	81%	82%
Algebra	76%	82%	82.5%	74%	65%	65%
Biology	95%	97%	96%	94%	95%	96%

Document 4

Excerpt of Teacher Survey

	Strongly Agree	Agree	Disagree	Strongly Disagree
I feel that I am effectively supported by the administration in my role.	15%	20%	43%	22%
Professional development is aligned to the actual needs of my classroom.	8%	30%	50%	12%
The curriculum is inclusive and aligned to the needs and capabilities of my students.	5%	20%	60%	15%
I feel overwhelmed by my workload.	40%	35%	15%	10%
I feel I am being pushed too hard to meet expectations.	30%	52%	8%	10%
Communication between the faculty and administration is effective.	20%	30%	30%	20%
Students are appropriately challenged, and content is neither too easy nor too difficult.	15%	12%	66%	7%

	Strongly Agree	Agree	Disagree	Strongly Disagree
The work that I am doing in my classroom is helping students to succeed in areas beyond state testing.	1%	8%	78%	13%

Excerpt of Student Survey

	Strongly Agree	Agree	Disagree	Strongly Disagree
My classes are engaging and informative.	36%	37%	15%	12%
My teachers provide support as needed.	52%	29%	12%	7%
The teachers primarily "teach to the test" and leave out other relevant and interesting information.	28%	57%	4%	11%
I feel comfortable communicating with teachers.	54%	31%	10%	5%
I am overwhelmed by the amount of homework assigned.	58%	27%	12%	3%
I feel pressured to perform well academically.	44%	36%	15%	5%

DOCUMENT 5

Excerpt of Observation Notes: ELA Department

Ms. G is a first-year ELA teacher at Crestview. I observed a lesson where she introduced the novel *The Great Gatsby*.

Domain 1: Planning and Preparation

- **1a: Demonstrating Knowledge of Content and Pedagogy**

    Ms. G did have some knowledge of American literature. She didn't connect *The Great Gatsby* to real life for the students in regard to themes. No contextual knowledge was given about the author and/or historical background.

- **1c: Setting Instructional Outcomes**

    Learning objectives were not clearly stated and not posted in the classroom. It did not appear that students understood what they should be able to do at the end of the lesson.

Domain 2: Classroom Environment

- **2a: Creating an Environment of Respect and Rapport**

    Ms. G was friendly but did seem to have minimal control of the classroom. Students did not follow requests to quiet down. A number of students were disrupting others.

- **2b: Establishing a Culture for Learning**

    The students were not very motivated by the content provided; many seemed detached and disengaged. Several were on their phones.

Domain 3: Instruction

- **3a: Communicating with Students**

    The directions for the assignment were unclear, and many students were confused. Ms. G did assist students but only after the initial introduction of the task.

- **3b: Using Questioning and Discussion Techniques**

    Ms. G did pose some questions; however, none were higher-order thinking questions. Most were closed-ended questions that required only short answers without explanation.

Mr. P is a sixth-year ELA teacher. I observed a lesson where he drew parallels between themes of *To Kill a Mockingbird* and modern issues in America.

Domain 1: Planning and Preparation

- **1a: Demonstrating Knowledge of Content and Pedagogy**

    Mr. P highlighted a number of literary concepts and was well-versed in their application within the text. Additionally, Mr. P drew connections to essential themes within the section of chapters the class was working with.

- **1c: Setting Instructional Outcomes**

    Mr. P clearly posted the learning objectives for the lesson on the smartboard in the classroom. He consistently looped back to the objectives as he progressed through the lesson to ensure student understanding and mastery.

Domain 2: Classroom Environment

- **2a: Creating an Environment of Respect and Rapport**

    Students were discussing issues of racism in the text. Despite the emotional and sometimes controversial nature of the topic, students engaged with one another in a respectful and insightful manner.

- **2b: Establishing a Culture for Learning**

    The classroom was lively and engaging. Mr. P promoted critical thinking and drew connections to the real world. Students were motivated and engaged in their learning.

Domain 3: Instruction

- **3a: Communicating with Students**

    Mr. P provided clear and easy-to-follow instructions. Additionally, all directions were posted on the smartboard so that students could reference them as needed. Furthermore, he utilized a variety of techniques to explain complex ideas, such as visual aids and examples.

- **3b: Using Questioning and Discussion Techniques**

    Mr. P used higher-level questions that encouraged meaningful discussion. He guided students in exploring important themes, encouraging them to elaborate on their thoughts and engage with their peers.

- **3c: Engaging Students in Learning**

    Students were actively engaged throughout the lesson. Small group discussion allowed for collaboration, and Mr. P moved around the room and worked to support conversations.

SHORT ANSWER QUESTIONS

From your school building leadership understanding and the information supplied, address the following tasks:

1. Write a response about 100-200 words long, in a format you prefer (e.g., an outline, a list of bulleted items, prose paragraphs), addressing this question and these prompts:

Question/Prompts: Based on the information above and your understanding of school building leadership, what is the most significant human capital concern at Crestview High School and how would you address it? Explain your reasoning.

Be very specific in your answer, being sure to clearly identify the situation, what you would do about it, and the evidence necessary to justify your answer.

2. Write a response about 100-200 words long, in a format you prefer (e.g., an outline, a list of bulleted items, prose paragraphs), addressing this question and these prompts:

Question/Prompts: Based on the information provided and your understanding of school building leadership, what are the two most important actions you would take to bring about long-term human capital improvements at Crestview High School? Explain why these actions would have long-term benefits.

Be very specific in your answer, being sure to clearly identify the situation, what you would do about it, and the evidence necessary to justify your answer.

3. Write a response about 100-200 words long, in a format you prefer (e.g., an outline, a list of bulleted items, prose paragraphs), addressing this question and these prompts:

Question/Prompts: Based on the information provided and your understanding of school building leadership, describe the actions you would take to ensure that Ms. G develops into a more effective teacher. Explain why you would take these actions.

Be very specific in your answer, being sure to clearly identify the situation, what you would do about it, and the evidence necessary to justify your answer.

4. Write a response about 100-200 words long, in a format you prefer (e.g., an outline, a list of bulleted items, prose paragraphs), addressing this question and these prompts:

Question/Prompts: Based on the information provided and your understanding of school building leadership, describe the professional growth opportunities you would suggest for Mr. P. Explain why.

Be very specific in your answer, being sure to clearly identify the situation, what you would do about it, and the evidence necessary to justify your answer.

SHORTER PERFORMANCE TASK
FAMILY AND COMMUNITY ENGAGEMENT

Use the information and documents below to complete the task that follows. You have 40 minutes to complete this assignment.

DESCRIPTION

You are the building principal at an urban high school that is one of seven high schools in the school district. You have been the building principal for the last four years but have worked for the district in various capacities including as vice principal, dean of students, and math teacher. Your building serves approximately 1,445 students in grades 9-12. The population of the school is diverse, as the student body is 42% black or African American, 27% Hispanic or Latino, 17% white, and 14% Asian or Pacific Islander. Additionally, many students come from households below the poverty line.

Over the summer, the school board decided to streamline special education services and voted to transport all students with significant cognitive disabilities to your school beginning this school year. Students will be enrolled in the newly developed Life Skills Program and take part in certain elective classes such as physical education and art in an inclusive setting. In all, 28 new students will be participating in the Life Skills Program in the fall. The school board and administrative staff believe that this will be cost-effective as well as ensure that students are provided with greater opportunities and transition services.

Many families are upset with the change and would like their children to maintain placement in their current academic setting. During the school board meeting when the change was approved, several parents spoke to voice their displeasure. The school board and members of the administration called a meeting for the families of all students in the Life Skills Program. They presented the program as one that would give students with cognitive delays a greater degree of engagement with their typically developing peers as well as greater employment and internship opportunities.

The superintendent has requested that, with the assistance of the special education director and several special education teachers, you develop another component of the Life Skills Program that will meet the needs of all students who engage with the program. Thus, in addition to the curricular change at the school, you and the rest of your team have decided to implement a co-op program for students in the Life Skills Program. The team will work to develop relationships with various businesses in the community so that students can develop essential vocational skills. Furthermore, you and the team have also decided to implement a cafe at the school in which students in the Life Skills Program will have the opportunity to serve in different roles. Typically developing students will serve as mentors in this program and assist the students with cognitive delays as they perform daily cafe operations.

DOCUMENT 1

Overview of Life Skills Program: Sample Courses

Course/Offering	Description
Cafe Program	Students will have the opportunity to carry out different tasks that would be expected of an employee at a restaurant, cafe, and/or coffee shop. Tasks will include toasting bagels, preparing coffee, cutting fruit, maintaining a clean work environment and good hygiene, and serving customers. Students will be assigned a peer mentor to help with task completion.
Partners in Physical Education	Students will participate in traditional physical education class activities in a smaller setting. Selected students from the greater school population will engage in games and activities as well.
Sculpting Basics	Students will create sculptures and art using a variety of different mediums. The basics of sculpting, decorating, and firing will be reviewed.
Social Skills	Students will review important social skills such as engaging with peers, adults, and those in the workplace.
Co-Op	Students will be transported to various employment opportunities throughout the community where they will be able to learn essential workplace skills required for life beyond high school.
Musical Innovations	Students will be able to learn the basics of several musical instruments including the drums, xylophone, and recorder. Students will work on the development of rhythm and beats.

DOCUMENT 2

Email from the Special Education Director to the Superintendent

Hello,

Please review the list below of potential employment/internship opportunities I have arranged for students in the Life Skills Co-Op. Just as a reminder, with the current lack of bus drivers, we are struggling to arrange transportation for all students to their co-op position.

- Shop-N-Go Grocery Store
    - Students will be able to work in various positions, including bagger and stocker.
    - Willing to pay students minimum wage after a brief trial period.
    - Positions Available: 4
- Smith's Pharmacy
    - Students will be able to stock items.
    - Internship opportunity, no pay available.
    - Positions Available: 2
- Wingz and Thingz
    - Students will be able to assist with bussing tables and washing dishes. Based on ability, prepping certain food items may also be a possibility.
    - Paid opportunity based on experience.

- - Positions Available: 3
- Sandy's Bakery
  - Students will be able to assist with washing dishes as well as stocking items in the grab and go area.
  - Internship opportunity, no pay available.
  - Positions Available: 1

SHORT ANSWER QUESTIONS

Using the information given above, write a response about 400-500 words long, in a format you prefer (e.g., an outline, a list of bulleted items, prose paragraphs). In addressing the items below, give very specific details and cite evidence from the description and data that appropriately support your answers.

1. What are two important issues at your school relating to the implementation of the Life Skills Program that could benefit from family, caregiver, and community involvement?

2. Explain why and how these issues could benefit from family, caregiver, and community involvement.

3. What actions would you take to work with families, caregivers, and the community to address each issue you identified in Part 1? Explain why you believe that these actions would be effective.

4. What additional challenges might your actions create and what are some ways you could manage those challenges?

MULTIPLE CHOICE QUESTIONS

Use the information and documents below to complete the task that follows. You have 60 minutes to complete these questions.

FAMILY AND COMMUNITY ENGAGEMENT

DESCRIPTION

Mr. F is the building principal of Central High School. Central is the only high school in a newly developed school district. For this upcoming school year, two small suburban school districts have been merged as a result of a feasibility study indicating that their combination would result in a more financially and academically viable school system. The high school will serve approximately 1,770 students from diverse backgrounds.

One of the high schools involved in the merger, Johnstown High, served students from relatively high socioeconomic statuses, and the student body was characterized by an overall lack of diversity. Conversely, the other school involved in the merger, Dougherty High, served students from overall lower socioeconomic statuses, and the student body reflected a higher rate of diversity.

The staff at the school is made up of individuals who have significant teaching experience, with most members having taught for 10 or more years. There is a general lack of diversity among staff members; over 98% of teachers at the school are white. Mr. F is holding a series of informal meet and greets over the summer so that the teaching staff has the opportunity to meet one another as well as members of the administrative team. Professional development days prior to the first student day will also focus primarily on team building and "getting to know you" type activities.

Mr. F and the district-level leadership team are focused on building relationships among students, staff, and the community at large, as well as ensuring the development of a positive environment for all. In June, before the start of the new school year, he was tasked with developing a plan of action that will outline the steps aimed at promoting a welcoming and inclusive learning environment and involving families and the community. To accomplish this task, Mr. F plans to create a school-based leadership team that will include students, staff, and community members that will identify any issues or concerns as well as determine activities and initiatives that can promote a positive and inclusive learning environment. In order to prepare fully for the start of the school year, Mr. F reviews student demographic data and family survey results to aid in his development of the plan of action.

Document 1

Demographic Data from the Previous School Year

	Johnstown High School	Dougherty High School
Total Enrollment	863	907
White	94%	38%
Black or African American	4%	31%
Hispanic or Latino	1%	26%
Asian or Pacific Islander	1%	5%
Students Diagnosed with Disabilities	9%	20%
English Language Learners (ELLs)	0.5%	22%
Students from Economically Disadvantaged Backgrounds	6%	46%

Document 2

Excerpt from Family Survey Results: July Before Start of New School Year

	Percent Who Agree	Percent Who Are Unsure	Percent Who Disagree
I feel that my child has been prepared and supported for the upcoming school year.	14%	44%	42%
The district has adequately communicated the transition plan for the new school year.	78%	6%	16%
My family felt supported and valued in our previous school/district.	76%	18%	6%

	Percent Who Agree	Percent Who Are Unsure	Percent Who Disagree
The district is prepared to create an inclusive and welcoming learning environment.	10%	32%	58%
The district has effectively solicited the input of students and families in the lead-up to this school year.	18%	14%	68%
I am confident that my child will be appropriately assisted in his or her transition to a new learning environment.	25%	44%	31%
My child is nervous about the upcoming school year.	86%	10%	4%
I am interested in joining a committee aimed at improving the school environment at Central High.	25%	30%	45%

Document 3

Excerpt from Mr. F's Notes on the Development of an Action Plan

School Leadership Committee

Membership

- Invite department chairs and grade-level leaders to participate in monthly meetings.
- Request that team captains and the presidents of clubs and organizations from both Dougherty and Johnstown join.
- Send out an informal email to families asking for interest—allow for virtual participation.
- Communicate with various business owners that may be willing to provide incentives or funding for student team-building activities. Reach out via email and invite to meetings.

Potential Agenda for First Meeting

- Discuss student and family concerns for transitioning to a new school.
    - Work as a team to identify solutions.
- Discuss school-wide assemblies and reward days.
- Welcome Back to School Dance or Carnival?

Establishment of Clubs and Activities

- Incorporate clubs from both schools.
- Which teachers/staff will sponsor?

Sports

- How to handle tryouts with students from both schools?
- Larger teams? A team vs. B team?
- Parent meeting to discuss implications and options.

Open House

- How to increase parent participation?
- Band performance and/or other student involvement?
- Food trucks?

Internship Opportunities

- Community partnerships will encourage students to engage with their expanded community.
- Provide job training and general employment experiences in fields related to students' areas of interest.
- Interested businesses could attend a "job fair" at the high school.
- Reach out to district families that own businesses.

1. Mr. F determines that the team can better meet the needs of students seeking job experience by improving relations with local businesses. This process will be most effective if he explores which of the following questions first?
   a. Does any overlap exist between the interests of the school and interests of the businesses the team is attempting to build relationships with?
   b. How can the program be expanded to include additional businesses and organizations?
   c. Which students should be considered for internship opportunities?
   d. How can the school ensure that students who are unable to drive reach their internship locations?

2. Based on the information presented in the family survey, which of the following should be most concerning to Mr. F and his team?
   a. The lack of familial confidence in the school's ability to effectively transition students
   b. Communication strategies for continued parental engagement
   c. Student discomfort regarding the upcoming school year
   d. Facilitating familial interest in joining the school leadership committee

3. Mr. F wants to ensure that families are engaged fully throughout the transition process and feel welcome in the school environment. What step could Mr. F take to best accomplish this goal?
    a. Send out an additional survey requesting feedback regarding how to best accomplish his goal.
    b. Hold meetings with the administration from the two schools where the students were previously enrolled to discuss familial interests and needs.
    c. Encourage greater student involvement in the transition planning process.
    d. Introduce a policy for parent-teacher conferences in which translation services are provided for families in need.

4. Although families feel that the school district has adequately communicated plans for the transition, they lack confidence in the ability of the new district to carry out the transition and provide support to students as necessary. Which of the following steps will be most effective in easing these concerns?
    a. Sending out a robocall welcoming students back to school and outlining plans for the first day
    b. Developing a forum on the district website where students and families can pose questions and concerns
    c. Incorporating weekly office hours over the summer where families can stop in and ask questions of the administrative team
    d. Holding orientations prior to the school year where students and families have the opportunity to meet teachers and familiarize themselves with the new environment

5. Which of the following pieces of information would be most beneficial in understanding essential needs for the upcoming school year at Central High?
    a. Student opinions on elective offerings at Central High
    b. Anecdotal teacher data about social groups and conflicts
    c. Demographic data for the upcoming school year
    d. Teacher survey data regarding the transition process

6. Based on the student demographic data, which of the following is the most important concern for Mr. F and his team to consider regarding the upcoming school year?
    a. The higher rate of ELLs coming from Dougherty High School
    b. The changing racial and cultural environment for all students enrolled at Central High
    c. The difference in prevalence of students diagnosed with disabilities between Dougherty and Johnstown Highs
    d. The large variation in the socioeconomic statuses of students between Dougherty and Johnstown Highs

7. Based on the upcoming changing cultural and linguistic dynamic at Central High School, all of the following are strategies Mr. F should incorporate to alleviate any potential growing pains EXCEPT:
    a. Incorporate culturally responsive training for staff during professional development.
    b. Ensure that the curriculum incorporates diverse authors and content.
    c. Develop clubs and organizations that promote acceptance and understanding of the various cultural backgrounds.
    d. Specifically schedule students into classes with similar peers based on their membership in various cultural and/or linguistic groups.

8. Which of the following is the largest issue with the development of the school leadership committee?
    a. The process by which students are invited to join the committee
    b. The overall purpose of the committee is flawed and does not take into account the true needs of the school.
    c. The lack of presence of district-wide administration on the committee
    d. The frequency at which the committee meets

9. As a means to promote increased community involvement at Central High, Mr. F hopes to introduce an internship program as well as incorporate business owners and community members into the school leadership committee. Which of the following is the most likely barrier Mr. F may face when attempting to reach this goal?
    a. Financial issues that prevent the program from being funded
    b. Lack of desire among business owners to partner with the district and provide internship opportunities or engage in the committee
    c. Student unwillingness to participate in such initiatives and engage with community members in this way
    d. Overwhelming support from the community that makes choosing partners difficult

10. Which of the following strategies discussed in Mr. F's notes has the best chance of promoting family involvement overall?
    a. Inviting families to participate in the school leadership committee
    b. Holding a parent meeting to discuss changes to sports teams resulting from the merger
    c. Improving the appeal of an open house
    d. Reaching out to local business owners that may have children in the district to discuss the internship program

OPERATIONAL SYSTEMS, DATA SYSTEMS, AND LEGAL GUIDELINES TO SUPPORT ACHIEVEMENT OF SCHOOL GOALS

11. A building leader is tasked with presenting attendance data pertaining to a district-wide attendance challenge at the next school board meeting. In order to best facilitate understanding of the effect of the programs, the building leader should incorporate which of the following?
    a. Images taken at each of the schools during the attendance activities
    b. Charts highlighting the attendance rates of the school district vs. state averages
    c. Personal anecdotes from teachers and families praising the impact of the initiatives
    d. Graphs detailing attendance rates before and after the initiatives were launched

12. A high school teacher learns last minute of an academic competition relevant to her courses and requests permission to attend from her building leader. The building has a policy that all field trips must be budgeted for in the previous school year; however, the building leader recognizes the academic merit of the competition and wants to provide students with the opportunity to attend. Which of the following is the most appropriate response by the building leader?

  a. Deny the field trip citing funding concerns.
  b. Approve the field trip but require students to pay the admission and transportation costs.
  c. Approve the field trip and request that funds to cover the cost be transferred from a different budget category by the school board.
  d. Approve the field trip using deficit spending, knowing the amount used can easily be covered in next year's budget.

13. A building leader is working to develop a new digital citizenship program for her middle school. The program should incorporate all of the following aspects EXCEPT:

  a. A lesson that focuses on appropriate communication on social media platforms
  b. An activity where students research news stories detailing catfishing schemes
  c. A workshop that teaches students to recognize and prevent cyberbullying
  d. A presentation that reviews the importance of safeguarding private information such as passwords.

14. A building leader and his team are applying for the New York State Education Learning Technology Grant to support the development of a new program for English language learners. The building leader should keep which of the following in mind when working on the grant application?

  a. The application must be submitted as part of a consortium of two or more school districts.
  b. All funds must be used within a given school year and may not be carried over.
  c. The funding will last a minimum of three years.
  d. A one-year budget summary must be included with the grant application.

15. Under New York State law, each public or private school must conduct:

  a. Eight evacuation drills and four lockdown drills during the school year
  b. Ten total emergency drills, of which building leadership may decide the type
  c. At least five lockdown drills, one for each type of emergency response
  d. Six lockdown drills and six evacuation drills

16. A district-wide school safety plan must include which of the following requirements?

  a. The policies and procedures for responding to implied and direct threats of violence
  b. The implementation of a district-wide school police force
  c. The process for providing training on school safety initiatives for new employees within 90 days of hire
  d. The guidelines for charging students involved in serious offenses with crimes

17. Following a test to determine water safety, an elementary school is found to have levels of lead in its water that exceed 5 micrograms per liter. All of the following are steps that must be undertaken by the school EXCEPT:
   a. Immediately ensure that water outlets utilized for drinking or cooking are removed from service.
   b. Provide complimentary drinking water for student and staff use.
   c. Report results to the health department.
   d. Immediately prevent student and staff use of impacted water supply for handwashing and cleaning.

18. The school resource officer (SRO) at a high school is alerted to the boys' bathroom by the vape detector alarm. Upon entering the bathroom, the SRO locates one male student in a stall, whom he brings to the office for questioning. The male student claims that he does not have a vape in his possession and that other students were involved and present in the bathroom. Which step should the building leader take?
   a. Request that the SRO search the student for contraband.
   b. Personally search the student for contraband.
   c. Contact the student's parents so that they can be present for the search.
   d. Gather statements from the other students who were in the bathroom before searching the student.

19. A middle school student who has been diagnosed with an emotional disturbance and receives special education services was recently suspended from school for 12 school days. A manifestation determination review is held. Which of the following best characterizes the purpose of the review?
   a. To determine if the child should be expelled permanently from the school district
   b. To review the child's need and identify appropriate outside placement options where he could be enrolled moving forward
   c. To update the child's IEP and determine if his goals and services should be changed
   d. To determine if the child's actions were the result of his disability or a failure by the school district to correctly implement the IEP

20. A building leader receives a complaint from a parent that a high school teacher has been recording students without parental permission while they are delivering speeches in their oral argumentation class. If true, this is a violation of the Staff Code of Conduct. The building leader must interview the teacher and investigate the claims. In order to abide by the collective bargaining agreement signed into place by teachers and administrators, the building leader should proceed in which of the following ways?
   a. Reach out to the parent who complained and explain that the teacher will be interviewed and potentially disciplined.
   b. Provide notice of the complaint in writing to the teacher.
   c. Allow the teacher to request union representation during the interview.
   d. Send an email to the union president detailing the charges against the teacher.

21. A physical altercation occurs on the school bus and is captured on bus surveillance video. Two male students are involved and several other students are bystanders in the conflict. The parent of one of the bystanders reaches out to the building leader and indicates that she would like to view the video as her son is upset by what he saw. How should the building leader respond?
   a. The building leader should deny the request as it would be a FERPA violation.
   b. The building leader should allow the parent to view the video in accordance with FERPA guidelines.
   c. The building leader should reach out to the parents of the students involved for permission.
   d. The building leader should deny the request as it violates the principles of IDEA.

22. Which of the following most accurately details the use of restraint in accordance with New York State Department of Education regulations?
   a. The use of all types of physical restraint is prohibited.
   b. Physical restraint may be used as a form of planned intervention in a student's IEP or 504 plan.
   c. The use of prone restraint is prohibited, except when carried out by trained officials.
   d. Physical restraint is permissible in situations where the student demonstrates imminent risk of serious harm to him- or herself or others.

23. A building leader is planning the purchase of new furniture for the cafeteria and auditorium. She wants to ensure that the furniture is durable and visually appealing while also falling within the predetermined budget. What strategy will best help the building leader to reach these goals?
   a. Request that the parent-teacher organization provide funds to support the purchase.
   b. Attempt to bargain with the supplier by offering to purchase items for other areas of the school.
   c. Engage in the competitive offering process with multiple furniture suppliers.
   d. Solicit donations from community members and local businesses.

24. The least restrictive environment can be best understood as which of the following?
   a. Promoting a model of instruction centered around inclusion for students with learning disabilities
   b. Ensuring that students with disabilities are included in the general education classroom to the greatest extent possible
   c. Eliminating behavioral restrictions and allowing students to engage in sensory activities and free play
   d. Removing students from self-contained learning support classrooms regardless of their academic and behavioral needs

25. A new student moves into a high school. He moved to the United States from India in second grade and has demonstrated English proficiency. However, his parents possess limited English proficiency. He gets into an altercation at school, and a parent meeting is scheduled to discuss disciplinary consequences. His parents indicate they would like a translator for the meeting. Which of the following best describes the responsibility of the building leader?

   a. The building leader must provide translation services to the student's parents.
   b. The building leader should request that the parents locate and bring a translator of their choice to the meeting.
   c. The building leader is only responsible for providing translated documents, not oral translation services.
   d. The building leader may ask the student to translate for his parents in lieu of a formal translator.

26. A teacher informs the building leader that a student is an alleged victim of cyberbullying. In accordance with the Dignity for All Students Act, the building leader should take which of the following actions first?

   a. Conduct a thorough investigation to determine if a material incident is present.
   b. Report the claim to the New York State commissioner of education for him or her to review and determine next steps.
   c. Provide protection and accommodations to the complainant, if deemed necessary.
   d. Contact the appropriate law enforcement officials and request that they investigate the allegations.

Answer Key and Explanations for Test #2

Part 1

EXTENDED PERFORMANCE TASK
INSTRUCTIONAL LEADERSHIP FOR STUDENT SUCCESS

Sample Response:

1. A strength is the pass rates for AP exams. When comparing the pass rates of students at Western High School to those of students across the state, a higher percentage of students attained a passing score at Western High School in each of the AP courses offered. Furthermore, many of the rates of passage are significantly higher than those across the state. For example, 73% of students passed the AP World History exam at Western, while only 49% passed the exam in New York State.

2. The number of students from the historically underperforming groups enrolled in AP courses was lower than that of the general student population. Only 5% of students enrolled in AP English Language and Composition were classified as historically underperforming, yet students from this group constitute 46% of the total school population. Beyond the lack of enrollment and exposure is the fact that few of these students perform well on the AP exams. The only exams passed by these students were AP World History and AP Biology, with only one student passing each exam. Furthermore, in the anonymous student survey, fewer than half of the historically underperforming students indicated that they feel confident in their ability to do well in the course (48%) or in their ability to pass the exam (38%).

3. The highest area of need would be increasing student perceptions of success. Only 48% of historically underperforming students feel that they will be successful in their AP courses, and only 38% feel that they will pass the exam. Encouraging enrollment in advanced classes will be futile if students are not equipped to succeed and don't feel confident in their ability to be successful.

4.

Part 1. Why do students feel that they are unable to find success in AP courses? About 46% of students in the school are from historically underperforming backgrounds, yet very few of them are enrolled in advanced courses. One may conclude that the content delivery style of educators in these courses not only leads students to feel that they will be unsuccessful but also deters students from attempting to participate in the classes. Determining what exactly is going on within these classrooms and why students have negative feelings regarding their participation and success may help to encourage confidence in the courses.

Part 2. What professional learning opportunities can be provided to educators to ensure that the higher-level courses are both accessible and attainable to students from historically underperforming groups? In the survey, only 36% of teachers responded that they have received the training necessary to meet the needs of all students. Furthermore, only 47% feel that they can effectively adapt and modify content for students with diverse needs. The school must focus more attention and resources on providing training to teachers so they can incorporate the appropriate scaffolding and modifications for all students. This will help to ensure accessibility to students of every background.

5.

Part 1. The administration should develop a focus group of students from both the historically underperforming groups and the general population of the high school. The group should focus on developing a list of tactics and best practices that could be utilized by teachers and staff to promote a greater rate of student success and comfort when participating in AP courses.

Part 2. The administration should work to determine what the specific areas are within adapting and modifying that teachers require the most assistance with. Furthermore, identifying which groups of students teachers find most difficult to differentiate for would also be helpful. From there a list of professional development opportunities should be provided to teachers so that they can select the options that will be most beneficial to their teaching practice.

6. The school should focus professional development time on introducing strategies to adapt and modify content in a way that benefits diverse learners. Additionally, incorporating professional learning communities through which teachers can discuss the implementation of new strategies and reflect on their effectiveness may prove helpful as well. By encouraging the development of new teaching practices and strategies in the classroom, the school will help students from historically underperforming groups find greater success and build confidence—a notion that will spread throughout the school community.

7. Overall, students from the general population perform well on AP exams. The administration should leverage this truth with their teaching staff to promote teacher buy-in. Also, overall, students performing well indicates that teachers are able to meet the needs of the traditional student. The administration should focus on this strength as well as the fact that by making minor adjustments to their teaching practices, educators can not only promote student confidence but also help all students find success in the classroom and on AP exams.

8. Teachers may be hesitant or unwilling to make changes to their teaching practices. For example, teachers of advanced level courses may feel that modifying or adapting content means reducing the rigor and thus ultimately defeating the purpose of the distinction of enrolling in an AP course. Furthermore, teachers may resist the notion of welcoming lower-level students into their classes. Many educators do not subscribe to the idea that exposing lower-level students to higher expectations and coursework can be beneficial to their long-term academic success.

These challenges can be managed by building an understanding of the real-world application of appropriate modifications and accommodations. Such examples of scaffolding do not necessarily mean that content must be eliminated; they just mean that students are provided with adequate supports so that they can perform at the level of their peers.

SHORTER PERFORMANCE TASK 1
SCHOOL CULTURE AND LEARNING ENVIRONMENT TO PROMOTE EXCELLENCE, EQUITY, AND SOCIAL JUSTICE

Sample Response:

1. The primary issue is that teachers and staff believe they are creating an environment where all students feel safe and valued, while students and their families disagree. The survey results indicate that in all categories, fewer than half of families agreed that equitable practices were utilized at the school. For example, only 38% of families agreed that the school is an accepting environment where all students are made to feel welcome, whereas 91% of teachers and staff agreed with that statement.

2.

Part 1. How can teachers and staff be made to understand the impact of their actions and the school environment on students? Based on the survey results, teachers and staff appear to be unaware of the way students feel. This trend will most likely continue until teachers and staff are made aware of students' feelings and learn effective strategies that can be utilized to better understand those feelings.

Part 2. How often are teachers and staff failing to respond appropriately when students are making disparaging remarks? Educators must ensure that all students feel safe, secure, and valued in the school community. Based on the description and the results of the survey, it is clear that minority students do not feel this way. It is important to determine how frequently and under what circumstances teachers and staff are allowing hateful actions to take place under their watch.

3.

Part 1. Teachers and staff may require additional training to build an understanding of culturally sensitive teaching practices. By doing such training, participants will gain a better understanding of the effects of discriminatory peer behavior on students as well as strategies to promote a more inclusive environment. Some teachers and staff may feel personally attacked by the notion that they are allowing discriminatory behavior to occur. Others may refuse to buy in and attempt to change their practices as they do not believe a problem exists.

Part 2. I would conduct more informal observations to determine how frequently teachers and staff fail to respond to such behavior. Additionally, observing students and teachers and staff in between class periods when poor behavior is more likely to occur would also be helpful. Teachers and staff may feel targeted or under additional pressure if informal observations are increased without warning or seem to focus on certain departments or individuals.

4. One possible finding is that negative behaviors such as disparaging remarks or microaggressions are less likely to occur under the observation of the building principal. Consequently, the increased observations may actually result in a false sense of security that such behaviors are limited, when in reality this is not the case. In this situation it may be helpful to implement a school-wide system of positive behavioral interventions and supports (PBIS) so that students have motivation to engage in positive actions even when they believe no one is watching.

Shorter Performance Task 2
School Culture and Learning Environment to Promote Excellence, Equity, and Social Justice

Sample Response:

1. Students are experiencing increased rates of bullying. The principal has experienced a 62% increase in disciplinary referrals as a result. The bullying occurs in multiple settings across the school building. A culture where bullying occurs and is increasing leads to a negative environment for students, who may avoid coming to school and/or develop negative perceptions about their academic experiences. The school environment should be one where all students feel safe and secure. An environment where bullying runs rampant does not cultivate such an environment.

2.

Part 1. What factors are leading to an increase in bullying and how can they be eliminated? In order to improve the situation, it is important to identify any factors that may be encouraging bullying.

For example, is there a new trend or technology that some students have access to while others do not? Is this disparity causing students to be singled out or bullied?

Part 2. How is the bullying carried out? Are students making comments to others, cyberbullying, or engaging physically with those they are bullying? Understanding the mode of bullying can allow teachers and administrators to better watch out for the behavior as well as develop strategies to prevent it from occurring in the first place.

3.

Part 1. Getting to the root cause of the bullying can prove challenging as students may be unwilling to share the justifications for their behavior. A potential tactic may be to develop small focus groups of students. In these groups, students can work with guidance counselors and other staff members to identify potential issues facing the student body. In a small setting where students are comfortable and familiar with their surroundings, they may be more likely to be honest and up-front.

Part 2. It is important to understand the mode of bullying so that appropriate steps can be taken to manage the behavior in the school setting. The administration should develop a spreadsheet or tool that will allow the mode of bullying to be tracked, and then the data can be analyzed on a regular basis. A potential challenge might be allocating the time to effectively analyze the data and develop a plan to address it.

4. A potential finding is that students are bullying economically disadvantaged children who are forced to wear dirty or unwashed clothing items. A potential action would be the development of a caring closet where staff and members of the community donate gently used clothing items that students in need can "shop" from.

MULTIPLE CHOICE QUESTIONS
INSTRUCTIONAL LEADERSHIP FOR STUDENT SUCCESS

1. B: Fourth-grade students scored better on both the mathematics and ELA assessments than the students in other grades. In mathematics, 32% of fourth graders achieved proficiency, while on the ELA assessment, 31% of them achieved proficiency. Students in the remaining grades achieved proficiency on the ELA assessment at an average rate of 16.4%. On the mathematics assessment, students in the remaining grades attained an average rate of proficiency of 15.3%.

2. C: Although all of the options provided are topics that should be focused on at Valley Elementary, the highest priority must be increasing attendance rates across all grade levels. Students who miss 10 days of school annually beginning in kindergarten will have missed nearly an entire academic year by the time they reach 12th grade. Overall, in the previous school year, 57.28% of students at Valley Elementary missed 10 or more days by the end of the fourth quarter. A direct correlation exists between poor attendance and poor academic performance. Consequently, one can assume that many of the academic problems at the school (e.g., poor assessment scores and grades) are directly related to the lack of time students spend in an academic setting. Therefore, Mr. J and his team must make improving attendance their highest priority before they can strive to improve academic performance.

3. D: During the elementary years, families play a major role in preparing their children for school and ensuring that they are present, on time, and ready to learn. Although providing reward options to students can certainly promote a desire to be in school, if a child's parents are unwilling or unable to bring the child to school, any such reward offerings will be futile. Often times, families, especially those in lower socioeconomic areas such as those near Valley Elementary School, face barriers that prevent them from ensuring their child's attendance at school. For example, a child may come from a single-family household in which the parent works long hours and is not home to ensure that the child makes his or her way to school. Consequently, Mr. J may need to think outside of the box to develop a program that will meet not only his students' needs but their families' as well.

4. C: When one is considering curriculum options, it is important to involve teachers and provide them with the ability to give feedback and engage in the decision-making process. That being said, surveying and involving the staff as a whole may be overwhelming and lead to options that do not meet budgetary or other district and/or building considerations. However, by presenting district-approved options to a focus group of grade-level teacher leaders, the staff as a whole will feel more involved and valued in the decision-making process. Ultimately, this will lead to greater buy-in by the teaching staff and a more successful curriculum implementation process overall.

5. A: Although many issues are evident in the data, Mr. J and his team should be most concerned with the low rate of proficiency on both the ELA and mathematics assessments for sixth-grade students. Only 7% of sixth-grade students demonstrated proficiency in mathematics, while only 9% did in ELA. These scores are far below state averages, which are 45.5% on the mathematics assessment and 44.8% on the ELA assessment. Furthermore, sixth-grade scores are also at a markedly lower performance level than the other grade levels at Valley Elementary. Although proficiency scores are low across grade levels at the school overall, sixth-grade scores are significantly lower. Mr. J and his team must delve into the data and determine why this group of students performed so poorly on the state assessment.

6. B: Mr. J has already acknowledged that a connection between academic performance and attendance exists. Although attendance does present a likely justification for the poor academic performance of many students, Mr. J and his team must work to ensure that other factors such as the curriculum itself or classroom practices of teachers are not also contributing to the situation. Before delving into possible solutions, Mr. J must fully understand the problem itself. For example, 49.7% of students in grades 2-6 passed their math courses in the fourth quarter last school year, which means that 50.3% of the students failed their math courses. In the same quarter, 46.9% the same group of students missed 10 or more days of school. If all of the students who missed 10 or more days failed their math courses, there must also have been some students (50.3% − 46.9% = 3.4% of all students) who missed 9 or fewer days but also failed their math courses. The team must uncover what factors beyond may have led to poor academic performance by the 3.4% of students who failed even though chronic absenteeism was not present in that group.

7. A: In order to perform a cohesive review of Valley Elementary's academic performance and student growth, Mr. J must review additional academic records and assessment scores. When developing a plan of action, Mr. J's team must ensure that they are proceeding in a way that meets all students' needs. To do so, they must be well-informed about the performance of the student body across time and place. For example, the fourth-grade class has performed better academically despite displaying similar levels of chronic absenteeism as the other grade levels. Mr. J must determine if this is a trend that has been displayed by every fourth-grade class annually or if it is just this particular fourth-grade class that has performed better. Understanding such trends will allow Mr. J and his team to make data-informed decisions that will have a greater likelihood of success.

8. D: When one considers the data presented, there appears to be a direct correlation between chronic absenteeism and poor academic performance for many students. This is highlighted when comparing the attendance rates and passing grades in the first quarter versus the fourth quarter of the school year. Although this correlation is evident for students in grades 2, 3, 5, and 6, the same cannot be said for fourth-grade students. For example, 30% of fourth-grade students missed 10 or more days in the first quarter, and 46% of them missed 10 or more days in the fourth quarter alone. Despite these relatively high numbers of chronic absenteeism, 90% of fourth graders passed ELA in the first quarter and 72% passed in the fourth quarter. Ultimately, these numbers do not demonstrate the same level of correlation as the other grade levels.

9. B: Although each of the steps indicated here could be included within a successful five-year plan aimed to improve both attendance and academic performance, communicating with families to determine their individual needs is the initial step that must be taken. Until Mr. J and his team better understand why students are chronically absent and what steps can be taken at home to better facilitate higher attendance rates, implementing a new curriculum or attendance programs will most likely lead to little success. The team must attempt to determine the root cause of the attendance problem before embarking on initiatives that may or may not meet the needs of their students.

INSTRUCTIONAL LEADERSHIP FOR STUDENT SUCCESS

10. B: The curriculum utilized in the school is largely outdated and has been deemed ineffective. For the school to ensure greater student progress and overall academic growth, it is essential to provide materials that reflect the latest pedagogical trends and content. One can assume that older materials do not fully align with current state learning standards. Furthermore, the use of outdated materials and curriculum is undoubtedly encouraging educators at the school to rely on more traditional, lecture-based delivery methods. Overall, teachers throughout the school are supportive of a potential transition to a new curriculum model, with 92% of survey respondents acknowledging the inadequacies of their materials and 93% interested in exploring new materials.

11. D: By breaking student assessment data down by various demographic factors such as economic and disability status, Ms. B and her team would be able to analyze the information at a high level of granularity. For example, if upon reviewing the data, Ms. B identifies that economically disadvantaged students are consistently unable to meet projected performance levels, she can ensure that improvement initiatives are focused on that particular group. This ensures that valuable time and resources are not wasted on students who are already experiencing appropriate rates of growth on assessments and beyond.

12. D: Throughout her walk-throughs, Ms. B observed a limited amount of student-centered learning. As mentioned in the description, Ms. B understands that teacher-centered instruction often leads to a lack of student engagement and less academic growth overall. One of Ms. B's goals is the promotion of further student-centered learning, but such activities were observed in only three out of 37 classroom walk-throughs. During post-observation conferences, Ms. B should provide encouragement and feedback to teachers to help them implement student-centered activities. This one-on-one guidance will promote the goals of Ms. B and her team.

13. C: Although 87% of the teaching staff indicated their openness to incorporating new teaching methods into their classroom practice, only 38% expressed interest in joining the team that will research and determine which curriculum should be incorporated across the building. Ms. B can better promote support for the curriculum development team by ensuring that the teaching staff understands that membership will not require additional work performed outside of regular school hours. Many educators struggle to keep up with the demands required of their position and would be hesitant to take on additional work. By allowing the team to work during professional development hours and the school day when substitute coverage is available, Ms. B will make joining the team more desirable for many members of her staff.

14. B: Based on the walk-through data, students in ELA courses are more likely to engage in academic discourse and be exposed to student-centered learning activities. Student-centered learning occurred in two of the 17 ELA classes and only in one of the 20 math classes. Academic discourse occurred in only three of the 37 classroom walk-throughs, and two of these instances occurred in the 17 ELA classes, while only one occurred in the 20 math classes. Although this lack of student-centered learning and academic discourse is problematic in both subject areas, students are more likely to engage in these tasks within their ELA courses.

15. D: The primary goal of the changes within the school is to ensure a higher rate of proficiency on state assessments. Although Ms. B plans to focus her efforts in part on the correlation between student-centered learning strategies and academic performance, her primary concern should be the overall outcome of those actions. By incorporating more effective teaching practices and updated curriculum, Ms. B can expect overall student performance on state assessments to increase. Consequently, improved student performance on state assessments is the most helpful factor in determining the overall effectiveness of the newly incorporated modifications.

16. A: Walk-through data indicates that the teaching staff largely relies on teacher-centered instructional practices; teacher-centered practices were being used in approximately 65% of classrooms. Although teacher-delivered content is at times necessary, research has proven that student-centered instructional activities, in which students hold greater responsibility for their own learning, are more engaging and effective in promoting growth and mastery. Many teachers at the school report a willingness to incorporate new strategies (87%) yet are unsure how to do so successfully; only 6% of respondents are confident that they have the skills to incorporate new approaches. Consequently, professional development opportunities on the use of such strategies will allow for greater improvement of instructional strategies across the building.

17. C: When Ms. B introduces new strategies and expectations to the staff, it is essential that she include justification and research to support her decision to institute change, especially for those teachers who are hesitant to alter their teaching practices. Since the majority of the educators in the building have been teaching for over 10 years, Ms. B must realize that many staff members feel that they are unable to make such changes, and are unsure that these changes would be positive if made. However, by providing real-world examples of student growth, Ms. B may be able to find a greater degree of success in promoting the importance of making such instructional modifications.

INSTRUCTIONAL LEADERSHIP FOR STUDENT SUCCESS

18. D: Although all of the options presented here are worrisome, Mr. S should be most concerned that overall proficiency rates of 11th-grade students in ELA have declined over the last five years. In general, all proficiency rates are significantly below the most recent statewide proficiency rates of 81%. Furthermore, student assessment scores do not appear to be trending upwards. In fact, for each of the subgroups studied, scores one year ago were either about the same or lower than they were five years ago. Mr. S must determine why test scores have decreased and what he and his team can do to support his students to ensure a greater degree of academic growth.

19. C: Only 32% of teachers report that they are aware of differentiation strategies that will meet the needs of their students. Furthermore, only 28% of teachers are confident in their ability to effectively differentiate in their classrooms. That being said, most teachers understand that they can improve in this area but are unsure how to proceed. Consequently, it is important to provide training to teachers that focuses on differentiation techniques that are relevant and effective for the ability levels of their students as well as applicable within teacher content areas. Raising awareness and providing training will help teachers gradually gain comfort and confidence in utilizing new strategies, and ultimately, they will understand the importance of utilizing such practices in their classrooms. The majority of teachers surveyed indicated a willingness to try new strategies (66%) as well as an understanding that their differentiation practices can be improved upon (88%). Mr. S must focus on teaching his staff how to utilize differentiation practices effectively as many of them are already open to doing so.

20. C: The overall number of students who receive special education services at Woodsen High School has increased 157.7% over the last five years. Meanwhile, the number of ELL students who receive special education services has increased 5,000% over the last five years. Given the rapid increase of ELLs in the school, as well as the increase in ELLs who have been identified as having disabilities, steps must be taken to ensure that students are properly identified. Mr. S must focus professional development opportunities on strategies and procedures aimed to build understanding of the proper identification of those students whose native language is not English. This will ensure that students who require special education services have them and those who simply need additional support with their English language acquisition also receive what they need.

21. B: By providing teaching staff with the ability to consider their responses and identify an area of focus, Mr. S is encouraging reflective practices that will benefit the teachers and their students alike. Learning to differentiate in a meaningful way can be overwhelming for many teachers. Breaking the practice into simple, streamlined tasks can make the process more accessible and ensure a greater degree of success in the classroom. When time permits, teachers can further unpack their focus area and explore new ways to incorporate it effectively into their daily classroom routines.

22. A: During the last school year, ELLs were 18% of the total student body population. However, ELLs accounted for 38% of students with IEPs. This means that a greater number of ELLs are diagnosed with a disability than would be expected from a statistical perspective. Across the United States, it is common to see this misidentification of ELLs. A number of reasons exist for this discrepancy, with one of the largest being the complexity of the tests used to measure student IQ and learning capabilities. The language barrier often makes it difficult for school psychologists and others to determine the true abilities of ELLs. Ultimately, the misidentification of ELLs is problematic, as identifying a student with a disability can be both unnecessary and stigmatizing. Furthermore, by identifying a student with a disability and providing services based on that need, the student may be missing out on the assistance that he or she truly requires to be successful.

23. D: Although determining the presence of barriers experienced by both students with IEPs as well as ELLs is important in bringing about growth for those two groups, the school is experiencing below average assessment performance overall. Mr. S is working to develop a plan in which all staff are trained in differentiation strategies to ensure that the needs of all students are met. In order to achieve his goal of improving assessment proficiency rates, Mr. S must be sure that differentiation alone will bring about these results. Thus, the team must consider any additional strategies that may also bring about academic gain in the area of assessment scores.

24. B: The goal of the program is to increase student proficiency results through improving the use of differentiation in the classroom. Improved differentiation could take years to be seen in test scores. Furthermore, increased assessment scores alone would not show that the differentiation program is effective, as score improvements could have other causes. To determine the effectiveness of the program after the first year, Mr. S must look at how well the teachers have implemented differentiation strategies. By analyzing walk-through data, Mr. S and his team can determine if teachers are effectively using the practices in their classrooms that have been promoted during professional development opportunities. As teachers grow more comfortable and confident in their use of the strategies, student academic performance will increase. However, Mr. S must first ensure that the new strategies are being used and used effectively before attempting to draw connections to academic performance.

25. C: In order to ensure that the needs of ELLs are being met, the school must ensure that the ESL program is well-developed and effective. The staff must be prepared to provide appropriate instruction to students and provide the tools needed to reach English proficiency, even if that process occurs at a slower pace than peers in the program. Furthermore, all applicable members of the team must be trained and well-versed in referral and evaluation protocols, especially as it applies to ELLs. Finally, Mr. S must work to ensure that classroom instruction overall is effective at meeting the needs of all students. This is where differentiation strategies come into play. Conversely, promoting the belief that under identifying ELLs in need of special education services is a better alternative to the overidentification of such students will not ensure equity within the special education program. Many schools prolong the process of identifying ELLs with disabilities out of fear that the services are unnecessary, and this ultimately causes more harm than good. Mr. S must promote an environment in which ELLs are effectively evaluated for special education services and provided with the program that best meets their needs regardless of the outcome of the evaluation.

SCHOOL CULTURE AND LEARNING ENVIRONMENT TO PROMOTE EXCELLENCE, EQUITY, AND SOCIAL JUSTICE

26. C: Ms. L is concerned not only with the increase of disciplinary referrals but also the fact that Hispanic or Latino students are disproportionately involved in disciplinary actions in comparison to other demographic groups. When a specific demographic group is apparently targeted and/or involved in behaviors that violate the student code of conduct, it is essential that that the administrative team and teaching staff work to identify the reasons behind this outcome as well as develop a solution to remedy the issue. The PBIS program is being instituted to combat both rising disciplinary problems and the disproportionate involvement of a singular demographic as well as improve the school culture and learning environment. Consequently, Ms. L must be able to determine if the program effectively reduces the higher rate of disciplinary referrals involving Hispanic or Latino students.

27. D: In order to be effective, a PBIS program must include a multitiered system of support for students. This ensures that the program meets the needs of the entire student body and provides additional behavioral support for students who need greater assistance. Tier 1 should include universal supports designed to meet the needs of the majority of students. Within this tier, clear behavioral expectations must be outlined and positive behavior rewarded. Tier 2 supports provide additional assistance for students who may require slightly more support than their peers. For example, social skills groups may be incorporated for the students who struggle in this area. The final tier, Tier 3, includes intensive supports for students who demonstrate major behavioral challenges. Behavior intervention plans may be put into place for students whose behaviors demonstrate needs that fall under this category of support.

28. A: Based on the disciplinary data, Hispanic or Latino students are both referred to the principal and ultimately disciplined at a higher rate than other demographic groups. Hispanic or Latino students were approximately 39% of the school population last year yet constituted nearly 70% of the disciplinary referrals. Furthermore, the survey data reflects that parents are aware of these discrepancies. For example, only 17% of families agree that the school punishes all students fairly, and only 22% believe that the school culture is positive and welcoming. Based on this information,

Ms. L can deduce that the disproportionate disciplinary rates of Hispanic or Latino students has led parents to feel that their children are being treated unfairly and are not welcomed into the school community.

29. C: Although student disciplinary referrals have increased across demographic groups, Hispanic or Latino students are a disproportionate percentage of all such referrals. By incorporating training for staff that includes culturally responsive practices, Ms. L can better ensure that the needs of all students are met. By working to meet the needs of students from various cultural backgrounds, the staff can ensure that students from all backgrounds feel valued and respected. Students who feel as if they, and their traditions, are part of the school community may be less likely to engage in certain poor behaviors and attention-seeking tactics. Ultimately, focused training will help staff better understand the cultural practices of students from various backgrounds and better confront any misunderstandings or biases that may lead to increased disciplinary referrals for certain demographics.

30. D: Ultimately, each of the concerns outlined is problematic and must be addressed by Ms. L and her team. However, the fact that one student group is disproportionately represented among the total number of disciplinary referrals and is most likely to be punished with either detention or suspension in comparison to other demographic groups is problematic. Hispanic or Latino students were approximately 39% of the population last year yet were nearly 70% of disciplinary referrals. Additionally, 90% of Hispanic or Latino students who were referred to the principal received either detention or suspension in comparison to approximately 77% of students from other demographic groups. This data indicates that Ms. L and her team must address discrepancies in both the handling of disciplinary referrals and the ultimate punishment of students from such groups to ensure that treatment of all students is fair and equitable.

31. C: In the parent survey, families indicated an overall concern with the school culture and disciplinary procedures at McDonald Elementary. It is important to ensure that families feel as if they are valued members of the school community and that their opinions and ideas regarding their children's education matter. Additionally, families may have unique perspectives about their children and background that will be beneficial in developing and promoting a welcoming environment for all students. By holding monthly feedback sessions with building administration, the school can allow families to make their voices heard and also provide meaningful contributions to any plans that Ms. L and her team plan to implement to improve the school culture. Although holding additional conferences, especially in the evening, may be helpful as well, typically teacher contract obligations dictate the number of conference days that educators are required to work, especially when those conferences fall outside of traditional school/work hours.

32. C: Given the somewhat sensitive implications of the data, it is important that Ms. L presents the information in an objective way and encourages teacher input in rectifying the issue. If Ms. L presents the data in an accusatory fashion or provides a solution that may not take into account the teachers' opinions or experiences, she will be less likely to attain teacher buy-in or support of her initiatives. By presenting the data objectively and allowing staff to develop their own conclusions and contribute ideas that may help to reduce the disproportions in the data, Ms. L will help her staff feel more valued, and they will be more willing to make changes to their practice. Additionally, the staff may have insights into the issue that Ms. L is unaware of and that could be overlooked should she propose forced solutions or justifications for the data.

33. B: Although all information may be helpful in determining the overall effectiveness of the PBIS program, the ultimate goal of the initiative is to reduce disciplinary referrals, especially those that disproportionately impact Hispanic or Latino students, as well as to improve the overall school culture. Consequently, Ms. L and her team will need data that details disciplinary referrals at the beginning of the school year before the program was implemented and data from during the program and the close of the school year. This information will assist the team in determining if disciplinary referrals are decreasing as a result of the newly implemented PBIS program.

SCHOOL CULTURE AND LEARNING ENVIRONMENT TO PROMOTE EXCELLENCE, EQUITY, AND SOCIAL JUSTICE

34. D: Ultimately, Mr. V may need to introduce new initiatives to ensure that the school climate is improving; however, he must first thoroughly consider the initiatives he has already introduced. Although based on the results of the most recent staff survey Mr. V's initiatives do not appear to have shifted teacher perception in a positive trajectory, the policies may simply take a greater amount of time to impact staff. Furthermore, Mr. V should not move on to the use of new strategies until he has ensured that he has adequately analyzed the impact of his current initiatives on the school climate. By adding additional initiatives, Mr. V may overwhelm the staff and/or be unable to determine which initiative is actually evoking a positive change within the building.

35. B: Based on the results of the two surveys and historical knowledge of staff perceptions, Mr. V should understand that it is important to present information that may be sensitive in a manner that is not seen as aggressive or targeting specific teachers. In general, one would assume that most teachers at Britton are in their position because they care about their students and want to create positive change and academic growth for them. Consequently, by reiterating to the staff the importance of meeting students' needs and connecting with the staff on a shared level of concern regarding student improvement and well-being, Mr. V could have more successfully transitioned into discussing strategies that help to improve communication and relationships overall.

36. A: In his email to staff, Mr. V identifies a number of changes in both practice and mindset. He outlines the establishment of both a school leadership team and a community leadership team to facilitate staff and community involvement and relationship building. The development of both teams, although they are not problematic in and of themselves, may lead to a number of issues for Mr. V. In the staff survey sent out prior to the start of the school year, 76% of staff reported that certain teachers are treated preferentially and are provided with opportunities that others are not. In his email plan, Mr. V does not detail that all members of the team will be chosen in an equitable manner nor does he provide the opportunity for teachers to volunteer for the position. Mr. V simply states that members will be chosen by the principal. This decision may indicate to staff that their opinions from the survey are not heard or valued, which already seems to have happened as the percentage of staff members who feel that certain teachers are treated preferentially increased from 76% in the old survey to 81% in the new one from the end of the first quarter.

37. B: Mr. V must be most concerned with the hesitancy of his staff to buy into his newly proposed initiatives. The other answers are issues that existed before Mr. V's tenure began at Britton. Mr. V surveyed staff and identified a number of primary issues of concern that he hoped to rectify in an attempt to improve the school climate. Consequently, Mr. V should be most concerned that the staff seem unwilling or unable to use the tools provided to adapt and grow. Although the initiatives are still new and not a great deal of time has passed since their initial implementation, Mr. V must pay close attention to the primary issues identified to determine if any improvements are being made or if he should adapt the initiatives or develop new ones.

38. C: Although concerns do exist regarding the hesitancy of teaching staff to reach out to the families of their students, most of the issues with the school environment stem from the interpersonal relationships among staff members and between staff members and administrators.

Mr. V introduced various initiatives throughout the school year with the aim of improving communication between administrators and staff as well as increasing workplace morale overall. The survey sent out at the end of the first quarter indicated that Mr. V's policies were not proving fully successful in the short term. As with any such change, improvements can take time to manifest. Therefore, Mr. V must review survey data from staff members at the end of the school year to determine if improvements have occurred. This will help to guide future initiatives and changes for the next school year.

39. D: The behavior demonstrated by Mr. K should be addressed as quickly as possible to prevent any further escalation or negative reactions by other staff members engaging in the training. Mr. V should discreetly pull Mr. K aside at an appropriate time to discuss any concerns he may have regarding the training as well as to reiterate the professional responsibilities of teachers at Britton. By addressing the behavior of Mr. K in a discreet manner, Mr. V can reduce the likelihood of a public spectacle in which greater attention is drawn to the situation. Furthermore, it is important to deal individually with the perpetrator of the behavior so that staff does not feel wrongfully accused of actions they did not engage in.

40. B: In general, the teaching profession is characterized by a lack of time during the school day to complete clerical tasks such as collaborating with coworkers and communicating with parents. Based on the results of the survey completed at the end of the first quarter, 85% of teachers feel that they lack the time to communicate effectively with parents as well as to meet with members of their school-based team, and that is unlikely to have changed by the end of the year. By organizing the master schedule so that staff members have additional time to complete these tasks, Mr. V will not only improve staff morale but also encourage greater communication with families and between members of the staff.

41. D: Overall staff perceptions of the school climate have not changed significantly over the course of the first quarter, despite the initiatives introduced by Mr. V. However, despite the lack of significant change, some positive improvements were indicated. For example, prior to the start of the school year, only 4% of staff felt that the administration communicated effectively with teachers. At the end of the first quarter, 8% felt that members of the administrative staff communicated effectively. Although this is not a large difference, it still is a positive change potentially brought about by Mr. V's policy changes.

Part 2

Extended Performance Task
Developing Human Capital to Improve Faculty and Staff Effectiveness and Student Achievement

1. Sample Response:

The most significant human capital concern is the four teachers who are identified as ineffective. One ELA teacher, one social studies teacher, and two noncore teachers fall into the ineffective category based on their evaluation data. Ineffective teachers are unable to educate students in a way that promotes overall mastery and academic success. As principal, it is essential to ensure that all students in the building have access to effective educators who meet the needs of students.

To be sure that the evaluation data was not a fluke or misrepresentation of the teachers' abilities or the result of another factor, I would review personnel information as well as previous observation and assessment data. If it appears that the teachers are in fact ineffective, or have demonstrated an inability to progress their craft, I would schedule a meeting with each individual to discuss the implementation of an improvement plan. Throughout the remainder of the school year, I would set up biweekly meetings to discuss goals, progress, and areas of need.

2. Sample Response:

First, I would revitalize the induction program at Crestview High School. The scenario details that 86% of new teachers leave Crestview within three years. It is important, especially given that many of the teachers are experienced and presumably could be retiring at some point in the near future, to focus on the development and retention of new teachers. Although the data provided does not indicate a reason for the loss of these teachers, a comprehensive induction program that provides a variety of services such as a school mentor and open lines of communication with the administration could prove helpful at reducing the number of losses.

Second, I would attempt to institute changes that reduce the workload of staff. In the survey, 75% of staff said they feel overwhelmed by their workload. Teachers who are overwhelmed and unable to balance home and work responsibilities will be less likely to provide effective instruction in the classroom. Such feelings also often lead to a reduction in workplace morale. To accomplish this goal, I would analyze expectations and requirements of staff that may be unnecessary. For example, as opposed to holding a biweekly staff meeting that requires staff to stay after school, I would develop a weekly communication that details must-know information and important dates that must be communicated.

3. Sample Response:

The first year of teaching can be a challenging time for many educators. Ms. G requires support

and may also need time to build confidence, especially during walk-throughs and formal evaluations, which can be nerve-racking for even the most seasoned educators. Based on the observation data, Ms. G seemingly lacked content knowledge, failed to control the classroom environment, and utilized lackluster questioning techniques.

In order to provide support to Ms. G and to help her grow as an educator, I would ensure that she has a department-level mentor that can guide her with content-based concerns and other challenging aspects of the teaching profession. I would also meet with Ms. G to determine what assistance she requires to be more successful, and together we would develop a plan of action to bring about professional success. To ensure that Ms. G is improving as the year progresses, I would continue to conduct formal and informal evaluations, some planned and some unplanned.

4. Sample Response:

Based on the observation data, Mr. P is a highly effective teacher who possesses a high level of content knowledge as well as the ability to engage his class in higher-level thinking skills. Despite his proficiencies, it is important to consider the fact that everyone can improve. Consequently, I would discuss both the successes of his lesson as well how he may be able to promote even further levels of growth with his students. I would also ask Mr. P if he would consider serving as a mentor for Ms. G, who is struggling in her role as a first-year teacher. Beyond that request, I would consider recommending Mr. P to serve on various leadership committees where other members of the staff could learn from his aptitudes.

SHORTER PERFORMANCE TASK
FAMILY AND COMMUNITY ENGAGEMENT

Sample Response:

1. One issue that could benefit from family, caregiver, and community involvement is the fact that although 28 students are enrolling in the program, the special education director has developed relationships with only four businesses. Collectively, these businesses are able to take in only 10 students. Consequently, many of the students in the program may be unable to participate in the co-op opportunity due to lack of availability.
A second issue is that the available opportunities may not be of interest to all students and must be diversified. Many of the positions offered are similar in nature despite being in different establishments. The team requires additional community support so that new relationships can be forged and new opportunities can be developed for students in the program.
1. These issues could benefit from the involvement of families, caregivers, and community members in different ways. Developing meaningful relationships with businesses in the community will increase co-op opportunities for students. The district will be able to ensure that each student interested in the program has multiple options to choose from. Providing more diverse opportunities for students will increase the likelihood that students will be matched with a position that is interesting and enjoyable.
2. I would first reach out to additional businesses and detail the abilities of students in the program. I would also highlight the fact that pay, although helpful, is not a requirement, as the overall goal of the program is to increase the skills and abilities of participants. I would also contact businesses that have worked with similar programs in other districts to learn more about their experiences and the benefits of such a program for both the employers and co-op participants so that I could share this information with potential participants. Additionally, I would survey potential co-op participants and their families to determine the types of employers and positions that may be of interest to them. These results would help guide the team as they decide which employers to pursue connections with.
3. One challenge I might encounter would be the hesitancy of employers to hire individuals with cognitive delays. Employers may be unsure that such individuals will be capable of carrying out the work required with various positions. I would work with families and previous teachers to develop resumes that detail the capabilities of student applicants. I would also propose that students have informal interviews with employers to assuage any concerns.
Another challenge may be the fear that students will require a level of support that is unattainable by the management team at the business. To combat these fears, I would assign paraprofessionals to each business so that they may help oversee student work and serve as intermediaries between the student participant and the management team.

MULTIPLE CHOICE QUESTIONS
FAMILY AND COMMUNITY ENGAGEMENT

1. A: In order for the team to develop the internship program and provide multiple opportunities for students to engage with, it is important to work with business owners in the community and determine what interests or needs they may have. It is very possible that businesses may have an unmet need that students at the school are able to fulfill. For example, Mr. F learns that a number of students are interested in careers in the field of education. He reaches out to a local daycare and discovers that it is unable to locate individuals to work in its childcare rooms during the early morning hours. The daycare is having trouble attracting employees who are willing to accept its current wage offerings, yet it does not want to increase the price of childcare for already enrolled families. By developing a partnership with the school, the daycare facility would be able to meet its employment needs, and the school's needs of providing education-related experiences would also be met.

2. C: One of the primary goals of any academic institution is to promote an environment that is welcoming and inclusive of all students. Children who are anxious or fearful about attending school, like those from the 86% of families that expressed nervousness, historically demonstrate lower attendance rates and poorer academic performance overall. Consequently, it is essential that Mr. F ensures that he do all in his power to reduce negative perceptions regarding the upcoming school year. Although change can be difficult for both children and adults, Mr. F and his team can take steps to ensure a reduction in negative views regarding the school year as well as an effective transition process overall.

3. B: Mr. F should meet with the administration from the two previous schools to determine how they effectively involved parents and guardians in the school community. The survey results indicate that 76% of families surveyed feel that their previous school valued and supported them. Mr. F should reach out to these individuals to identify what policy decisions they incorporated to attain this sentiment among families at their school. He can then use this information to guide his action plan and provide future training opportunities for his own staff.

4. D: Although all of the strategies listed may prove helpful in assuaging the concerns of students and their families regarding the upcoming transition, holding orientations provides the best alternative. A back-to-school orientation will allow students the opportunities to walk through their schedules, meet their teachers, and learn more about what the new school year will actually look like. By allowing students access to the school and district plans prior to the first day, Mr. F and his team will be giving them a better understanding of what to expect and a sense of familiarity with their new learning environment.

5. C: Mr. F has access to demographic data for both Johnstown and Dougherty High Schools. However, as a result of natural matriculation as well as new enrollments from outside of both initial school districts, the data from last year is most likely inaccurate. Access to updated demographic data will help ensure that Mr. F and his team are prepared to meet the needs of all students. For example, enrollment of ELLs or students with Individualized Education Programs (IEPs) may have increased since last school year. This shift may necessitate the hiring of additional teachers certified in those particular areas.

6. B: Regardless of the location of initial enrollment, all students attending Central High this upcoming school year will experience shifts in their school environment. Students coming from Johnstown High are accustomed to an environment of limited diversity, where 94% of the student body was white, and only 0.5% were ELLs. Conversely, the student body at Dougherty was far more diverse, and 22% of the students were ELLs. Consequently, all students will be exposed to a different learning dynamic that encompasses new students as well as potentially new cultural and linguistic backgrounds. Mr. F and the leadership team must be prepared to support students through this process to ensure that all members of the student body feel included and valued.

7. D: Specifically scheduling students into classes based on their demographic group is counterproductive to promoting acceptance and understanding. Placing students into groups where they may easily assimilate means that Central will be more likely to have issues regarding acceptance of those who come from different backgrounds. The school should instead focus on ways to build an understanding of student differences and encourage the valuation of students' cultural backgrounds. The alternative options are effective ways that both students and staff can better comprehend and appreciate differences within the student body.

8. A: The process by which Mr. F plans to select student members of the school leadership committee is flawed. In his notes, Mr. F indicates his desire to invite student leaders from clubs and organizations within each school to serve on the committee, as well as captains of each sport team. Although these students will most likely serve as willing and vocal participants, generally speaking, students from these categories are already involved in their school-wide community and enjoy engaging with their peers. By including only students from these categories, Mr. F is missing the opportunity to pull in the opinions and feedback of students who tend to lack school-wide engagement and often slip through the cracks. Also, it is more than likely that students who do not have the support of a team or preexisting club or organization will struggle more with the transition to a new academic environment. Mr. F must work to include such students in the committee if he wishes to ensure a smooth transition period for all students.

9. B: The most likely barrier facing Mr. F is the lack of desire among business owners to participate. Unless specific entities have a stake in the initiative (e.g., have children in the district or another factor), participation in the program or committee may seem cumbersome or not worth the effort. For example, businesses may worry that students working in internship roles will require additional oversight or more support than can be provided. Mr. F must work with these individuals and organizations to demonstrate the benefits that will come from participating in the program.

10. C: The process of improving the appeal of an open house will have the greatest chance of promoting family involvement across the student body. In most districts, open houses at the high school level are poorly attended in comparison to elementary and middle school offerings. By scheduling student performances and promoting a greater degree of student involvement in general, or by offering incentives such as food or coffee trucks, Mr. F may be able to encourage greater participation by high school families. Although the alternatives may encourage some families to engage further in the school community, by virtue of their design, they do not have the ability to reach the number of families that an improved open house, an event which all building families are invited to, would.

OPERATIONAL SYSTEMS, DATA SYSTEMS, AND LEGAL GUIDELINES TO SUPPORT ACHIEVEMENT OF SCHOOL GOALS

11. D: Although images and anecdotes may be helpful in engaging the school board and community members in attendance, the use of graphs detailing attendance rates before and after the initiatives were introduced will be most effective in ensuring the understanding of the data. This strategy will provide a helpful visual aid that will allow school board members to determine the overall rate of improvement as a result of the initiatives. While statewide data may also be pertinent in building an understanding of attendance rates overall, it is not immediately helpful in showing the effects of district-wide attendance initiatives on district attendance.

12. C: Given the academic relevance of the academic competition, it is important that the building leader approves the field trip if fiscally possible. As long as funds are available in an appropriate budget category, the school board is able to authorize the transfer of funds to support the costs associated with the competition. This is the most effective strategy to provide students with the opportunity while maintaining fiscal responsibility for the school and economic equity for students who may not be able to afford the costs associated with the trip. Although some may argue that using deficit spending is also an appropriate response, borrowing money from the next year's budget is not a fiscally responsible practice. Ultimately, unexpected events or expenses could reduce the amount of funds available, which could place the school and district in a negative light, especially if an external audit were to take place.

13. B: As the world has grown more technologically advanced, and students of younger ages have become increasingly involved on social media platforms and online in general, the need to provide instruction in digital citizenship has also grown. Without explicit instruction, many middle school children lack the maturity to understand how to engage with the internet in an appropriate manner that supports their emotional and general well-being. Digital citizenship programming at the middle school level should focus on teaching appropriate communication, the prevention and recognition of cyberbullying, and the protection of secure information. Although the outcome of meeting up with an individual that one connected with through social media platforms is often poor and can result in devastating consequences, news stories detailing these occasions may not be developmentally appropriate for middle school students. News stories may include graphic or inappropriate details that younger students may find upsetting. Such an activity would be more appropriate for high school students.

14. B: The New York State Education Learning Technology Grant is designed overall to support the development of programs that use various learning technologies to personalize and increase access to rigorous academic programming. The grant period lasts a maximum of two and a half years, but any funding after year one is reliant upon performance and availability of funds from the New York State Legislature. There are different requirements for the application process depending upon the type and location of the school district. In general, school districts may apply either individually or in consortium with other school districts, with the exception of the Big Four public school districts that are required to apply individually. When applying, a two-and-a-half-year budget, in which the allocation of funds is detailed, must be included. Any funds provided must be used within the year they have been allotted and may not be carried over.

15. A: New York State Education Law Section 807 requires that all public and private schools hold eight evacuation drills and four lockdown drills. The drills must be conducted between September 1 and June 30. Furthermore, at least eight of the total drills must be conducted by December 31. Additionally, schools must conduct two additional drills if summer school is held at the building. Conducting drills is an essential practice by which both students and staff can be better prepared for emergency situations.

16. A: A district-wide school safety plan must include an overview of the policies and procedures that will be undertaken in the event of both implied and direct threats of violence. This should include the way in which such threats by students, staff, and school visitors will be handled at a district level. The plan should also include how the district will handle threats of self-harm or suicide by students. The plan must be reviewed annually and approved by the school board no later than September 1. The district must provide the opportunity for students, families, and the community at-large to comment on the plan for a minimum of 30 days prior to the formal adoption of the plan. Upon approval, the district must post the plan to the district web page, as well as submit the plan to the New York State Education Department.

17. D: To ensure that the water used in school is clean and free of contaminants such as lead, New York State requires compliance testing every three years. Schools must collect samples at all water outlets that have the potential to be utilized for drinking or cooking purposes. If the collected samples exceed the response-to-action level of 5 micrograms of lead per liter, a number of steps must be undertaken by the school. Any water outlets that may potentially be utilized for cooking or drinking must be immediately taken out of service. Outlets that are used for cleaning or handwashing may continue to operate but only with proper signage indicating that such water may not be used for cooking or drinking purposes. Schools must also offer drinking water free of charge to students and staff until the situation has been rectified. Finally, schools must report levels to the appropriate health department within one business day of receiving results.

18. B: Based on the evidence presented, the building leader has reasonable suspicion that the student is in possession of contraband. Students have a degree of protection under the Fourth Amendment to be free from unreasonable searches and seizures. However, the protections provided are limited in comparison to those provided outside of the school setting. According to the 1985 Supreme Court ruling *New Jersey v. T.L.O.*, although Fourth Amendment protections extend to students in schools, searches performed by school officials are subjected to fewer restrictions. For example, a school official performing a search requires only reasonable suspicion, not the probable cause required of law enforcement officials. Consequently, most school districts institute policies for searches that allow only school officials to search students, as SROs, who are typically sworn officers of the law employed by local police departments, must have probable cause to search.

19. D: A manifestation determination review (MDR) is held when a child with an Individualized Education Program (IEP) is suspended for more than 10 school days. The purpose of the MDR is to determine if the behavior is the result of the student's disability and/or the failure of the school district to effectively implement the IEP as written. If through the course of the MDR, the team determines that the behavior was in fact a result of the student's disability, the team must complete a functional behavior analysis (FBA) designed to determine the reasoning behind a child's behavior. Based on the results of an FBA, the team may develop a behavior intervention plan to meet the needs of the student.

20. C: The building leader must be certain that any meetings or disciplinary proceedings are carried out in compliance with the collective bargaining agreement. A collective bargaining agreement is an important document that governs relations between teachers and administrators. Such a document may include teacher expectations and rights, guidelines regarding disciplinary proceedings, and expected work hours and after-school responsibilities. The best way to ensure compliance with the collective bargaining agreement is to provide the impacted teacher with the ability to request union representation throughout the investigative process. This ensures that no violations of the collective bargaining agreement occur throughout the interview and investigation or when any disciplinary measures are administered.

21. A: The building leader should deny the parents access to the video as it constitutes a FERPA violation. FERPA, or the Family Educational Rights and Privacy Act, is a piece of federal legislation that protects the education records of students. The act is designed to ensure that, in certain situations, parents have some control over whether their child's education records can be disclosed and have the ability to request an amendment to those records. Additionally, parents are allowed access to education records that are maintained by the school and are directly related to their child. Although the child in question does appear on the bus video, he is not directly involved in the conflict. Furthermore, the video may include sensitive information about the students involved that may not be released. Consequently, the video should not be released to the parent of the bystander child.

22. D: Physical restraint should only be used in situations where the student demonstrates an imminent risk of serious physical harm to him- or herself or others. Staff involved in restraint must undergo formal training to ensure that the process is carried out correctly and in a way that does not pose harm to the student involved. There are many guidelines that govern the use of restraint in schools. For example, the least restrictive method should be used, and the student's ability to breathe or communicate should never be restricted. Additionally, students should never be restrained in the prone position, and parents must be notified if their child has been restrained. Furthermore, restraint should never be utilized by school officials as a planned intervention within a student's IEP or 504 plan to control behavior.

23. C: The New York State Advertising Law requires that purchases over $20,000 be subject to competitive bidding or offering. The competitive offering process will allow the building leader to ensure that she is provided with the lowest price while also considering the value of the product offered. In order to engage in the process, the building leader and/or her purchasing agent must create and post a public request for proposals for the furniture items, evaluate any responses received, and then make a decision based on the best price or value. The values used to select the winning offer must be quantifiable or objective, or there must be a written justification that explains the reason for the choice.

24. B: The least restrictive environment (LRE) is a key component of the Individuals with Disabilities Education Act (IDEA.) It is important to recognize that, as with other components of the IEP, the LRE must be considered on an individual level. What may be considered restrictive for one child may be considered inclusive for another. Ultimately, the purpose of the LRE is to ensure that students with disabilities are educated in the general education classroom alongside typically developing peers to the greatest possible degree.

25. A: Federal law, including the Civil Rights Act of 1964 and the Equal Educational Opportunities Act of 1974, requires that schools provide translation services to students and their families who do not demonstrate English proficiency. This ensures that students and families are provided equal access to the same educational opportunities as their English-speaking peers. The school is required to locate a well-trained translator and may not request that the student serve in the role or that the parents procure their own translation services.

26. C: The Dignity for All Students Act (DASA) is a piece of legislation that works to ensure the protection of students from harassment, bullying, and discrimination. The act provides a framework that outlines how school districts should respond to reports of such behavior. When a report is made by a student, witness, or parent, the incident must be reported to the DASA coordinator verbally within one day and in writing within two days. Building leadership must then work to ensure that the complainant is protected while the team conducts an investigation. The investigation may entail interviews with the complainant, the accused, or witnesses, as well as reviews of any pertinent evidence. The team then determines if a material incident is present. If the complaint is found to be true, the district will move forward with appropriate disciplinary measures. Both sides have the right to appeal the findings of the investigation to the school board or state. The school is responsible for reporting all material incidents to the New York State commissioner of education at the end of the school year.

How to Overcome Test Anxiety

Just the thought of taking a test is enough to make most people a little nervous. A test is an important event that can have a long-term impact on your future, so it's important to take it seriously and it's natural to feel anxious about performing well. But just because anxiety is normal, that doesn't mean that it's helpful in test taking, or that you should simply accept it as part of your life. Anxiety can have a variety of effects. These effects can be mild, like making you feel slightly nervous, or severe, like blocking your ability to focus or remember even a simple detail.

If you experience test anxiety—whether severe or mild—it's important to know how to beat it. To discover this, first you need to understand what causes test anxiety.

Causes of Test Anxiety

While we often think of anxiety as an uncontrollable emotional state, it can actually be caused by simple, practical things. One of the most common causes of test anxiety is that a person does not feel adequately prepared for their test. This feeling can be the result of many different issues such as poor study habits or lack of organization, but the most common culprit is time management. Starting to study too late, failing to organize your study time to cover all of the material, or being distracted while you study will mean that you're not well prepared for the test. This may lead to cramming the night before, which will cause you to be physically and mentally exhausted for the test. Poor time management also contributes to feelings of stress, fear, and hopelessness as you realize you are not well prepared but don't know what to do about it.

Other times, test anxiety is not related to your preparation for the test but comes from unresolved fear. This may be a past failure on a test, or poor performance on tests in general. It may come from comparing yourself to others who seem to be performing better or from the stress of living up to expectations. Anxiety may be driven by fears of the future—how failure on this test would affect your educational and career goals. These fears are often completely irrational, but they can still negatively impact your test performance.

Elements of Test Anxiety

As mentioned earlier, test anxiety is considered to be an emotional state, but it has physical and mental components as well. Sometimes you may not even realize that you are suffering from test anxiety until you notice the physical symptoms. These can include trembling hands, rapid heartbeat, sweating, nausea, and tense muscles. Extreme anxiety may lead to fainting or vomiting. Obviously, any of these symptoms can have a negative impact on testing. It is important to recognize them as soon as they begin to occur so that you can address the problem before it damages your performance.

The mental components of test anxiety include trouble focusing and inability to remember learned information. During a test, your mind is on high alert, which can help you recall information and stay focused for an extended period of time. However, anxiety interferes with your mind's natural processes, causing you to blank out, even on the questions you know well. The strain of testing during anxiety makes it difficult to stay focused, especially on a test that may take several hours. Extreme anxiety can take a huge mental toll, making it difficult not only to recall test information but even to understand the test questions or pull your thoughts together.

Effects of Test Anxiety

Test anxiety is like a disease—if left untreated, it will get progressively worse. Anxiety leads to poor performance, and this reinforces the feelings of fear and failure, which in turn lead to poor performances on subsequent tests. It can grow from a mild nervousness to a crippling condition. If allowed to progress, test anxiety can have a big impact on your schooling, and consequently on your future.

Test anxiety can spread to other parts of your life. Anxiety on tests can become anxiety in any stressful situation, and blanking on a test can turn into panicking in a job situation. But fortunately, you don't have to let anxiety rule your testing and determine your grades. There are a number of relatively simple steps you can take to move past anxiety and function normally on a test and in the rest of life.

Physical Steps for Beating Test Anxiety

While test anxiety is a serious problem, the good news is that it can be overcome. It doesn't have to control your ability to think and remember information. While it may take time, you can begin taking steps today to beat anxiety.

Just as your first hint that you may be struggling with anxiety comes from the physical symptoms, the first step to treating it is also physical. Rest is crucial for having a clear, strong mind. If you are tired, it is much easier to give in to anxiety. But if you establish good sleep habits, your body and mind will be ready to perform optimally, without the strain of exhaustion. Additionally, sleeping well helps you to retain information better, so you're more likely to recall the answers when you see the test questions.

Getting good sleep means more than going to bed on time. It's important to allow your brain time to relax. Take study breaks from time to time so it doesn't get overworked, and don't study right before bed. Take time to rest your mind before trying to rest your body, or you may find it difficult to fall asleep.

Along with sleep, other aspects of physical health are important in preparing for a test. Good nutrition is vital for good brain function. Sugary foods and drinks may give a burst of energy but this burst is followed by a crash, both physically and emotionally. Instead, fuel your body with protein and vitamin-rich foods.

Also, drink plenty of water. Dehydration can lead to headaches and exhaustion, especially if your brain is already under stress from the rigors of the test. Particularly if your test is a long one, drink water during the breaks. And if possible, take an energy-boosting snack to eat between sections.

Along with sleep and diet, a third important part of physical health is exercise. Maintaining a steady workout schedule is helpful, but even taking 5-minute study breaks to walk can help get your blood pumping faster and clear your head. Exercise also releases endorphins, which contribute to a positive feeling and can help combat test anxiety.

When you nurture your physical health, you are also contributing to your mental health. If your body is healthy, your mind is much more likely to be healthy as well. So take time to rest, nourish your body with healthy food and water, and get moving as much as possible. Taking these physical steps will make you stronger and more able to take the mental steps necessary to overcome test anxiety.

Mental Steps for Beating Test Anxiety

Working on the mental side of test anxiety can be more challenging, but as with the physical side, there are clear steps you can take to overcome it. As mentioned earlier, test anxiety often stems from lack of preparation, so the obvious solution is to prepare for the test. Effective studying may be the most important weapon you have for beating test anxiety, but you can and should employ several other mental tools to combat fear.

First, boost your confidence by reminding yourself of past success—tests or projects that you aced. If you're putting as much effort into preparing for this test as you did for those, there's no reason you should expect to fail here. Work hard to prepare; then trust your preparation.

Second, surround yourself with encouraging people. It can be helpful to find a study group, but be sure that the people you're around will encourage a positive attitude. If you spend time with others who are anxious or cynical, this will only contribute to your own anxiety. Look for others who are motivated to study hard from a desire to succeed, not from a fear of failure.

Third, reward yourself. A test is physically and mentally tiring, even without anxiety, and it can be helpful to have something to look forward to. Plan an activity following the test, regardless of the outcome, such as going to a movie or getting ice cream.

When you are taking the test, if you find yourself beginning to feel anxious, remind yourself that you know the material. Visualize successfully completing the test. Then take a few deep, relaxing breaths and return to it. Work through the questions carefully but with confidence, knowing that you are capable of succeeding.

Developing a healthy mental approach to test taking will also aid in other areas of life. Test anxiety affects more than just the actual test—it can be damaging to your mental health and even contribute to depression. It's important to beat test anxiety before it becomes a problem for more than testing.

Study Strategy

Being prepared for the test is necessary to combat anxiety, but what does being prepared look like? You may study for hours on end and still not feel prepared. What you need is a strategy for test prep. The next few pages outline our recommended steps to help you plan out and conquer the challenge of preparation.

STEP 1: SCOPE OUT THE TEST

Learn everything you can about the format (multiple choice, essay, etc.) and what will be on the test. Gather any study materials, course outlines, or sample exams that may be available. Not only will this help you to prepare, but knowing what to expect can help to alleviate test anxiety.

STEP 2: MAP OUT THE MATERIAL

Look through the textbook or study guide and make note of how many chapters or sections it has. Then divide these over the time you have. For example, if a book has 15 chapters and you have five days to study, you need to cover three chapters each day. Even better, if you have the time, leave an extra day at the end for overall review after you have gone through the material in depth.

If time is limited, you may need to prioritize the material. Look through it and make note of which sections you think you already have a good grasp on, and which need review. While you are studying, skim quickly through the familiar sections and take more time on the challenging parts.

Write out your plan so you don't get lost as you go. Having a written plan also helps you feel more in control of the study, so anxiety is less likely to arise from feeling overwhelmed at the amount to cover.

STEP 3: GATHER YOUR TOOLS

Decide what study method works best for you. Do you prefer to highlight in the book as you study and then go back over the highlighted portions? Or do you type out notes of the important information? Or is it helpful to make flashcards that you can carry with you? Assemble the pens, index cards, highlighters, post-it notes, and any other materials you may need so you won't be distracted by getting up to find things while you study.

If you're having a hard time retaining the information or organizing your notes, experiment with different methods. For example, try color-coding by subject with colored pens, highlighters, or post-it notes. If you learn better by hearing, try recording yourself reading your notes so you can listen while in the car, working out, or simply sitting at your desk. Ask a friend to quiz you from your flashcards, or try teaching someone the material to solidify it in your mind.

STEP 4: CREATE YOUR ENVIRONMENT

It's important to avoid distractions while you study. This includes both the obvious distractions like visitors and the subtle distractions like an uncomfortable chair (or a too-comfortable couch that makes you want to fall asleep). Set up the best study environment possible: good lighting and a comfortable work area. If background music helps you focus, you may want to turn it on, but otherwise keep the room quiet. If you are using a computer to take notes, be sure you don't have any other windows open, especially applications like social media, games, or anything else that could distract you. Silence your phone and turn off notifications. Be sure to keep water close by so you stay hydrated while you study (but avoid unhealthy drinks and snacks).

Also, take into account the best time of day to study. Are you freshest first thing in the morning? Try to set aside some time then to work through the material. Is your mind clearer in the afternoon or evening? Schedule your study session then. Another method is to study at the same time of day that you will take the test, so that your brain gets used to working on the material at that time and will be ready to focus at test time.

STEP 5: STUDY!

Once you have done all the study preparation, it's time to settle into the actual studying. Sit down, take a few moments to settle your mind so you can focus, and begin to follow your study plan. Don't give in to distractions or let yourself procrastinate. This is your time to prepare so you'll be ready to fearlessly approach the test. Make the most of the time and stay focused.

Of course, you don't want to burn out. If you study too long you may find that you're not retaining the information very well. Take regular study breaks. For example, taking five minutes out of every hour to walk briskly, breathing deeply and swinging your arms, can help your mind stay fresh.

As you get to the end of each chapter or section, it's a good idea to do a quick review. Remind yourself of what you learned and work on any difficult parts. When you feel that you've mastered the material, move on to the next part. At the end of your study session, briefly skim through your notes again.

But while review is helpful, cramming last minute is NOT. If at all possible, work ahead so that you won't need to fit all your study into the last day. Cramming overloads your brain with more information than it can process and retain, and your tired mind may struggle to recall even previously learned information when it is overwhelmed with last-minute study. Also, the urgent nature of cramming and the stress placed on your brain contribute to anxiety. You'll be more likely to go to the test feeling unprepared and having trouble thinking clearly.

So don't cram, and don't stay up late before the test, even just to review your notes at a leisurely pace. Your brain needs rest more than it needs to go over the information again. In fact, plan to finish your studies by noon or early afternoon the day before the test. Give your brain the rest of the day to relax or focus on other things, and get a good night's sleep. Then you will be fresh for the test and better able to recall what you've studied.

STEP 6: TAKE A PRACTICE TEST

Many courses offer sample tests, either online or in the study materials. This is an excellent resource to check whether you have mastered the material, as well as to prepare for the test format and environment.

Check the test format ahead of time: the number of questions, the type (multiple choice, free response, etc.), and the time limit. Then create a plan for working through them. For example, if you have 30 minutes to take a 60-question test, your limit is 30 seconds per question. Spend less time on the questions you know well so that you can take more time on the difficult ones.

If you have time to take several practice tests, take the first one open book, with no time limit. Work through the questions at your own pace and make sure you fully understand them. Gradually work up to taking a test under test conditions: sit at a desk with all study materials put away and set a timer. Pace yourself to make sure you finish the test with time to spare and go back to check your answers if you have time.

After each test, check your answers. On the questions you missed, be sure you understand why you missed them. Did you misread the question (tests can use tricky wording)? Did you forget the information? Or was it something you hadn't learned? Go back and study any shaky areas that the practice tests reveal.

Taking these tests not only helps with your grade, but also aids in combating test anxiety. If you're already used to the test conditions, you're less likely to worry about it, and working through tests until you're scoring well gives you a confidence boost. Go through the practice tests until you feel comfortable, and then you can go into the test knowing that you're ready for it.

Test Tips

On test day, you should be confident, knowing that you've prepared well and are ready to answer the questions. But aside from preparation, there are several test day strategies you can employ to maximize your performance.

First, as stated before, get a good night's sleep the night before the test (and for several nights before that, if possible). Go into the test with a fresh, alert mind rather than staying up late to study.

Try not to change too much about your normal routine on the day of the test. It's important to eat a nutritious breakfast, but if you normally don't eat breakfast at all, consider eating just a protein bar. If you're a coffee drinker, go ahead and have your normal coffee. Just make sure you time it so that the caffeine doesn't wear off right in the middle of your test. Avoid sugary beverages, and drink enough water to stay hydrated but not so much that you need a restroom break 10 minutes into the test. If your test isn't first thing in the morning, consider going for a walk or doing a light workout before the test to get your blood flowing.

Allow yourself enough time to get ready, and leave for the test with plenty of time to spare so you won't have the anxiety of scrambling to arrive in time. Another reason to be early is to select a good seat. It's helpful to sit away from doors and windows, which can be distracting. Find a good seat, get out your supplies, and settle your mind before the test begins.

When the test begins, start by going over the instructions carefully, even if you already know what to expect. Make sure you avoid any careless mistakes by following the directions.

Then begin working through the questions, pacing yourself as you've practiced. If you're not sure on an answer, don't spend too much time on it, and don't let it shake your confidence. Either skip it and come back later, or eliminate as many wrong answers as possible and guess among the remaining ones. Don't dwell on these questions as you continue—put them out of your mind and focus on what lies ahead.

Be sure to read all of the answer choices, even if you're sure the first one is the right answer. Sometimes you'll find a better one if you keep reading. But don't second-guess yourself if you do immediately know the answer. Your gut instinct is usually right. Don't let test anxiety rob you of the information you know.

If you have time at the end of the test (and if the test format allows), go back and review your answers. Be cautious about changing any, since your first instinct tends to be correct, but make sure you didn't misread any of the questions or accidentally mark the wrong answer choice. Look over any you skipped and make an educated guess.

At the end, leave the test feeling confident. You've done your best, so don't waste time worrying about your performance or wishing you could change anything. Instead, celebrate the successful completion of this test. And finally, use this test to learn how to deal with anxiety even better next time.

Review Video: Test Anxiety
Visit mometrix.com/academy and enter code: 100340

Important Qualification

Not all anxiety is created equal. If your test anxiety is causing major issues in your life beyond the classroom or testing center, or if you are experiencing troubling physical symptoms related to your anxiety, it may be a sign of a serious physiological or psychological condition. If this sounds like your situation, we strongly encourage you to seek professional help.

Additional Bonus Material

Due to our efforts to try to keep this book to a manageable length, we've created a link that will give you access to all of your additional bonus material:

mometrix.com/bonus948/nystcescbl109110